Church Music in America

1620–2000

MERCER
UNIVERSITY PRESS

Endowed by
TOM WATSON BROWN
and
THE WATSON-BROWN FOUNDATION, INC.

Church Music in America,

1620–2000

John Ogasapian†

MERCER UNIVERSITY PRESS

MACON, GEORGIA

MUP/H720

© 2007 Mercer University Press
1400 Coleman Avenue
Macon, Georgia 31207

First Edition.

Books published by Mercer University Press are printed on acid free paper that meets the requirements of American National Standard for Information Sciences—Permanence of Paper for Printed Library Materials.

The publisher wishes to thank Lisa Ellrott, for her countless hours spent assisting the press in the copyediting her father's work and her dedication to her father's scholarship.

Library of Congress Cataloging-in-Publication Data

Ogasapian, John.
Church music in America, 1620 to 2000 / John Ogasapian. -- 1st ed.
p. cm.
Includes bibliographical references (p.   ) and index.
ISBN-13: 978-0-88146-026-1 (hardcover : alk. paper)
ISBN-10: 0-88146-026-5 (hardcover : alk. paper)
1. Church music—United States. I. Title.
ML2911.O43 2007
781.7100973--dc22
2007001902

Contents

To my granddaughter Hollis Marion Ellrott

born 14 January 2005

Preface

The history of American church music is a particularly fascinating and challenging subject, if for no other reason than because of the variety of diverse religious groups that have immigrated and the movements that have sprung up. Indeed, for the first time in modern history—possibly the only time since the rule of medieval Iberia under the Moors—different faiths have coexisted here with a measure of peace—sometimes ill-humored, occasionally hostile, but more often amicable or at least tolerant—influencing and even weaving their traditions into the fabric of one another's worship practices even as they competed for converts in the free market of American religion.

I have attempted an overview of some of the more prominent threads in that fabric, but by no means could I touch on all of them. Indeed, anyone who attempts a single-volume survey of so broad a subject as the history of American church music must make hard decisions as to what must be left out and how deeply to address the subject matter that is included. Having made those decisions, I have observed them carefully, albeit not always comfortably. Some readers will doubtless be disappointed with the omissions of specific contexts, composers, and works. By way of some little compensation, however, I have attempted to provide a generous amount of bibliography in the footnotes for any who might be inclined to pursue a particular subject in depth.

Since this book is not a critical study of the repertoire, I have limited myself to general stylistic comments about the music. There are no analyses of particular pieces. I have not attempted to engage such aspects as music in the Spanish colonies, synagogue music, or the liturgical music of Eastern Orthodoxy, partly because such music is part of an ethnically or culturally discrete worship practice, but largely because such areas call for a distinctive and special expertise to which I make no pretense. Finally, I have limited the subject matter to actual church music and its composers and compilers; that is, I have endeavored to preserve the distinction eighteenth- and nineteenth-century Americans made between sacred music—concert music with sacred texts—and church music—music regularly and customarily employed in worship. As a result, there is no mention of pieces like Bernstein's *Mass* for instance.

Like its predecessors, Leonard Ellinwood's *The History of American Church Music* and Robert Stevenson's *Protestant Church Music in America*, this study aims at compact synthesis rather than original archival research. Apart from my own area of expertise, American organs and organ-building, I have had to rely on the accumulated scholarship of others, whose work is listed in the bibliography, and I acknowledge my debt of gratitude to them.

It is my good fortune that so much has been done in the two decades since the bicentennial heightened scholarly interest in American music and culture. Of course, Ellinwood's and Stevenson's books both antedated that post-bicentennial surge of scholarship. They worked unaided by the kinds of bibliographic resources and scholarly amenities published since 1976, which I have been able to take for granted and to turn to as needed. I am also grateful to live and work in close proximity to several research collections, especially those of the American Antiquarian Society and the Mugar and School of Theology Libraries at Boston University. As always, the staff of O'Leary Library at the University of Massachusetts, Lowell, has been of immeasurable assistance, especially Richard Slapsys, the university's music librarian, and Deborah Friedman of the Interlibrary Loan Department.

Many people have played a role in this book's development. Barbara J. Owen, Stephen L. Pinel, and Edward C. Wolf, in particular, provided information and items I needed at one time or another. Karl D. Kroeger and N. Lee Orr read over early drafts and were especially generous with their comments and criticisms. Errors and infelicities surely remain, but they are mine alone.

In a sense, this book began its development some fifty years ago, when my father, Karekin Ogasapian, was pressed into service as organist of our family's church on the death of his predecessor, my mother's uncle. His interest in church music and the organ was passed on to me, and though he has been gone these past ten years, he is very much in my thoughts. It was he who (unwittingly and reluctantly, it must be said) launched me on a lengthy odyssey of studying, thinking about, writing about, practicing church music, and ultimately the writing of this book. As always, my wife Nancy has been a source of love and support. Without her, none of this could have been done—or would have seemed worth doing. Our daughter Lisa was in elementary school when I first drafted a rough outline for this study. In the intervening years, Lisa has finished college and graduate school, married, and she and our son-in law, Thomas, have presented us with a grandson and granddaughter, Nolan and Hollis Ellrott. To them, and to my mother Marion Ogasapian, in her ninety-ninth year as I write, I express my love. To my granddaughter Hollis especially, this book is dedicated.

John Ogasapian

Prologue

In the last decade of the fifteenth century, two European courts honored Genoese explorers who had planted their respective flags in the new world. Christopher Columbus—designated Admiral of the Ocean Sea, whose voyages in the name of those Most Christian Rulers, Ferdinand and Isabella, opened Spain's way to what would become Central and South America—was designated viceroy and governor general of the lands he discovered, and he was entitled to a tenth of the riches he brought back. John Cabot, who in 1497 had crossed the Atlantic in the name of Henry VII of England and sailed down the coast of what is now Newfoundland, received from that tight-fisted monarch the substantial—if far less generous—gift of ten pounds and an annual pension of twenty pounds. Cabot's second and last voyage failed the next year. Thereafter, except for the rich fishing banks off its coast, England lost interest in America for a century.

Spain, on the other hand, dispatched fortune-hunting soldiers and colonists along with missionaries. In the midst of their countrymen's greed and cruelty, Franciscans established schools and taught the natives a new faith and its music. On 6 January 1494—the Feast of the Epiphany—mass was sung in the New World for the first time, and in 1512—the year Ponce de Leon discovered Florida—the first cathedral charter was granted for the New World. The city of Santo Domingo on the island of Hispaniola—today shared by Haiti and the Dominican Republic—was to have the full panoply of a metropolitan cathedral, including its own music establishment patterned on the Spanish model.

Five years later, an ocean and part of a continent away, Martin Luther nailed his ninety-five theses to the Castle Church door in Wittenberg. Over the next two centuries and more, European Christianity would divide and subdivide into warring factions. A generation of English dissenters would flee to John Calvin's Geneva, and a later one who shared John Wintrop's vision would plant its own "city upon a hill" in North America.

That British presence still lay decades in the future in spring 1564, when a group of Huguenots, French Calvinist Protestants, began building a settlement they called Fort Caroline at the mouth of the James River, near what is now Jacksonville, Florida. The next summer, an expedition from Spain established its own outpost, St. Augustine, some forty miles south of Fort Caroline. The Spaniards easily captured the Huguenots' timber-and-sod fortifications and put its defenders to the sword, sparing only two musicians whose professional services were apparently required at St. Augustine. For years thereafter, local Indians who had learned some of the Huguenots' psalm tunes sang them to white men they met as a means of discovering whether the strangers were the relatively friendly French or the hostile Spanish.

Translations of the psalms into verse had appeared in Europe early in the sixteenth century. The earliest were probably intended for recreational singing to popular airs of the day, but they quickly found a place in the worship practice of Reformed Protestantism. Metrical psalms set to unison melodies would become the only music for many churches on the Continent, in England, and subsequently in America.[1]

A number of sprightly chanson-like metrical translations of selected psalms by the popular poet Clement Marot (1496/1497–1544), groom of the chamber to French king Francis I, were circulating among the French nobility. Marot had sent copies to foreign courts, among them that of the Holy Roman Emperor Charles V, so he was probably neither surprised nor displeased to learn that the translations were also making their way into Protestant worship. Indeed, Marot himself had been suspected of having Lutheran sympathies as early as the 1520s, and there is at least the possibility that some of his earliest psalm versifications were made at

---

[1] Nicholas Temperley, *The Music of the English Parish Church* (Cambridge: Cambridge University Press, 1979) 98 points out that such singing of psalms to well-known tunes had a didactic purpose in that it facilitated their familiarization.

the behest of the reformer John Calvin, whom he had first met in 1531.[2] Even as those first psalms were circulating in 1534, Marot was forced into exile for a brief period for suspected Protestant activities.

Calvin's first Psalter, titled *Aulcuns pseaulmes et cantiques mys en chant*, printed in Strasbourg in 1539 and thus referred to as the Strasbourg Psalter, contained nineteen metrical psalm texts—thirteen of them by Marot—and eighteen unharmonized melodies by German composers in Strasbourg. The next year a collection titled *Souterliedekins* appeared in Antwerp. Its metrical psalm texts were set to popular tunes harmonized by Jacobus Clemens non Papa, a Catholic composer, albeit one who may have had Protestant leanings. In Paris in 1542, Marot published a set of thirty metrical psalm texts, *Trente Pseaulmes de David*, to be sung to popular airs. The ensuing uproar drove him to seek refuge in Geneva, which in September of the previous year had welcomed Calvin back as minister and virtual dictator. In 1542, under Calvin's leadership, the press in Geneva published a Psalter, all but seven of whose thirty-nine texts were Marot's, and a 1543 collection containing fifty psalms and other texts, all by Marot.

Either because Marot's Protestantism was not especially fervent or because his free-wheeling ways did not sit well with the city's dour ministers, he left Geneva in 1543 for Italy where he died the next year. But many of his translations lived on in the 1562 Genevan Psalter, formally titled *Les Pseaumes mis en rime française*, from which the Florida Huguenots sang. Marot's verses, together with psalm translations by Theodore Beza (1519–1605), were set to tunes compiled and in many cases composed by Louis Bourgeois (c1510–1560). The Genevan Psalter eventually went through 225 editions in some twenty languages.

Meanwhile England was in the throes of religious reformation, at this stage political and economic rather than confessional. Henry VIII's marital and dynastic concerns brought on the Act of Supremacy of November 1534, ending the authority of the pope in

---

[2] Friederich Blume, *Protestant Church Music* (New York: W. W. Norton, 1974) 133–34.

English religious affairs and vesting that authority in the king. Although he now governed a church that was still essentially Catholic in faith and practice, Henry sought a political alliance with Lutheran princes in Germany. Around 1535, Myles Coverdale published his *Goostly psalmes and spirituall songes*, forty-one metrical psalms, hymns, and canticles with unharmonized melodies, largely adapted from Lutheran sources. By 1539, Henry's negotiations with the Germans had turned sour. Lutheran interests in England were suppressed, and Coverdale's collection was among the books burned in September 1546. It thus had minimal effect on subsequent publication of English metrical psalmody.[3]

With Henry VIII's death in January 1547 and the accession of his nine-year-old son Edward VI under the protectorship of Edward Seymour, Duke of Somerset, the Protestant party—including Thomas Cranmer, Henry's appointed Archbishop of Canterbury, who would correspond with Calvin in Geneva as he drafted the services in the first Book of Common Prayer—was able to influence the direction of the Church of England and its music. As early as 14 April 1548, a royal injunction to the Dean and Chapter of Lincoln Cathedral directed that the service music be clear and understandable: "Not in Latin but...they shall turn the same into English setting thereunto a plain and distinct note for every syllable one."[4]

The Act of Uniformity was passed and Cranmer's Anglican Prayer Book published in 1549. That same year, the first complete set of English metrical psalms—Robert Crowley's *Psalter of David*—appeared. The music consisted of a single tune, labeled "Playn Song," adapted from the Gregorian seventh tone and set

---

[3] On the background and content of Coverdale's collection, see Robin Leaver, *"Goostly Psalmes and Spirituall Songes": English and Dutch Metrical Psalms from Coverdale to Utenhove, 1535–1566* (Oxford: Clarendon Press and New York: Oxford University Press, 1991) 62–108.

[4] Gustave Reese, *Music in the Renaissance* (New York: W. W. Norton, 1959) 796–97.

Faburden-style with melody in the tenor harmonized with voices above and below.[5]

But it was another—earlier and more modest—publication that would, with additions and revisions, become the standard collection for English congregations. About 1547, a set of nineteen metrical psalm translations, grandly titled *Certayne Psalmes Chosen out of the Psalter of David and Drawen into English Metre by Thomas Sternhold, Groome of Ye Kings Maiesties Roobes*. Sternhold, born about 1500, had evidently been a favorite of Henry VIII, for he received from him a legacy of 100 marks. His collection was dedicated to the king, and its preface made clear Sternhold's pious intent. The style and language were plain and straightforward, and each psalm was preceded by an extra stanza summarizing its moral content.[6]

By the end of 1549, Sternhold was in his grave, but a second edition of his psalms had already been issued with eighteen more translations, plus another seven by John Hopkins. Subsequent editions—over 600 of them, to as late as 1828—would contain translations by a number of others, culminating in a full metrical Psalter; however, the collection in all its subsequent editions to the end of its active use would still be known as Sternhold and Hopkins and commonly referred to as the Old Version.

With the death of Edward and accession of his Catholic half-sister Mary and her Archbishop of Canterbury, Cardinal Reginald Pole, many of the leading English Protestants went into exile in Geneva, taking with them the enlarged 1553 version of the Sternhold and Hopkins. A new edition was published in Geneva in 1556 as a separately titled appendix to the English version of Calvin's *The*

---

[5] Peter Le Huray, *Music and the Reformation in England, 1549–1660* (New York: Oxford University Press, 1967) 371–72. See also Temperley, *The Music of the English Parish Church*, 34–35.

[6] This first publication bears no year. A tentative dating of 1549 is suggested both by Temperley, *The Music of the English Parish Church*, 23; and Percy Scholes, *The Puritans and Music in England and New England* (London: Oxford University Press, 1934, repr. Oxford: Clarendon Press, 1967) 254. More recent research by Robin Leaver points to the earlier date of 1547. See Leaver, "*Goostly Psalmes*," 120–21. Appendix IV (p. 300) contains the full text of Sternhold's introduction.

Forme of Prayers and Ministration of the Sacraments, &c.... It contained revised versions of forty-four Sternhold and Hopkins texts, along with seven new texts and a metrical setting of the Ten Commandments by William Whittingham, brother-in-law of Calvin and John Knox's associate as minister of the English congregation in Geneva. For the first time, tunes were provided, but no composers were named.[7] Most of the texts were in alternating eight- and six-syllable lines with four and three accented syllables respectively, typical of the secular English ballad of approximately the same time and thus termed common meter. Other texts were in long or short meter, consisting respectively of four eight-syllable lines per stanza, and two six-syllable lines, one of eight syllables and another of six syllables.[8]

Ironically, Whittingham later became Dean of Durham Cathedral under Elizabeth and in that capacity built an elaborate music establishment with "the best songs and anthems that could be got out of the queen's chapell, to furnish the quire withall." But in 1556, his Geneva preface warned against trained choirs: "Satan hath...most impudently abused this notable gift of singing, chiefly by the papists...in disfiguring it, partly by a strange language [Latin]...and partly by...hiring men to tickle the ears and flatter the fantasies."[9] A second, 1558 edition of this Geneva service book and Psalter accompanied the exiles when they returned to England with the accession of Elizabeth later that year. The next year saw the first known instances of sung metrical psalmody in English worship.[10]

A 1562 version of Sternhold and Hopkins titled *The Whole Booke of Psalmes, Collected into Englyshe Metre* was published in London by

---

[7] For a full discussion of this 1556 collection, see Leaver, *"Goostly Psalmes,"* 123–29.

[8] Temperley doubts that "common metre" was indeed common in secular ballads before Sternhold, but he suggests that his settings were the cause of the metre becoming common because most such common metre ballads date from later than Sternhold's psalm texts. See Temperley, *The Music of the English Parish Church,* 33–37; Leaver, *"Goostly Psalmes,"* 119–20.

[9] Scholes, *The Puritans and Music,* 255. Temperley, *The Music of the English Parish Church,* 29. Le Huray, *Music and the Reformation,* 373.

[10] Temperley, *The Music of the English Parish Church,* 42–43.

John Day and is thus commonly referred to as Day's Psalter. It contained English metrical translations of the complete Psalter along with forty-six tunes. The next year Day published a polyphonic version in four part-books titled *The Whole Booke of Psalmes in Foure Partes*. Its tunes, taken from the 1562 publication with some additional ones, appear for the most part in the tenor with harmony supplied by the other three voices. Although tunes would come and go with subsequent editions of the Old Version, some three-dozen specific tunes would persist in every edition between 1562 and 1687. Of those, few were in general use from church to church. In 1594, the printer Thomas Est opined that "in most churches of this realm" four tunes sufficed to sing all the psalms.[11]

The accession of Elizabeth, a Protestant, brought the English reformers home from Geneva, and Parliament quickly became Protestant. Indeed, its tendencies were so Puritan that it began its sessions with a psalm, much to Elizabeth's disgust. She loathed metrical psalms, which she referred to with contempt as "Geneva jigs." But she was generally tolerant and was self-disciplined and pragmatic as few monarchs before or since. She saw clearly and immediately the need for compromise and wisely followed that course.

Elizabeth retained an appreciation for ritual, and the preface to the 1559 Prayer Book decreed that "chauncels shall remain as they have done in times past." On the other hand, a musical concession was made to the Puritan wing in the matter of clear text settings: "Repeating of notes with words and sentences...shall not be used." Had she had the resources, Elizabeth might have commanded the reinstitution of elaborate music establishments in cathedrals and collegiate churches; however, her reign saw an economic inflation such as to make the restoration of most music establishments, whose endowments had been confiscated during her father's reign, impracticable.[12] Indeed, even in the queen's own St. George's Chapel, Windsor, the choirboys were forced to take part in stage

---

[11] Temperley, *The Music of the English Parish Church*, 59–60, 68.

[12] David Wulstan, *Tudor Music* (Iowa City: University of Iowa Press, 1986) 314.

plays in order to support themselves because their stipend was so scanty.[13]

Still, cathedrals and large churches in Elizabethan England managed to preserve and rebuild their choirs. Smaller parish churches, which heretofore had little—if any—music in general, took to psalmody for its ease and practicality. Psalmody was congregational music that was simple, scriptural, and singable. The short repeated stanzas in clear English, set syllabically to easy tunes in familiar style, were popular and accessible. In other words, two different traditions developed side by side in English church music: on one hand, the full cathedral service of polyphonic choral music (with some metrical psalms, probably sung in parts by the choir), and on the other, the plain unison congregational psalmody of the modest parish church. The latter tradition, of course, was the one brought to America by British colonists.

[13] Neville Wridgway, *The Choristers of St. George's Chapel, Windsor Castle* (Slough, Berkshire: Chas. Luff, 1980) 27–35.

1.

Psalmody in the English Colonies

The earliest recorded instance of English music in North America dates to the summer of 1579. Sir Francis Drake had beached his vessel, the *Golden Hinde*, for repairs on the California shore north of modern-day San Francisco. Back in London, the expedition's chaplain, Francis Fletcher, recalled the local natives' fascination with the Englishmen's singing of Sternhold and Hopkins' psalms, probably from Day's 1562 Psalter: "They took such pleasure in our singing of psalmes, that whensoever they resorted to us...they entreated that we should sing."[1]

By 1607, when Jamestown, the first permanent English colony, was established in Virginia, Anglicans were singing their Old Version, Sternhold and Hopkins psalms from one of several collections of harmonized tunes that appeared in England toward the end of the sixteenth century. Among the most popular was London printer Thomas Est's *The Whole Booke of Psalmes: With Their Wonted Tunes, as They Are Song in Churches, Composed into Foure Partes*, printed in 1592. Est's collection contained fifty-eight tunes "compiled by sundry authors," among them the Catholic composer of lute songs John Dowland. Est had set each psalm to a tune; however, many tunes were used more than once and two of them more than thirty

---

[1] Sir Francis Drake and Francis Fletcher, *The World Encompassed by Sir Francis Drake* (London: Printed for Nicholas Bourne, 1652) 72.

times each. The melody, or air, was in the tenor, printed at the left of a two-page spread with a treble part above it. Similarly, the bass was printed on the right page, below the alto. The first stanza was printed with the music; the remainder of the text was printed at the bottom of the two pages.[2]

The Plymouth Colony

In 1607, the year of Jamestown's founding, a company of religious separatists, who had abandoned the established church and formed themselves into an independent congregation only a year earlier, abandoned their homes in Scrooby, Nottinghamshire, for Amsterdam, where they might enjoy religious liberty. Another congregation of English separatists was already settled in Amsterdam. Its pastor was Henry Ainsworth (1570/1571–1622/1623), Cambridge scholar, Hebraist, theologian, and arguably the finest mind among the English separatists.[3]

Ainsworth was engaged in preparing his own metrical translation of the psalms for the use of his church. By the time his *The Booke of Psalmes: Englished Both in Prose and Metre* was printed in Amsterdam by the Englishman Giles Thorp in 1612, the Scrooby congregation had removed from Amsterdam to Leiden. Nevertheless, they too adopted the Ainsworth Psalter, doubtless with a sense of satisfaction

---

[2] Leonard Ellinwood, *The History of American Church Music* (New York: Morehouse-Gorham, 1953; repr., New York: Da Capo, 1970) 12. Peter Le Huray, *Music and the Reformation in England, 1549–1660* (New York: Oxford University Press, 1967) 381; Nicholas Temperley, *The Music of the English Parish Church* (Cambridge: Cambridge University Press, 1979) 68–74. The main resource on New England psalmody remains George Hood, *A History of Music in New England* (Boston: Wilkins, Carter, & Co., 1846; repr., New York: Johnson, 1970). Other resources include Richard Crawford, *The Core Repertory of Early American Psalmody*, vols. 11–12 of *Recent Researches in American Music* (Madison: A-R Editions, 1984) and Henry Wilder Foote, *Three Centuries of American Hymnody* (Cambridge: Harvard University Press, 1940; repr., Hamden CT: Shoe String Press, 1961). See also, but with extreme care, Hamilton C. MacDougall, *Early New England Psalmody* (Brattleboro: Stephen Daye Press, 1940; repr., New York: DaCapo, 1969) 13.

[3] Edmund S. Morgan, *Visible Saints* (Ithaca: Cornell University Press, 1975) 54–56.

at having cut off yet another tie to the established church in England by discarding the ubiquitous Old Version.

Ainsworth's Psalter provided both metrical and prose translations for each psalm, printed side by side on the page, along with commentary on the psalm. He employed some sixteen different metrical schemes and supplied forty-eight tunes, nine of them duplications. Several were drawn from Day's 1562 collection, but a larger number were from continental sources, including the Genevan Psalter. Ainsworth wrote in his preface: "Tunes for the Psalmes, I find none set of God: so that e[a]ch people is to use the most grave, decent, and comfortable manner of singing that they know, according to the general rule.... The singing notes therefore I have most taken from our former Englished psalms, when they will fit the measure of the verse; and for the other long verses, I have also taken (for the most part) the gravest and easiest tunes of the French and Dutch psalmes."[4]

Where a tune was provided, a portion of the metrical text was underlaid, and the rest was printed in the column below the music. Where no tune appeared with a psalm, a reference was provided to one printed with another psalm in the book. Moreover, alternates were even suggested for some psalms already supplied with their own tunes. All in all, the length of the tunes chosen by Ainsworth and the variety of meters in his Psalter attest to the musical skill of at least some in his congregation. The translations of Psalm 8 provide an illuminating example. The psalm begins in the King James Version, "O Lord, our Lord, how excellent is Thy name in all the earth! who has set Thy glory above the heavens." Thomas Sternhold's Old Version metrical translation is in a regular common meter with eight syllables and four accents alternating with six syllables and three accents in each four-line stanza:

---

[4] See Lorraine Inserra and H. Wiley Hitchcock, *The Music of Henry Ainsworth's Psalter (Amsterdam, 1612)* (Brooklyn: I.S.A.M., 1981) 3. Edward Winslow, *Hypocrasie Unmasked* (London: Richard Cotes for John Bellamy, 1646) 91 termed "many of the Congregation very expert in musick." On the English and continental styles of psalm tunes, see Emily Brink, "Metrical Psalmody: A Tale of Two Traditions," *Reformed Liturgy and Music* 23/1 (Winter 1989): 3–8.

O God our Lord, how wonderful
are Thy works ev'ry where!
Thy frame surmounts in dignity
the highest heav'ns that are.

Henry Ainsworth's translation, by contrast, employs an irregular pattern that overlaps the verses, which he fits to an especially fine tune of five ten-line syllables, probably by Louis Bourgeois, used in the Genevan Psalter as well as the Scottish Psalter as a setting for Psalm 124: "Jah our Lord, how excellent-great is/ Thy name in all the earth; Thou which hast given/ thy glorious-majestie above the heauen."[5]

In 1620 the Leiden church again moved. Part of the congregation departed Delfthaven for England and late that summer sailed for America. The Pilgrims, as history would name them, dropped anchor at what was to become Plymouth, Massachusetts, in late fall and set about planting their colony. Unlike the Puritans who would begin settling the Bay Colony to their north ten years later, few of the Plymouth settlers were educated. Most were farmers and artisans. Their minister had stayed back in Leiden, and their worship was led by elder William Brewster. Yet they managed to sing their psalmody in Ainsworth's complex meters and tunes until 1682, by which time their settlement had been joined with the Bay Colony.

The Bay Colony Puritans

As early as 1628, a small company of non-separatist Puritans led by John Endecott settled at Salem. Like the Plymouth settlers, they sang their psalmody from Ainsworth, but in fact they were the vanguard of a great immigration that began in spring 1630, when the first of their countrymen sailed into Massachusetts Bay. Over the next decade, some 80,000 Puritans left England, a third of them bound for New England and intent on building a godly commonwealth in and

---

[5] Inserra and Hitchcock, *The Music of Henry Ainsworth's Psalter*, 46.

around Boston. Unlike their neighbors at Plymouth, most were literate, and they brought their ministers with them, a university-educated intellectual class.[6]

Although the Puritans, unlike the Plymouth separatists, had remained within the Church of England, they distrusted any kind of elaborate worship ritual that might be a distraction from the serious business of scriptural preaching and be a detriment to true worship. Other than their use of the Old Version, rather than Ainsworth, the worship in the meetinghouses of the Bay Colony was like that of the settlers at Plymouth, and their polity was one of independent churches whose members called and ordained their own ministers. The service in general and the two-hour sermon in particular were an occasion for teaching, intellectual stimulation, and even entertainment, in a manner of speaking.[7] The building was not to be thought of, or termed, a "church." Two generations later, Boston's leading minister Cotton Mather wrote, "A meeting house is the term that is most commonly used...[there being] no just ground in Scripture to apply such a trope as *church* to a place for assembly."[8]

As for music, the Puritan ministers harkened to the writings of the early church fathers. They feared music's ability to arouse inappropriate feelings and to lull the sinner's fear of eternal damnation, to "mistake the natural Effects of *Musick*, for the Comforts of the Holy Spirit."[9]At best, they felt, it might be useful in communicating with those who lacked the intellectual capability to respond to their preaching.[10] Nevertheless, scripture mandated the congregational singing of psalms, and scripture was their infallible guide. Choirs were considered both unscriptural and a Roman

---

[6] David Hackett Fischer, *Albion's Seed* (New York: Oxford University Press, 1989) 13–39.

[7] See Larzer Ziff, *Puritanism in America* (New York: Viking, 1973) 53; and Darrett B. Rutman, *American Puritanism* (New York: Norton, 1977) 12–13.

[8] Cotton Mather and Increase Mather, *Ratio Disciplinae Fratrum Nov-Anglorum* (Boston: S. Gerrish, 1726) 5.

[9] Thomas Symmes, *The Reasonableness of Regular Singing, or, Singing by Note* (Boston: B. Green for Samuel Gerrish, 1720) 18.

[10] Temperley, *The Music of the English Parish Church*, 41.

corruption, as were instruments, especially organs. The psalms were to be sung in unison, plainly and by all. They had no aesthetic significance as music; their role was to instruct by virtue of their scriptural authority.

To be sure, cultured Puritans enjoyed music, and even dancing, as much as other Englishmen of the era. They were not averse to singing and playing psalms in parts for their own recreation. In New England homes, one might find Day's 1563 collection with tunes "in foure parts which may be song to al musicall instruments" or Est's 1592 collection, Richard Allison's *Psalmes of Dauid* (1599), with the melody in the upper-most voice, rather than the customary tenor, and parts that could "be sung and plaide vpon the Lute, Orpharyon, Citterne or Base Violl, severally or together…in fowre voyces," or especially Ravenscroft's 1621 publication *The Whole Booke of Psalmes: With the Hymns Evangelicall, and Songs Spirituall. Composed into 4 Parts by Sundry Authors*. Ravenscroft included ninety-seven tunes, several of them new, set in parts by major composers of the era, including two Catholics, Dowland and Morley.[11]

The Bay Psalm Book

The Bay Colony's ministers, with their thorough knowledge of Hebrew and Latin and their obsessive fidelity to a literal and accurate rendition of scripture, were uneasy about the Sternhold and Hopkins psalm translations. Most agreed with John Cotton of Boston's First Church, who considered the Old Version translations too free with the literal meaning of the texts in Hebrew. The ministers were consistently on guard against scriptural and doctrinal deviations. Indeed, at least part of their eagerness for a new translation may well have been by way of response to the wave of independence, usually termed the Antinomian Controversy, that had flared up in Cotton's own congregation and subsequently resulted in the trial and exile of Anne Hutchinson in 1637.

---

[11] See Percy Scholes, *The Puritans and Music in England and New England* (London: Oxford University Press, 1934; repr., Oxford: Clarendon Press, 1967) 260–61.

In any event, once they had established their college in nearby Cambridge, thirty "pious and learned Ministers" embarked on a new and careful translation of the psalms from the original Hebrew into metrical English. Published in 1640 by Stephen Daye on a press at Harvard College in Cambridge, it became the first book produced in the Colonies. The lengthy formal title was *The Whole Booke of Psalmes Faithfully Translated into English Metre*; however, it has more generally been referred to as the Bay Psalm Book. A preface, possibly by John Cotton, set forth the scriptural case for congregational psalmody and for metrical versification, reminding his readers that the psalms were poetry in their original language. On the inadequacies of previous translations, he wrote:

> For although wee have cause to blesse God in many re-spects for the religious indeavours of the translaters of the psalmes into meetre usually annexed to our Bibles, yet it is not unknowne to the godly learned that they have rather pre-sented a paraphrase then the words of David...and that their addition to the words, detraction from the words are not sel-dome and rare, but very frequent and many times needles....
>
> We have therefore done our indeavour to make a plaine and familiar translation of the psalmes and words of David into english metre, and have not soe much as presumed to paraphrase....
>
> If therefore the verses are not always so smooth and elegant as some may desire or expect; let them consider that Gods Altar needs not our pollishings...for wee have respected ra-ther a plaine translation, then to smooth our verses with a sweetnes of any paraphrase, and so have attended Conscience rather than Elegance, fidelity rather than poetry, in trans-lating the hebrew words into english language, and Davids poetry into english meetre, that so we may sing in Sion the Lords songs of prayse according to his owne will....[12]

---

[12] A relatively accessible source for the text is Elwyn A. Weinandt, *Opinions on Church Music* (Waco: Baylor University Press, 1974) 28–35. Henry Wilder Foote,

The 1640 preface makes mention of "the difficulty of *Ainsworths* tunes" as a second justification for the new translation. Indeed, the number of meters called for in the Bay Psalm Book was reduced to six from the seventeen in Day's complete Old Version and fifteen in Ainsworth, in use in both the Salem and Plymouth churches. By far the most frequently represented was common meter. One hundred and twelve of the texts were so set, plus one in double common meter. Another fourteen were in short meter, fifteen in long meter, and the remaining eight were in other schemes. No tunes were included; however, "An Admonition to the Reader" recommended using those from the Ravenscroft collection as well as "our english psalme books."

The Bay Psalm Book translation of Psalm 8 is in the same common meter as the Old Version, quoted above.

O Lord our God in all the earth
how's Thy name wondrous great.
who has Thy glorious majesty
above the heavens set.

The angular character of the translations prompted Henry Dunster, who provided alternate translations and other scriptural texts, to rework some of the earlier Bay Psalm Book verses with "a little more of Art." His 1651 version was reissued in over fifty subsequent editions; however, no music was printed with the texts until the ninth edition of 1698. Its thirteen tunes—all but four of which were in common meter—were taken without acknowledgement directly from John Playford's *Brief Introduction to the Skill of Musicke*[13] and printed

---

Three Centuries of American Hymnody (Cambridge: Harvard, 1940; repr. Hamden: Shoe String, 1961) 40ff. In passing, he attributed the preface to Richard Mather, rather than Cotton, on the basis of a draft apparently in Mather's hand in the Boston Public Library (p. 43, n.7). Foote's chapters on American hymnody in the seventeenth and eighteenth centuries, while not without flaw, are a valuable and readable reference, nearly sixty years after their publication.

[13] John Playford, *Brief Introduction to the Skill of Musicke* (London, Printed by

in two-voices, melody over bass, with Playford's solfege letters, F[a], S[ol] [La] and M[i].[14]

Lining Out

At the very time the New England churches were abandoning the Old Version for the Bay Psalm Book, the quality of their congregational psalmody was in decline; and the introduction of new translations must have exacerbated the problem. Unsupported by any instrument, congregations found themselves able to sing fewer and fewer tunes.[15] The introduction or imposition of the new Bay Psalm Book translations, to be sung to the same tunes as their accustomed Old Version psalm texts, can only have added to the frustration and confusion of the common people in the pews. John Cotton published his treatise, *Singing of Psalmes a Gospel-Ordinance*, suggesting the temporary implementation of a custom that had evidently originated in Scotland, whereby a deacon or precentor read the psalm text out, line by line, as the congregation sang.[16] Cotton was not especially enthusiastic about the idea, but he was willing to tolerate lining out the psalms as a temporary expedient. He wrote:

William Godbid, 1655),

[14] Henry Dunster, *The Psalms Hymns and Spiritual Songs of the Old & New Testament: Faithfully Translated into English Metre* (Boston: B. Green and J. Allen, 1698). For a list of tunes, facsimiles, and discussion, see Richard G. Appel, *The Music of the Bay Psalm Book* (Brooklyn: I.S.A.M. Monographs, 1975). On Playford, see also Charles Edward Lindsley, "Scoring and Placement of the 'Air' in Early American Tunebooks," *Musical Quarterly* 58/3 (July 1972): 365–82. Irving Lowens, "The Bay Psalm Book in 17th Century New England," *Music and Musicians in Early America* (New York: Norton, 1964) 36–38 suggested that an earlier edition, possibly an unknown sixth or seventh edition published in London by Chiswell, also contained tunes.

[15] Things had deteriorated even earlier in England. Este was claiming as early as 1594 that most congregations sang psalms to but four tunes (see Temperley, *The Music of the English Parish Church*, 68).

[16] John Cotton, *Singing of Psalmes a Gospel-Ordinance* (London: Printed by M. S. for Hannah Allen, 1647).

It will be a necessary helpe, that the wordes of the *Psalme* be openly read before hand, line after line, or two lines together, that so they who want either books or skill to reade, may know what is to be sung, and joyne with the rest in the dutie of singing....

We for our parts easily grant, that where all have books and can read, or else can say the *Psalme* by heart, it were needlesse there to read each line of the *Psalme* before hand in order to sing.[17]

In practice, the actual lining out varied among congregations. In some, the deacon or minister read the psalm line by line and a strong-voiced precentor "raised the tune," followed by the congregation. In other churches, the text and tune were lined out together, the congregation repeating each line. Or the deacon might read each line and then raise the tune with the congregation.[18] In any

---

[17] On lining out, see Foote, *Three Centuries of American Hymnody*, 370–82. The practice appeared about the same time in England and for the same reasons; see Nicholas Temperley, "John Playford and the Metrical Psalms," *Journal of the American Musicological Society* 25/3 (Fall 1972): 331–78. It is worth noting that in the service, the psalm was usually read in prose and expounded on by the minister before the congregation sang it. Ainsworth's Psalter, it will be recalled, printed the prose and metrical versions side by side, as well as a comment below on the page. Temperley, *The Music of the English Parish Church*, 82 notes that lining out would also facilitate the learning of a new translation of the psalms, such as the more faithful but nevertheless unfamiliar translations of the Bay Psalm Book.

[18] See *The Diary of Samuel Sewall, 1674–1729*, 3 vols. (vols. 4–7), Collections of the Massachusetts Historical Society, series 5 (Boston: Massachusetts Historical Society, 1878–1882) 6:39. "This day I set Windsor Tune..." and Foote, *Three Centuries of American Hymnody*, 374–86; also Scholes, *The Puritans and Music*, 262–65. For an especially illuminating commentary on the musical data in Sewall's diary, see David W. Music, "The Diary of Samuel Sewall and Congregational Singing in Early New England," *The Hymn* 41/1 (January 1990): 7–15. See also David McKay and Richard Crawford, *William Billings of Boston* (Princeton: Princeton University Press, 1975) 13. Especially valuable is Alan Clark Buechner, *Yankee Singing Schools and the Golden Age of Choral Music in New England, 1760–1800* (Boston: Boston University, 2003) 17–40. Allen P. Britton, "Theoretical Introductions in American Tune-Books to 1800" (Ph.D. diss., Michigan, 1949) 83–84, distinguishes between lining out and setting the tune, and remarks that the latter practice was English and came into use

case, as happens so often the temporary and expedient became a tradition and custom. Only a few relatively educated and sophisticated urban congregations were able to dispense with it.

Lining out was by no means restricted to New England; the practice could be found, for instance, in New Amsterdam's Dutch Reformed churches. But among New England congregations, it is worth noting that the practice seems to have been related to the use of the Bay Psalm Book. For instance, the Brattle Square Church, which adopted the Tate and Brady Psalter, or New Version, shortly after its founding in 1698/1699, seems never to have adopted the practice of lining out.[19]

The New Version

Outside of New England and in the Anglican churches, the Bay Psalm Book gained no real foothold. Scottish and Ulster immigrants in the Middle Colonies held to their own Scottish Psalter of 1635. In English churches, the Old Version remained in use. In 1696, Nahum Tate and Nicholas Brady published their *New Version of the Psalms of David, Fitted to Tunes Used in Churches* in London. Several Colonial Anglican congregations, many of them founded only recently, adopted this New Version, among them Trinity Church in New York (1707) and King's Chapel in Boston (1713). The Puritans of New England and the Scottish Presbyterians regarded the elegant, but far less strict, translations in the New Version as dangerously close to paraphrase, although a few of the more liberal Puritan congregations, notably Boston's Brattle Square Church, which was founded shortly after the New Version appeared, chose it over the scrupulously accurate but hard-edged translations in the Bay Psalm Book. For example, the New Version translation of Psalm 8 is in common meter, like the Old Version and Bay Psalm Book

---

in America toward the end of the eighteenth century.

[19] In passing, the conservative ministers of Boston regarded Brattle Street as dangerously close to Anglicanism. Their suspicions can only have been confirmed by that congregation's refusal to adopt the practice of lining out and its rejection of the Bay Psalm Book in favor of Tate and Brady's far less literal New Version, favored by Anglican congregations.

translations above. The translators have taken minor liberties with the text; however, the poetry is somehow more fluid, graceful, and even personal.

> O Thou, to whom all creatures bow
> within this earthly frame,
> Through all the world how great art Thou!
> How glorious is Thy name.

Whatever the ministers of Boston might have thought of it, the New Version was well received by Anglican congregations in America, to say nothing of England. Several musical supplements were printed from 1700 on, and many of its graceful verses gained a permanent place in the standard hymn repertoire, for instance William Croft's "St. Anne."[20]

Regular Singing

Most of the ministers in late seventeenth- and early eighteenth-century New England would regard the deterioration of psalm singing in the churches as one sign of the degraded state to which the colony had sunk and a portent of greater evil to come. The children and grandchildren of the colony's venerable founders had lost their forbears' zeal, as the ministers never ceased to remind their congregations, lamenting and exhorting from their pulpits in sermons they called Jeremiads, after the model of the Old Testament prophet.

As if to underscore the fears and warnings, New England's Indians rose up in 1675/1676 to raid outlying settlements in a firestorm that has come to be known as King Philip's War. In 1684, London revoked the Bay Colony's charter so that other religious groups, especially the dreaded Church of England, could now intrude upon the sacred precincts of the original Puritan founders' "city upon

---

[20] NicholasBrady and Nahum Tate, *Supplement to the New Version* (London: Printed by John Nutt, 1708) no. 18. See W. Thomas Marrocco and Harold Gleason, *Music in America* (New York: Norton, 1964) 21–22. See also Crawford, *The Core Repertory of Early American Psalmody*, 11, 12.

a hill." Possibly worst of all from the ministers' perspective, the devil himself seemed to be taking advantage of the situation and invading the Puritans' Godly Commonwealth, when in 1692, several hysterical young girls in an outlying village of Salem, north of Boston, began to cry out against women they claimed were tormenting them by witchcraft. In such things, the ministers of New England discern the signs of God's displeasure, and many began to fear that God was at last turning his face against that Commonwealth.

Psalm singing in the churches of Massachusetts had been on the decline since mid-century. North of Boston, the Salem church had given up on the Ainsworth and adopted the Bay Psalm Book in 1667, not because of the latter's scriptural fidelity, but because of "the difficulty of the tunes and because we could not singe them so well as formerly." South of Boston, the Plymouth colonists had held out a good bit longer against the adoption of the Bay Psalm Book and continued to sing their psalms to Ainsworth's complex meters and melodies without the need for lining out. But on 17 May 1685, the elders decided to sing another version of Psalm 130 because the Ainsworth "tune was soe difficult few could follow it." Seven years later, on 19 June 1692, the congregation finally decided to abandon Ainsworth because it "had such difficult tunes as none in the church could sett," and on 7 August, the church ratified its previous decision, voting that "wee should sing the Psalmes now in use in the neighbour-churches in the Bay."[21]

Put simply, the problem was that most congregations in New England and indeed, the English-speaking colonies, now used but a few tunes that they sang line by line as the deacon gave out the psalm text. Individual singers in the congregation moved at their own speed, coming together only at the beginning and end of lines. Precentors and some singers improvised their own turns and ornaments to fill leaps in the melodic line, and at the ends of lines and verses as they waited for slower members of the congregation to catch up. Minister Thomas Symmes called attention to the problem

---

[21] Robert Stevenson, *Protestant Church Music in America* (New York: W. W. Norton, 1966) 13–14.

in his 1721 pamphlet *The Reasonableness of Singing*: "Most [notes are] too *long*, and many *Turnings of*, or *Flourishes with* the Voice, (as they call them) are made where they should not be, and some are wanting where they should have been."[22] Two years later, he described the deplorable state of singing in his treatise *Utile Dulci*:

> Some affect a quavering flourish on one note, and others upon another which…they account a grace to the tune; and while some affect a quicker motion, others affect a slower and drawl out their notes beyond all reason….
>
> Tunes that are already in use in our Churches; which, when they first came out of the Hands of the Composers of them, were sung according to the Rules of the *Scale of Musick*…are now miserably tortured, and twisted, and quavered, in some Churches, into an horrid medley of confused and disordered *Noises*…. Yea, I have my self heard (for Instance) *Oxford* Tune sung in three Churches…with as much difference as there can possibly be between *York* and *Oxford*, or any two other different Tunes.[23]

A modern ethnomusicologist might see such a singing style as a genuine folk tradition in which the tunes were treated, consciously or unconsciously, in Stevenson's words, "as mere melody-types that…could be embellished at will, and transform the psalmody into song tunes."[24] More to the point, the ministers themselves could have argued with a good bit of consistency that such a singing style was

---

[22] Symmes, *The Reasonableness of Regular Singing*, 10.

[23] Thomas Symmes, *Utile Dulci, or A Joco Serious Dialogue Concerning Regular Singing* (Boston: B. Green for S. Gerrish, 1723) 17; Thomas Walter, *The Grounds and Rules of Musick Explained: or An Introduction to the Art of Singing by Note Fitted to the Meanest Capacities* (Boston: J. Franklin for S. Gerrish, 1721) 3.

[24] Stevenson, *Protestant Church Music in America*, 22. Stevenson cites Thomas Symmes's *Utile Dulci*, 44: "*Most* of the *Psalm-Tunes* as Sung in the *Usual Way*, are much more like Song-tunes, than as Sung by Rule." On the issue of a folk practice, see Britton, "Theoretical Introductions," 86–88; and McKay and Crawford, *William Billings*, 14–15.

proper for a theological system that valued individual existential praise and that organized, harmonious congregational singing veered rather closely toward the shoals of unreformed ritualism. Except for a dissenting voice here and there, primarily from rural ministers like the Reverend Samuel Niles of South Braintree, they did not.

For whatever reason, most of New England's ministers, and virtually all the prominent ones in Boston, chose to ignore such theological implications. On the contrary, they went so far as to condemn the freedom of the so-called "usual style'" as a departure from the orthodox tradition of the tunes as handed down and as a lapse into the heterodoxy of individual and uneducated interpretation. As one of them wrote, "Our *Psalmody* has suffered the like Inconveniences which our *Faith* has laboured under, in case it had been committed and trusted to the uncertain and doubtful Conveyance of *Oral Tradition*."[25]

It is difficult to assess the influence on at least some of the New England clergy that the recently established Anglican churches nearby might have had. Places like King's Chapel with New Version psalmody were growing, and much of their growth was at the expense of the older Puritan churches. There had long been Anglican churches to the south of New England, of course, but the New England clergy were well aware of the vast differences between their own settled ministries and the itinerant Anglican clergy of Virginia, who more often than not served at the pleasure of rural vestries among whose churches they circulated.

Secure in their parsonages, the Puritan clergy preached to congregations whose homes were usually clustered within a half-mile or so of the meetinghouse, and midweek services as well as Sunday ones were usual. In Virginia, on the other hand, Anglican ministers had read prayers and sermons to plantation folk who were dispersed over wide distances from the church and who often attended worship once or twice a month, rather than once or twice a week as in New

---

[25] Walter, *Grounds and Rules*, 3. In *William Billings*, McKay and Crawford suggest that "usual" style singing may have verged too close to secular practice for their taste (15).

England. The New England ministers, Harvard- and Yale-educated, knew they constituted a social aristocracy of sorts, whereas the ministers of Virginia were essentially servants to a planter aristocracy.

When it came to psalmody, the ministers of New England knew and could demonstrate from scripture that psalmody was—in Cotton's words—"a Gospel ordinance." In the rural churches of Anglican Virginia, sung psalmody had heretofore more often been an option than an ordinance. In some places, it was done more or less adequately; in many, it was not done at all. Instead, the psalms were read out of a book, as were the appointed scripture readings, prayers, and sometimes even the sermons. The Anglican clergy, lacking anything like the power and influence of the Puritan clergy to their north, could do nothing about congregational psalm singing, if indeed they even noticed or cared.

Yet around the turn of the century, some of these very parishes had begun importing psalm books and singing teachers from London, almost certainly to help teach their congregations the New Version psalmody.[26] In Virginia during December 1710, William Byrd II was given a book each for himself and his wife and shortly thereafter quarreled with her "about learning to sing Psalms." But ten days later, "we began to give in to the new way of singing Psalms."[27]

We cannot know if the ministers of New England took their cue from the established churches in their own backyard, let alone in Virginia. On one hand, they would certainly have given no consideration to emulating King's Chapel, which in 1714 became the first church in the colonies to make regular use of an organ to improve congregational singing. But few, if any, could have objected to the idea of engaging a singing teacher to improve congregational psalmody. In 1720, Thomas Symmes (1678–1725), minister in the town of Bradford, north of Boston, published *The Reasonableness of Regular Singing, or Singing by Note*.[28] In his pamphlet, Symmes

---

[26] Nicholas Temperley, "The Old Way of Singing," *Journal of the American Musicological Society* 34/3 (Fall 1981): 538.

[27] William Byrd II, *The Secret Diary of William Byrd of Westover 1709–1712* (Richmond: Dietz, 1941) 272, 276.

28 Thomas Symmes, *The Reasonableness of Regular Singing, or Singing by Note*

affirmed yet again that the singing of psalms was commanded by the Bible, observing that music had been part of the Harvard curriculum from the first. Yet, he lamented, psalm singing had of late fallen on bad days. Worse, there was resistance within most congregations to any *"Reformation in their Singing"* admittedly arising most often from *"Misapprehensions & Mistakes* [among] honest and well-meaning" members.

Symmes went on to answer several of the most usual objections, among them that "papists" sang by note and that such regular practice corrupted young people, who would become "too light, profane and airy while they are learning the Tunes." His solution to the problem was the promotion of formal singing schools and teachers. "People that want *Skill* in *Singing*, would procure a *Skillful Person* to *Instruct* them, and meet *Two* or *Three* Evenings in the Week, from *five* or *six* a Clock, to *Eight*, and spend the Time in Learning to Sing. Would not this be an innocent and profitable *Recreation?*"

In fact, Boston had its first singing school in 1714, and not long after, the battle for regular singing was joined by no less a personage than Cotton Mather (1663–1728), Boston's leading clergyman. In 1717 he had to dispense with a psalm in domestic devotions, "so indifferent at singing" had his household become.[29] Nor was the singing much better among his congregants at Boston's largest church, the Second or North Church. As if justifying the singing school begun in the parish, he wrote in his 13 March 1721 entry: "Should not something be done towards mending the *Singing* in our Congregation?" Evidently, the school's results were less than he had anticipated, for on 5 June, he wrote again, "I must of Necessity do something that the Exercise of *Singing* in the sacred *Psalms* in the flock may be made more beautiful."[30]

(Boston: B. Green for S. Gerrish, 1720) under the pseudonym, 'Philomusicus.' The text may be found in Hood, *A History of Music in New England*, 91–104. See also Britton, "Theoretical Introductions," 96–100.

[29] Kenneth Silverman, *The Life and Times of Cotton Mather* (New York: Columbia, 1985) 305.

[30] Cotton Mather, *Diary of Cotton Mather 1709–1724*, vol. 8 of Massachusetts

That year he published his pamphlet *The Accomplished Singer*. In it, Mather threw all the authority and prestige of his position behind the cause of improved congregational singing by means of training in the "rules" of music, characterizing such Regular Singing as all but divinely ordained. He wrote:

> The Skill of *Regular Singing* is among the *Gifts* of GOD unto the Children of Men, and by no means unthankfully to be Neglected or Despised. For the Congregations, wherein 'tis wanting, to recover a *Regular Singing*, would be really a *Reformation* and a Recovery out of an *Apostacy*, and what we may judge that Heaven would be pleased withal. We ought certainly to Serve our GOD with our *Best*, and *Regular Singing* must needs be better than the confused Noise of a Wilderness.

As to any objections that the notes to be used in the Regular Singing of psalms were the same as those used by the Roman Catholics, Mather replied, "And what if they were? Our *Psalms* too are used there."[31] By 1722, a Society for Promoting Regular Singing had been established in Boston. On 1 October 1723, Reverend Joseph Green wrote approvingly of "ye delightful exercise of singing performed at the New Brick Church...only by ye masters of it, viz. men and women seated in the front Gallery."[32] But a few ministers and laymen, mostly from rural congregations, put up a spirited resistance, occasionally referring to the solidly Calvinistic theological basis that undergirded the Usual Way. As one correspondent wrote to the *New*

Historical Society Collections, series 7 (Boston: Massachusetts Historical Society, 1912) 560, 660.

[31] Cotton Mather, *The Accomplished Singer...How the Melody of Regular Singing, and the Skill of Doing It, according to the Rules of It, May Be Easily Arrived Unto* (Boston: B. Green for S. Gerrish, 1721). An excerpt may be found in Perry Miller and Thomas H. Johnson, eds., *The Puritans* (New York: Harper & Row, 1963) 452–53.

[32] Quoted in Nicholas Tawa, *From Psalm to Symphony: A History of Music in New England* (Boston: Northeastern University Press, 2001) 28–29.

England Chronicle in 1723, "Truly I have a great jealousy that if we once begin to sing by rule, the next thing will be to pray by rule, and preach by rule; and then comes popery."[33]

Other objections were made on the grounds of custom, and feelings ran high. In a letter to Thomas Bradbury dated 22 April 1724, Mather referred to a "Little Crue at a Town Ten miles from the City of Boston...sett upon their old Howling in the public Psalmody, that being rebuked for the Disturbance they made, by the more Numerous Regular Singers, they declared They would be for the Ch[urch] of E[ngland] and would form a little assembly for that purpose." Mather was almost certainly talking about the Reverend Samuel Niles's South Braintree congregation, where—as *The New England Courant* for 10 February 1724 reported—twenty "opposers of Regular Singing...have publicly declared for the Church of England."[34] Their indignation may have been heightened by Thomas Symmes's *Utili Dulci*, published in 1723. Symmes cast his pamphlet in the form of a humorous dialogue between a minister and his "neighbor." Among other things, Symmes ridiculed his opposition by abbreviating the characterization Anti-Regular Singers as "ARSes."[35]

The Regular Singing movement and singing schools caught on quickly in some places. Jonathan Edwards wrote of his Northampton congregation's singing during the Great Awakening, beginning in 1734, that they carried "regularly and well, three parts of music, and the women a part by themselves."[36] In Worcester, on the other hand, not until August 1779 did the congregation finally vote to drop lining out, at the same time seating the singing school class not in the

---

[33] Quoted in Foote, *Three Centuries of American Hymnody*, 383. The letter is dated 20 March 1722 and signed by one Ephraim Rotewell.

[34] Mather, *Diary*, ser. 7, vol. 8, p. 796–97. See also Foote, *Three Centuries of American Hymnody*, 383–86; Stevenson, *Protestant Church Music in America*, 23; and Ellinwood, *History of American Church Music*, 21. The absurdity of deserting to the prescribed ritual of the Prayer Book to avoid Regular singing scarcely needs to be pointed out.

[35] See Irving Lowens, "Music in the American Wilderness," *Music and Musicians in Early America*, 19.

[36] Ellinwood, *History of American Church Music*, 25.

congregation, but together in a front gallery. The next Sunday, the deacon read out the first line as usual; however, the singers continued without pause and in parts. The poor man at first tried to shout the next line over the din, but became so mortified that he left the church in tears.[37]

Singing Schools

Singing schools became widespread after 1720 partially because they provided young people a social outlet. The schools sometimes met in the local schoolhouse, but were most often held in local taverns, the community center of the time where people socialized and swapped news.[38] Most made use of one or the other of two books. The *Boston News-Letter* for 2–9 January 1721 carried a notice by Samuel Gerrish, a Boston bookseller: "A Small Book containing 20 Psalm Tunes with Directions how to Sing them, contrived in the most easy Method ever yet Invented…[and] may serve as an Introduction to a more Compleat Treatise for Singing which will Speedily be published."[39]

John Tufts (1698–1750) was a first cousin of Cotton Mather and minister of the church in Newburyport. Like similar manuals that would follow over the next century or more, his 1721 publication, *An Introduction to the Singing of Psalm-Tunes, In a Plain & Easy Method*…began with an explanation of the rudiments of singing, musical notation, intervals, scales, and time. The tunes that followed were printed in three voice parts, as they appeared in John Playford's *Whole Book of Psalms* of 1677, and included Playford's syllable letters along with dots indicating the duration of each note.[40] Tufts's book,

---

[37] Ralph T. Daniel, *The Anthem in New England Before 1800* (Evanston: Northwestern, 1966; repr. New York: DaCapo, 1979) 16–17. By 1775 only the Scottish and Scotch-Irish, who emigrated from about 1720 and settled away from the cosmopolitan urban centers along the seaboard, clung to the custom of the deacon lining out with a clerk to "raise the tune."

[38] Stanley R. McDaniel, "Church Song and the Cultivated Tradition in New England and New York" (DMA diss., University of Southern California, 1983) 54–73.

[39] See Irving Lowens, "The First American Music Textbook," *Music and Musicians in Early America*, 39–57.

[40] To date, the earliest known is a copy of the third edition, in the library of

measuring three by five inches or so, was often bound with copies of the Bay Psalm Book. It was reissued in eleven editions, to 1744.

In July 1721 Gerrish issued his "more Compleat Treatise" titled *The Grounds and Rules of Musick Explained: Or An Introduction to the Art of Singing.*[41] It was prepared by Thomas Walter (1696–1725), assistant minister at his father's church in Roxbury. Walter was a nephew of Cotton Mather. His grandfather, the venerable and highly respected dean of Boston's ministers, was Increase Mather. The elder Mather added his seal of approbation to the collection by signing its "Recommendatory Preface" along with thirteen of Boston's other prominent ministers. It contained an introductory essay on music rudiments and sixteen pages of three-part music. The psalm tunes were printed in the middle voice accompanied by a bass part below and a countermelody above. Walter's *Grounds and Rules* remained in use for the next forty years. Indeed, except for a handful of American publications and a few imported collections from England, the manuals of Tufts and Walter held a virtual monopoly in the New England singing school movement for American singing schools for about fifty years. To the point, Walter's format of instructional essay followed by the music itself became a model for numerous compilations and manuals that began appearing in the late 1700s.

It seems clear that by supporting the institution of singing schools, New England's ministers expected that young people from their congregation, having been taught psalmody in a singing school organized in their town or church, would return to their assigned places in the congregation and lead others with their singing. Things did not work out in quite the manner the ministers anticipated, for singers frequently insisted on sitting together in their own pew, or gallery. In effect, singing school classes became choirs, an institution

---

Pittsburgh Theological Seminary. This edition has tunes in two, rather than three voices, and it is evident from Gerrish's notices, quoted in Lowens, "The First American Music Textbook," that the first and second editions, now apparently lost, had tunes only. See Allen Perdue Britton, Irving Lowens, and Richard Crawford, *American Sacred Music Imprints before 1810* (Worcester MA: American Antiquarian Society, 1991) 584–86.

[41] Symmes, *The Reasonableness of Regular Singing*, 18.

particularly abhorrent to strict Puritan sensibilities. The controversy surrounding choirs, along with its ramifications, properly belongs in a subsequent chapter. For the moment, however, it is well to bear in mind that the seeds of that controversy were inadvertently sowed and nurtured by the singing school movement, even though that movement had been intended solely as a means of improving congregational psalmody.

The first issue that surfaced in regard to these incipient choirs was the matter of seating. Colonial churches were generally "seated" each year; that is, each worshiper was assigned a particular seat, determined in accordance with social or perceived spiritual status in the community. Those who were most successful financially, politically prominent, venerable because of great age, or especially exemplary in conduct (and therefore most likely to be among the "elect") were allocated the best pews. The younger, less prominent, less successful, and so on were assigned less desirable places. Moreover, men were generally seated apart from the women and children. Clearly, neither of these patterns could be maintained if the singers—of different sexes, ages, and social status—were to be allowed to sit together.

The second issue was more subtle, but it was also more significant: a phenomenon that might properly be characterized as the destabilization of traditional Puritan ministerial authority, at least as perceived by the congregation. Briefly, the traditional Puritan image of "God's schoolhouse"—with the minister as teacher standing in the sole position of leadership authority over the congregation of passive pupils, who are seated as directed, listening, and even taking notes during his sermon—would be offset by a competing group of singer-teachers, who are seated together in their own pew and sharing leadership in the process of worship. Surely Cotton Mather and his fellow Boston ministers, secure in their status as an intellectual aristocracy, would have been far less enthusiastic about the singing school movement—and possibly far more willing to heed the concerns of their colleague Samuel Niles regarding the theological superiority of singing in the "usual" way, however untidy its musical effects—had they foreseen the unintended cultural consequences of regular singing.

2.

Choirs, Anthems, and Tunesmiths

In a sense, the early eighteenth century marked the weakening of ministerial power and the displacement of the ministers' intellectual aristocracy as the primary influence in New England culture and society. To be sure, the orthodox Puritan clergy resisted the trend, but the spirit and events of the era were arrayed against them. Theologically, they were whipsawed by pietism on one side and the rationalism of the Enlightenment on the other. Among members of their educated class, earthly concerns were displacing spiritual ones. Whereas thoughtful men and women of the seventeenth century debated issues of soul and salvation, those of the eighteenth century debated issues of government and economics. Culturally, the exclusive place of honor the ministers had held in New England society came to be shared with prominent men of commerce, the law, and politics.

Music, of course, was not a cause of this shift, or even a contributing factor, but it was surely one of many signs of underlying ferment. More to the point, musical developments of the era and the controversies that boiled around them serve as a perspective from which we may view the changing culture of New England's churches. A salient element was that the singing school class maintained its identity within the parish rather than dispersing back into assigned seats in the congregation once the singing school ended. By the middle of the eighteenth century, singers were being seated together as a choir in their own special pew, often in the gallery. As such, they constituted a visible shift in the ritual control of worship that had heretofore been exercised exclusively by the ministers.

The singers generally arranged themselves not by vocal part, but rather by age, with younger singers at the ends and older ones in the center. In some cases, the front row stood and turned to face the back row when it came time to sing. In other cases, the singers were seated in a square pew around the table that held their singing books. Since men almost always outnumbered women in the group, they sang the melody, which music books of the era printed in the tenor voice, as well as the alto and bass parts. The women joined the tenors singing the melody, doubling at the octave. If there was a fourth voice, the treble, some of the women and children (if there were any) would sing it, with a few men doubling an octave lower.[1]

During the years before 1760, successive editions of Tufts's *Introduction* and especially Walter's *Grounds and Rules* were printed, but little else by way of books for Colonial singing schools and choirs beyond a handful of compilations by other men. Two collections of psalm tunes, similar in style to Tufts's and meant to be bound with metrical Psalters, appeared in Boston. James Turner (d.1759) issued an untitled supplement of forty-nine three-voice pieces in 1752. Thomas Johnston's similarly untitled collection of fifty-one three-voice tunes first appeared in 1755 and was reissued until 1767. As usual for the era, the melody or "air" was placed in the tenor. The two other parts supplied block harmony, over and under the melody.[2] In practice, the air in the tenor could be sung alone, or the tenor and bass only could be sung, the air being accompanied by the implied

---

[1] Stanley R. McDaniel, "Church Song and the Cultivated Tradition in New England and New York" (DMA diss., University of Southern California, 1983) 54–73.

[2] Allen Perdue Britton, Irving Lowens, and Richard Crawford, *American Sacred Music Imprints before 1810* (Worcester: American Antiquarian Society, 1991) 104–105, 242–43, 590–91, 374–79 (hereafter cited as *ASMI*). In addition to works cited herein, this chapter, like similar works on the subject, relies heavily on Allen Perdue Britton's landmark study, "Theoretical Introductions in American Tune-Books" (Ph.D. diss., University of Michigan, 1949).

harmony of the bass underneath. The uppermost part was essentially a countermelody to the air.

The Great Awakening, Watts, and the Wesleys

Even as the repertoire of tunes increased, the exclusive status of metrical psalm texts in congregational worship diminished. The principal cause—or at least the occasion—for this was a wave of religious fervor, mirroring the rise of pietism in Europe. The movement in America reached its height in the Great Awakening of the 1730s and 1740s; however, it continued to smolder in rural areas. Maine and Nova Scotia underwent a period of revival as late as the Revolutionary War (1776–1783). Pietism focused on individual response and personal emotion. Preaching exhorted listeners about their souls' health, as opposed to the traditional Puritan sermon with its systematic and carefully structured exposition, interpretation, and application of a particular scripture passage on the one hand, and the rationalism of the newly fashionable Enlightenment on the other.[3]

From the first, congregational song played a major role in the revivals. In fact, revival and hymnody were synergistic. The emotional and personal exhortations of the New Light preachers did not lend themselves to the sort of scripture-based metrical psalmody associated with the tightly reasoned scriptural expositions of the so-called Old Light orthodox ministers.[4] The first great revivalist

---

[3] Alan Clark Buechner, *Yankee Singing Schools and the Golden Age of Choral Music in New England, 1760–1800* (Ph.D. diss., Harvard, 1960) 41; Joanne Grayeski Weiss, "The Relationship Between the 'Great Awakening' and the Transition from Psalmody to Hymnody in the New England Colonies" (DA diss., Ball State, 1988) puts the case persuasively that the rapid adoption of Watts's texts in America, even by anti-revival Old Light Congregational and Old Side Presbyterian congregations, was part of a change implicit in the Great Awakening itself from the rigid theocentrism of Puritan theology and worship to a new spirit of anthropocentrism.

[4] See George Hood, *A History of Music in New England* (Boston: Wilkins, Carter, 1846; repr., New York: Johnson, 1970) 138–39. In fact, two constant complaints against the revivals were that there was too much singing at the meetings, and that the singing was "hymns of human composure," rather than psalms. For a political context and perspective, see Rochelle A. Stackouse, "Hymnody and Politics: Isaac Watts's 'O God Our Help in Ages Past' and Timothy Dwight's 'I Love Thy

George Whitefield (1714–1770) brought with him from England hymns by Isaac Watts (1674–1748), which were set in the usual meters and therefore usable with the very tunes congregations were accustomed to sing metrical psalms. A friend of John (1703–1791) and Charles Wesley (1707–1788) from student years at Oxford, Whitefield also introduced their *Hymns and Sacred Poems*.[5] Though the collection was reprinted a year later in Philadelphia, Whitefield preferred the restrained texts of Watts to the more personal and emotional poems of the Wesleys. Indeed, nearly half the hymns in John Wesley's earlier collection *A Collection of Psalms and Hymns*,[6] published during his brief stay in America, between early 1736 and late 1737, were by Watts.[7]

Watts, the pastor of an independent London congregation, had published two collections for congregation's use.[8] The twenty-two texts in *Hymns and Spiritual Songs*[9] were in the usual meters and thus fit tunes the people already knew and sang. In Boston, no less a personage than Cotton Mather endorsed them and used them in his own family's devotions, as he assured Watts. In fact, Mather was in likelihood instrumental in having *Hymns and Spiritual Songs* reprinted in Boston in 1720. But Mather withdrew his approbation from the next set of texts Watts sent him from London, together with a letter dated 17 March 1717/1718. "Tis not a translation of David I pretend;

Kingdom, Lord,'" in *Wonderful Words of Life: Hymns in American Protestant History and Theology*, ed. Richard J. Mouw and Mark A. Noll (Grand Rapids: Eerdmans, 2004) 42–66.

[5] John Wesley and Charles Wesley, *Hymns and Sacred Poems* (London: Printed by W. Strahan, 1739)

[6] John Welsey, *A Collection of Psalms and Hymns* (Charleston: Lewis Timothy, 1737).

[58] On hymnody during Wesley's America period, see David W. Stowe, *How Sweet the Sound: Music in the Spiritual Lives of Americans* (Cambridge: Harvard University Press, 2004) 17–30.

[8] An earlier work, Isaac Watts, *Horae Lyricae* (London: Printed by S. and D. Bridge for J. Lawrence, 1706) was essentially a literary endeavor and not intended for use in worship. None of its contents appear in the later publications.

[9] Isaac Watts, *Hymns and Spiritual Songs* (London: J. Humphreys for John Lawrence, 1707).

but an imitation of him so nearly in Christian hymns…. If I may be so happy as to have your free censure and judgment of 'em it will help me in correcting others by them. I entreat you, Sir, that none of them may steal out into public."[10]

Psalms of David Imitated in the Language of the New Testament appeared in 1719. Watts clearly intended them for congregational use in worship. The texts were intended to invoke more piety and personal relevance for congregations by paraphrasing the psalms and infusing them with New Testament doctrines and Christian contexts in a graceful and engaging style. His setting of Psalm 8 may be compared with the earlier translations:

> O Lord, our Lord, how wondrous great
> Is thine exalted name!
> The glories of thy heav'nly state
> Let men and babes proclaim.

But Old Lights like Mather bristled at the liberties Watts took in such conflating of the Old and New Testament as occurs in the fourth and fifth verses, to say nothing of the imagery:

> That thine eternal son should bear
> To take a mortal form;
> Made lower than his angels are
> To save a dying worm

> Yet while He lived on earth unknown,
> And man would not adore,
> The obedient seas and fishes own
> His godhead and His power.

Mather, who viewed the Old Testament, including the psalms, as containing essential prophecies of Christ, deplored the collection

---

[10] Hood, *A History of Music in New England*, 155.

as lacking "any Air of the Old Testament."[11] In 1718, doubtless by way of response to the advance texts Watts had sent him, he had published his own 464-page *Psalterium Americanum* containing a set of translations in blank verse "fitted to the *Tunes* commonly used in the Assemblies of our *Zion*."

Mather's Psalter did not gain much of a following, nor, for that matter, did an edition of Watts's *Psalms of David Imitated* reprinted by Benjamin Franklin in Philadelphia in 1729. Franklin complained of the number of copies remaining on his shelves for several years, but the Watts texts quickly gained favor with many congregations, and by 1741, Franklin was able to publish another edition of Watts's hymns at a profit. That same year Jonathan Edwards ordered an edition of Watts's *Psalms of David Imitated* to be printed in Boston for use alongside the Bay Psalm Book in his Northampton church. So popular did the new texts become that, much to his dismay, Edwards found on his return from a journey the next year that his congregation had begun using only Watts.

Other churches introduced Watts's texts alongside their usual psalmody. Brattle Square Church in Boston, where there was little sympathy for the revival, printed an *Appendix, Containing a Number of Hymns, Taken Chiefly from Dr. Watts's Scriptural Collection* for their New Version Psalter. Similarly, Boston's Old South Church allowed its pastor, Thomas Prince, to revise and supplement the Bay Psalm Book they used in 1758. Prince's *The Psalms, Hymns, and Spiritual Songs, of the Old and New Testaments, Faithfully Translated...Revised and Improved with an Addition of Fifty other Hymns* included forty-two texts by Watts.[12]

The conservative Consistory of New York's Dutch Reformed Church, where as late as 1764 the only source for congregational psalmody had been Datheen's Dutch translation of the Genevan Psalter, commissioned the prominent Philadelphia lawyer and

---

[11] Kenneth Silverman, *The Life and Times of Cotton Mather* (New York: Columbia, 1985) 304. On Mather and Watts, see Henry Wilder Foote, *Three Centuries of American Hymnody* (Cambridge: Harvard, 1940; repr. Hamden: Shoe String, 1961) 50–68.

[12] Weiss, "The Relationship," 145, 162–64.

amateur musician Francis Hopkinson (1737–1791) to prepare an English-language Psalter whose texts could be sung by English speaking worshipers along with, and to the same tunes as, Datheen's texts.

The problem, of course, was that the Genevan Psalter texts were in a larger variety of meters than Hopkinson, who was used to the Tate and Brady New Version, had probably anticipated. In the event, Hopkinson's 479-page *The Psalms of David...For the Use of the Reformed Protestant Dutch Church of the City of New York*[13] actually turned out to be an adaptation of New Version texts to Dutch psalm tunes, although not necessarily the particular tunes to which the corresponding psalms in Dutch were sung.[14] Given the problems Hopkinson must have encountered and the not altogether satisfactory results he achieved, it is not surprising that Watts's texts all but displaced strict metrical psalms among New York's English speaking Reformed by the last decade of the century. In 1794, Henry Wansey, a traveler from Britain and himself a Unitarian, recorded his impressions of the English-language service he had attended at the North Church on 1 June 1794: "In the afternoon I went to hear Dr [William] Lynn at the Dutch Reformed Church: this is a large handsome meeting house, with an organ in the gallery.... They use Dr. Watts's Psalms mixed with some others of Heidelburgh composition."[15]

As may be imagined, the introduction of new texts for congregational singing provoked wide controversy. During his brief and unsuccessful ministry in Georgia, John Wesley produced *A*

---

[13] Francis Hopkinson, *The Psalms of David...For the Use of the Reformed Protestant Dutch Church of the City of New York* (New York: James Parker, 1767).

[14] See Daniel Meeter, "Genevan Jigsaw: The Tunes of the New-York Psalmbook of 1761," in *Ars et Musica in Liturgia: Essays Presented to Casper Honders on His Seventieth Birthday*, ed. Frans Brouwer and Robin A. Leaver (Metuchen NJ: Scarecrow, 1994) 150–66. Hopkinson was paid £145 for his efforts.

[15] Henry Wansey, *The Journal of an Excursion to the United States of North America in the Summer of 1794*, repr. (New York: Johnson, 1969) 84–85. The term "Heidelburgh" is a reference to the Datheen Psalter in use by New York churches at the time. Petrus Dathenus (1531–1588) had translated the Geneva Psalter into Dutch during the 1560s while ministering to the Dutch Reformed exiles in Heidelberg.

Collection of Psalms and Hymns.[16] The collection contained fourteen "psalms" by Watts and five of Wesley's own translations of German hymn texts. In late August 1737, Wesley was summoned before a Grand Jury in Savannah to answer for "changing...the version of the Psalms publicly authorized to be sung in the church" and "introducing...psalms and hymns...not inspected or authorized."[17]

Fifty years later, in 1783, there appeared a thirty-three-page pamphlet by a conservative Albany minister, the Reverend Thomas Clark, titled *Plain Reasons Why Neither Dr. Watts' Imitations of the Psalms...Nor Any Other Human Composition, Ought to Be Used in the Praises of the Great God.*[18] Clark's arguments took the form of an answer to the query from a "young Minister" about using Watts's *Psalms of David Imitated.* His points exemplify the objections raised by many Old Lights.

To begin with, Clark asserted that free translations such as those of Watts were not warranted in scripture or history since not even the apostles altered the psalms or imitated them. And in any case, such texts were both unnecessary and superfluous, not to mention superstitious. Clark took aim squarely at choirs: "[Congregations] are dumb before the Lord, all except a few *concillators* [sic] or *singing boys and girls* in the gallery," all of which reminded him of a "Mass-house in Dublin" rather than a professed Protestant congregation. Such a practice was "Grievous and Offends God's people," as well as blasphemous. Clark found Watts's description of the "dull indifference" toward singing among congregations to be "daring impudence" asserting that Watts was in essence blaming God's word for the indifference of sinners. And finally, Clark maintained, such imitations of the psalms violated the biblical admonition against

---

[16] *A Collection of Psalms and Hymns* was often referred to as the "Charlestown Collection," and actually the first set of hymns, along with metrical psalms for use in the Anglican churches.

[17] Robert Stevenson, "John Wesley's First Hymnbook," *Patterns of Protestant Church Music*, 116–17. See also and especially Carlton R. Young, "John Wesley's 1737 Charlestown Collection of Psalms and Hymns," *The Hymn* 41/4 (October 1990): 19–27.

[18] Copy in the American Antiquarian Society, Worcester MA.

adding to the scriptures. Thus, he concluded, the use of such hymns was contrary to the tenets of religious orthodoxy.

Even some of the New Lights had their reservations about hymnody. In England, Charles Wesley's texts had been sung to popular and well-known melodies—folk tunes, operatic airs, ballads, and the like—for private meditation and instruction or at meetings of Methodist societies whose members retained their Anglican identity and attended regular worship in Anglican churches on Sundays.[19] But once Methodism was formally established in America as an independent denomination, the Methodists placed a set of strictures on denominational hymnody. Eight years after the Baltimore Christmas conference of 1784 that established the Methodist Episcopal Church, the *Discipline* of 1792 specifically admonished, "Sing no hymns of your own composing."[20]

Anthems and Choirs

Around the 1730s, the music of English parish churches became somewhat more complex and ornate, with melodic turns and simple imitation in place of plain and unrelieved syllabic tunes. During the 1750s, this newer style appeared in America with imported collections published by William Knapp (1698/1699–1768), John Arnold (c1720–1792), and especially William Tans'ur (1700–1783).[21]

Tans'ur's *The Compleat Melody, or Harmony of Sion* of 1734 was reissued in 1755 as *The Royal Melody Compleat*, and it quickly became popular. As early as 1740, Tans'ur's contemporary John Arnold had

---

[70] John Wesley, *A collections of Hymns for the People Called Methodists* (London: J. Paramore, 1780) was organized didactically, including such headings and subheadings as "Exhorting," "Convincing," "Praying," etc. John Wesley's introduction described it as containing "all the important truths of our most holy religion...directions for making our calling and election sure: for perfecting holiness in the fear of God."

[20] Robert Stevenson, *Protestant Church Music in America* (New York: W. W. Norton, 1966) 69–70.

[21] See Irving Lowens, "The Origins of the American Fuging-Tune," in *Music and Musicians in Early America* (New York: W. W. Norton, 1964) 243–44; and David McKay and Richard Crawford, *William Billings of Boston* (Princeton: Princeton University Press, 1975) 22.

pronounced him one of the "best Authors...of the present Age."[22] Daniel Bayley of Newburyport, Massachusetts, reprinted the introduction from Tans'ur's collection in the second book of his own publication, *A New and Compleat Introduction to the Grounds and Rules of Musick in 2 Books* (1764).[23] Three years later Bayley reprinted the third edition of *The Royal Melody Complete*.[24] Its contents included "many fuging chorus's,...Hymns, Anthems and Canons...set by the greatest Masters of the World...in Two, Three, Four, and Five Musical Parts,...set in score for Voices or Organ." Bayley published new editions of Tans'ur's collection as late as 1774.[25]

Tans'ur's most striking feature was his fuging choruses: optional imitative sections for trained singers attached to the end of congregational psalm tunes in traditional block chordal style. They provided models for native composers.[26] In addition to plain and ornate psalm tunes and fuging choruses, Tans'ur and his fellow composers of music for rural parishes also wrote anthems and set-pieces. The distinction is somewhat of a fine one. Strictly speaking, anthems intended for rural choirs (as distinct from cathedral choirs) were multi-sectional single movement pieces on a prose text from scripture; the latter were similar multi-sectional pieces on a metrical text, either a psalm or hymn. Both anthems and set pieces included solos, duets, trios, and choral passages in homophonic and simple polyphonic texture intended for a trained choir. Tans'ur's introduction on the principles of harmony, rhythm, and tempo provided a model for Americans, especially William Billings of Boston. Similarly, Tans'ur's compositional style is reflected in

---

[22] Quoted in Stevenson, *Protestant Church Music in America*, 60.

[23] Leonard Ellinwood, *The History of American Church Music* (New York: Morehouse-Gorham, 1953; repr., New York: Da Capo, 1970) 27–28; *ASMI*, 140. The first book of Bayley's pair reprinted the introduction from Walter's *Grounds and Rules of Music*. For biographical information on Bayley, see Frank J. Metcalf, *American Writers and Compilers of Sacred Music* (New York: Abingdon, 1925; repr., New York: Russell & Russell, 1967) 23–29.

[24] William Tans'ur, *The Royal Melody Complete* (Boston: W. M'Alpine, 1767).

[25] The spelling was changed in the American edition. See *ASMI*, 115–34.

[26] On English fuging tunes, see Nicholas Temperley, *The Music of the English Parish Church* (Cambridge: Cambridge University Press, 1979) 173–76.

Billings's music; indeed, Billings went so far as to paraphrase passages in the music of Tans'ur in his own pieces.[27]

By the late 1750s, many city churches in the colonies had established choirs, and over the next two decades, they appeared in town churches as well. Whereas English country parish churches could look to a history of Anglican cathedral worship in which anthems and choirs held a clear place, American churches had no such tradition. Nevertheless, American collections from the 1760s began to include what were essentially anthems, ostensibly as recital pieces with which singing scholars displayed their prowess at "graduation" concerts. Since singing classes tended to remain together after graduation and to sit together as a choir in their own pew, gallery, or separate area of the church, it was natural that they also cultivate their own distinctive repertoire to be presented at occasional services.

As might be expected, controversy continued unabated over the presence of choirs and their music in regular worship. The matter of seating choir members together—without regard to age, social class, or sex—raged on in some quarters. Parishioner Ezra Barker expressed indignation in a letter dated 1780:

> When our singing wanted to be revived, ...they so suddenly exchanged old tunes for New ones...it was but a few could bear a part in the delightful part of Divine Worship.... The Meeting House was Seated as much in favour of promoting the Singing as could be convenient with decency as to Age and Birthright,... Now Seats are Shifted, Some of the males have Stretched a Wing over upon the Female Side and have intruded upon their Right.[28]

---

[27] See Karl Kroeger, "William Tans'ur's Influence on William Billings," *Inter-American Music Review* 11/2 (Spring–Summer 1991) 1–12; and Kroeger, *American Fuging Tunes, 1770–1820: A Descriptive Catalogue* (Westport CT: Greenwood, 1994).

[28] Ezra Barker to Moses Stebbins, 1780, quoted in Kenneth Logan, "Living Issues in Early American Psalmody," *Reformed Liturgy and Music* 23/1 (Winter 1989): 10. Logan's source is Vinson Bushnell, "Daniel Read of New Haven (1757–1836): The Man and His Musical Activities" (Ph.D. diss., Harvard University, 1979) 36–37.

A 1764 letter to a Boston newspaper signed as F. B. highlights a particular disdain for the fuging tune: "Instead of those plain and easy Compositions...away they get off, one after another, in a light airy jiggish Tune.... The matter of the Psalm has very little Share in their Attention."[29]

The first comparable collection by an American appeared in 1761. James Lyon's (1735–1794) *Urania* was published in that year in Philadelphia. There is some evidence that Lyon, a 1759 graduate of the College of New Jersey (now Princeton) had taught a singing school in Philadelphia in 1760, during the time he would have been preparing the collection. Once ordained to the Presbyterian ministry in 1764, he apparently abandoned musical activity in order to care for his churches, first in Nova Scotia and then in 1772 in Machias, Maine.[30]

Urania's twelve pages of introductory text provided a clear explanation of tempo and rhythm. There followed ninety-six pieces of music beautifully engraved on 198 pages. There were twelve pieces for two, three, and four voices, including six fuging tunes, the first published in America. Most of the music was by European composers; however, there were also works by William Tuckey (1708–1781), a native of Bristol who had emigrated to New York and taken charge of the music at Trinity Church; the Italian immigrant Giovanni (John) Palma (fl. 1757), who worked in Philadelphia at the time; Lyon himself; and Hopkinson.

In 1763, Hopkinson published *A Collection of Psalm Tunes with a few Anthems and Hymns...for the Use of the United Churches of Christ Church and St. Peter's Church in Philadelphia*, where he was a vestryman and warden. That year a new organ had been installed in

---

[29] F. B. to the *Boston News Letter*, quoted in Logan, "Living Issues in Early American Psalmody," 11, from Bushnell, "Daniel Read of New Haven," 34–35.

[30] James Lyon, *Urania, or A Choice Collection of Psalm-Tunes, Anthems and Hymns, from the Most Approv'd Authors, with Some Entirely New: in Two, Three, and Four parts...Adapted to the Use of Churches, and Private Families* (Philadelphia: Henry Dawkins, 1761; repr., New York: Da Capo, 1974). See *ASMI*, 444–48. On Lyons, see Metcalf, *American Composers and Compilers*, 32–42.

St. Peter's, and Hopkinson's collection included pieces for two treble voices and bass with keyboard accompaniment, among them his own setting of Tate and Brady's twenty-third psalm. Hopkinson's music was written in the graceful style adopted by contemporary English composers under the influence of Italian opera, so popular in England at the time.[31]

Choirs continued to demand anthems, and entrepreneurial singing masters and compilers supplied them. Over the remainder of the century, about a thousand pieces of choral music were printed. Numerous collections, heavily derivative from one another, were issued by American singing masters who organized and taught singing schools. In a relatively short time, these semi-amateur musicians had become the closest thing to a native-grown musical profession that America would see for many years. Most of them carried on their teaching practice part time and in conjunction with trades they practiced at least part of the year.

The Tunesmiths

During the second half of the eighteenth century, singing masters were expanding their musical activities from teaching singing schools to compiling and composing their own music. These composers—tunesmiths, as they have come to be called—represent the beginnings of a distinctive Colonial American school of composers. Their pieces consisted of congregational tunes for use with metrical psalms and Watts texts, but they also wrote set pieces and anthems, also usually to texts by Watts. The term "anthem" first

---

[31] Stevenson, *Protestant Church Music in America*, 47; *ASMI*, 333–34. This piece appears, unsigned and without figures in the bass in the Library of Congress manuscript, Francis Hopkinson's Lessons: a facsimile edition of Hopkinson's personal book: an anthology of kepboard compositions and arrangements copied in his own hand (Washington DC: C. T. Wagner, 1979). It concludes with an untexted passage for one treble and bass, and an instrument may thus be inferred. The ending is shown in Elwyn A. Weinandt and Robert H. Young, *The Anthem in England and America* (New York: The Free Press, 1970) 176. *Urania* contains the same piece without the keyboard part but with an added fourth voice, or 'counter.' Lyon, of course, was a Presbyterian, and organs, as will be seen, were virtually unknown in non-Anglican churches in the English-speaking colonies during the 1760s.

appears in America in connection with a simple three-voice setting in James A. Turner's psalm-tune supplement of 1752.[32] A manuscript in the hand of Francis Hopkinson, now in the Library of Congress, contains "An Anthem from the 114th Psalm" by "F. H. 1760."[33]

Among the singing masters who were producing their own collections of anthems and fuging tunes by the last quarter of the century was Bostonian Josiah Flagg (1737–1795). A jeweler and engraver by trade, Flagg ran singing schools, organized band concerts using British regimental musicians, and actively promoted the music of George Frederick Handel in America. His compilation, *A Collection of the Best Psalm Tunes…To Which Are Added Some Hymns and Anthems, the Greater Part of Them Never before Printed in America,* was engraved and printed by Paul Revere in 1764. In addition to a number of psalm tunes borrowed from English sources and Lyon's *Urania*, including one from a Handel opera, Flagg's collection contained two brief unattributed anthems. Two years later, Flagg himself engraved and printed a volume of twenty-five pieces, psalm tunes, and anthems by minor English composers, titled *Sixteen Anthems*.

If Flagg was a compiler, his fellow Bostonian William Billings (1746–1800) became the best known and most influential American composer of the late eighteenth century. Billings may briefly have been a pupil of Flagg, but he appears to have been largely self-taught.[34] As early as 1769, he was conducting singing schools from greater Boston and Providence to as far away as Maine.[35] Billings was somewhat of an eccentric: a tanner by trade who had a booming voice, one eye, a withered arm, and a stunted leg. He must have been a remarkable presence when he stood before a class. Between 1770

---

[32] Ralph T. Daniel, *The Anthem in New England Before 1800* (Evanston: Northwestern, 1966; repr., New York: DaCapo, 1979) 39.

[33] Francis Hopkinson's Lessons. The piece is scored for two treble voices and bass with figures. See Daniel, *The Anthem in New England before 1800*, 97.

[34] The description is from Nathaniel Gould, *Church Music in America* (Boston: A. N. Johnson, 1853; repr., New York: AMS Press, 1972) 46.

[35] See Nym Cooke, "William Billings in the District of Maine, 1780," *American Music* 9/3 (Fall 1991) 243–59.

and 1800, Billings published six major collections of his own music, along with a scattering of psalm tunes and individual anthems in pamphlet form, for a total of at least 340 pieces over his thirty-year career.

Approximately a third of Billings's pieces are anthems, fuging tunes, rounds, and set pieces for a trained choir.[36] In general, the anthems and set pieces are sectional, the music changing with sections of text. Earlier anthems usually have sharper tempo contrasts between sections than later ones. Billings's distinctive triadic and diatonic harmonies contain few chromatic alterations, but they do make marked use of unorthodox doublings and harmonic progressions, much like Tans'ur's harmony. Passages labeled as solos were actually intended by Billings to be sung by small groups rather than individual singers.[37]

Most of Billings's pieces are congregational hymn tunes. Like Tans'ur, his primary interest was clearly in the melodic motion of the parts, rather than the vertical harmony. Accordingly, Billings appears to have composed them part by part. He evidently began with the melody or "air," which he placed in the tenor. His melodies' modal character suggests influences from the numerous popular and well-known folk airs to which ballads of the era were sung. In other words, there seems to have been a sort of convergence between the relatively tonal character of psalm melodies and the modal character of folk melodies as they had generally developed along their separate courses over the previous two centuries or so. Billings then apparently wrote his bass line for harmonic support, followed by a countermelody for the soprano and possibly a filler part for alto. As was customary at the

---

[36] See Karl Kroeger, *Catalogue of the Musical Works of William Billings* (New York: Greenwood Press, 1991); Karl Kroeger and Hans Nathan, *The Complete Works of William Billings (1746–1800)* (Charlottesville: University Press of Virginia, 1977–1990). On the subsequent reprinting of Billings's music as an index of the practical aims of compilers, see Richard Crawford, "William Billings (1746–1800) and American Psalmody: A Study of Musical Dissemination," in *The American Musical Landscape* (Berkeley: University of California Press, 1993) 111–50.

[37] See Daniel, *The Anthem in New England*, 102–19 for a fuller discussion of Billings's style.

time, sopranos and tenors shared both the air and countermelody, thus doubling those two voices at the octave.

Billings's *The New-England Psalm-Singer*, the first collection of music by a single American composer, appeared in 1770. Its "Introduction to the Rules of Musick" also drew on Tans'ur. But Billings also declared his independence:

> Perhaps it may be expected by some, that I should say something concerning the Rules for Composition; to these I answer that *Nature is the best Dictator*, for all the hard dry studied Rules that ever was prescribed, will not enable any Person to form an Air any more than the bare Knowledge of the four and twenty [*sic*] Letters, and strict Grammatical Rules will qualify a Scholar for composing a Piece of Poetry, or properly adjusting a Tragedy, without a Genius. But it must be Nature, Nature must lay the Foundation, Nature must inspire the Thought.

The New-England Psalm-Singer contained psalm tunes for the most part, but there were also four anthems, one set-piece, and three canons. The 126 pieces include some of his best and best-known work, like the lyrical canon, "When Jesus Wept." The British military presence in Boston had become odious, and the fiercely patriotic Billings indicated his sympathies with the defiant "Chester":

> Let tyrants shake their iron rod
> And slavery clank its galling chains
> We fear them not, we trust in God
> New England's God forever reigns.[38]

---

[38] In addition to the definitive work by McKay and Crawford, *William Billings of Boston*, and works by Kroeger and Crawford previously cited (Kroeger, *Catalog*, and Kroger and Nathan, *Complete Works*), see Metcalf, *American Writers and Compilers*, 57–64; *ASMI*, 173–86. See also Kenneth Silverman, *A Cultural History of the American Revolution* (New York: Thomas Y. Crowell, 1976) 199–207; Michael Broyles, *Mavericks and Other Traditions in American Music* (New Haven: Yale University Press, 2004) 13–38.

The collection was a success; however, Billings was evidently dissatisfied with it, at least judging from the preface to his next publication.[39] Or he may have simply been trying to drum up sales for his new collection. In any case, he wrote:

> After impartial examination, I have discovered that many of the pieces in that Book were never worth my printing, or your inspection; therefore in order to make you ample amends for my former intrusion, I have selected and corrected some of the Tunes which were most approved of in that book, and have added several new pieces which I think to be very good ones...I make no doubt but you will readily concur with me in this sentiment, viz. that the *Singing Master's Assistant*, is a much better Book, than the *New-England Psalm-Singer*.[40]

The Singing Master's Assistant contained seventy-one pieces, including eight anthems and one set-piece, and closed with a glossary of 140 musical terms. Among the new works were "Judea" with its Christmas text "A Virgin Unspotted," the lyrical "David's Lamentation," and the anthem "I Am the Rose of Sharon." "Chester," by now a patriotic call-to-arms, this time had four more stanzas. *The Singing Master's Assistant* was very popular and went through four editions, the last of them in 1786.

Billings himself printed and sold *Music in Miniature* (1779). Its seventy-two four-voice congregational psalm tunes included several from his own earlier collections as well as ten tunes from English sources, the only music not by him in any of his books. The book's smaller size and vertical shape allowed it to be bound in a metrical Psalter. *The Psalm-singer's Amusement* (1781) and *The Suffolk Harmony* (1786) were also printed and sold by Billings himself. The first of

---

[39] William Billings, *The Singing Master's Assistant* (Boston: Draper and Folsom, 1778).

[40] See Britton, "Theoretical Introductions," 348–49.

these contained twenty-four pieces, among them six anthems, five set-pieces, and five fuging tunes, all for four voices and clearly intended for experienced singers, rather than students. A later edition, published anonymously after the composer's death, contains supplemental psalm tunes and an added preface with the usual instructions on reading music and singing. *The Suffolk Harmony* shows a more refined compositional style. The twenty-five psalm and hymn tunes were coordinated with specific texts, and the three anthems and four fuging tunes show a marked tendency toward a smoother texture and more cohesiveness. Clearly, Billings was sensitive to the changing preferences of Americans for more fashionable European musical style.

Billings was in financial straits when his last collection appeared.[41] The collection was published in his behalf by a committee. Two years earlier, the *Massachusetts Magazine* had carried an appeal for subscriptions for a "volume of Original American Musick, composed by William Billings, of Boston.... The distressed situation of Mr. Billings' family has so sensibly operated on the mind of the committee as to induce their assistance in the intended publication."

Of the fifty-one pieces in the volume, fourteen were fuging tunes, seventeen were anthems, and one was a set piece, all for four voices and evidently written at different times during his career. The collection opened with an introduction reprinted from *The Singing Master's Assistant*, to which had been added a discussion of musical "rules," set as a dialogue between master and disciple. At one point, Billings defended the fuging tune against the increasing preference for music patterned on more cultivated and sophisticated European models: "*Variety is always pleasing*, and...there is more variety in one piece of fuging music, than in twenty pieces of plain song."

But the trend was away from Billings and the fuging tune as the century waned. Andrew Law (1749–1821) of Cheshire, Connecticut, was a graduate of Brown University, an ordained minister, and

---

[41] William Billings, *The Continental Harmony* (Boston: Isaiah Thomas and Ebenezer Andrews, 1794)

singing master. He taught singing schools as far afield as Pennsylvania, Maryland, and the Carolinas. Law was more a compiler than a composer, and his eight major collections went through several editions. His first compilation, *Select Harmony* (1779), was reissued in a much revised version in 1782. It combined tunes by English and American composers in equal proportion.

Law made a number of departures from the Billings style. He moved the melody from the tenor to the soprano voice. He included Anglican chants along with psalm tunes in his *Rudiments of Music* (1789), and in the first edition of his *The Musical Primer* (1793), he declared his preference for quality European music and refined singing voices:

> In a word, our singing in general is extremely harsh; and this harshness produces its natural effects, it renders our psalmody less pleasing and less efficacious; but it does more; it vitiates our taste and gives currency to bad music. A considerable part of American music is in reality faulty. It consists more of the sweet and perfect cords [harmonies], than European music, which aims at variety and energy, by introducing the perfect cords less frequently; and therefore American music will better bear with the harshness of our singing. Hence the great run it has taken to the exclusion of European composition. But it was the roughness of our singing that ought to have been smoothed and polished, and not the compositions of Madan and Handell [*sic*].[42]

---

[42] *ASMI*, 421. The definitive study is Richard Crawford, *Andrew Law, American Psalmodist* (Evanston: Northwestern University Press, 1968; repr., New York: Da Capo, 1981). See also Silverman, *A Cultural History of the American Revolution*, 477; Metcalf, *American Writers and Compilers*, 69–79. Law's allusion is to George Frederick Handel (1685–1759) and to Martin Madan (1726–1790), an Anglican clergyman who had compiled an extremely popular collection of music to be sung in parish churches by charity children in 1769. An edition of *The Collection of Psalm and Hymn Tunes Sung at the Chapel of Lock Hospital* was published in Boston by West & Blake and Manning & Loring in 1809. See Elwyn A. Weinandt and Robert H. Young, *The Anthem in England and America* (New York: Free Press, 1970) 156–58.

Law's own music and his direct influence were limited largely because of his stubborn insistence on a method of musical notation—"additions and improvements...printed upon a new plan"—he introduced in his fourth edition of *The Art of Singing* (1803). In essence, the system employed four shape notes that followed the flow of the melody, but they were printed on empty staves, rather than regular ones of lines and spaces.

Daniel Read (1757–1836) may have attended singing schools taught both by Billings and by Law. Read kept a store in New Haven, Connecticut, and ran occasional singing schools, but he seems to have been more interested in composing and compiling music. He published ninety-four of his own pieces in four collections, the third of which, *The Columbia Harmonist*, was issued in three volumes between 1793 and 1795. His earlier works, beginning with *The American Singing Book* (1785, subsequent editions to 1796), include fuging tunes with folk-like character and incomplete triadic harmonies.

Although Read continued publishing fuging tunes until 1807, by 1795, the year he issued the last volume and the combined three volumes of *The Columbia Harmonist*, he had moved toward a smoother cultivated European style. In a letter dated 3 February 1829, Read characterized his earlier music as "chiefly ephemeral," and in another letter, dated 2 May of that year, he recorded his preference for European musical style as based "on the broad ground of settled principles, rather than the narrow one of individual taste."[43]

In February 1795, the press of Isaiah Thomas and Ebenezer T. Andrews in Boston printed a collection of seventy-eight compositions, at least seventy of them by non-American composers. The preface to *The Massachusetts Compiler*—signed by the Danish

---

[43] In addition to Bushnell, "Daniel Read," see Irving Lowens, "Daniel Read's World: The Letters of an Early American Composer," in *Music and Musicians in Early America*, 159–77; also Metcalf, *American Writers and Compilers*, 94–103. On his style, see Daniel, *The Anthem in New England*, 124–26. Like most of his contemporaries, Read was an admirer of Handel and even named a son after the master.

immigrant musician Hans Gram and by two native New Englanders, Samuel Holyoke and Oliver Holden—said in part: "Many American votaries of sacred music, have long since expressed their wishes for a compendium of the genuine principles of that science. At the present period it becomes necessary that greater attention be paid to every mean for improving that important part of divine worship, as good, musical immigrants are daily seeking an asylum in this country."

Among the composers represented in the collection were the Englishmen Thomas A. Arne, Charles Burney, and Henry Purcell; the continental masters Handel and Haydn; and the British immigrant musicians George K. Jackson and William Selby, both of Boston. Holden, Holyoke, and Gram each contributed one piece. The contents included one anthem, nine set-pieces, and two doxologies for two, three, and four voices, in addition to hymn tunes. In the preface to the collection, Holden, Holyoke, and Gram pointed out that "with respect to the selection of music, it is necessary to observe, that several of the pieces were not originally composed for sacred words; they were chosen and adapted for furnishing a variety of style from the most modern compositions."[44]

Samuel Holyoke (1762–1820) and Oliver Holden (1765–1844) represented the new generation of musicians who looked not to Billings but to Law and the Europeans for their inspiration and indeed their music. Holden was a native of Shirley, Massachusetts, but from 1787 on he made his home in Charlestown. Holyoke was born in Boxford, Massachusetts, of an old family and was a graduate of Harvard. Holden taught singing schools during from 1792 to 1807; Holyoke also taught singing schools. In spite of his educational background and cosmopolitan tastes, to say nothing of his prolific output of some 650 pieces, Holyoke remained a provincial figure. Holden, on the other hand, is better known, largely because of his tune, "Coronation," which still appears in virtually every denominational hymnal set to the text "All hail the power of Jesus' name" and on almost every congregation's list of favorite hymns.

---

[44] *ASMI*, 292–93.

Although he produced a number of fuging tunes himself, Holden wrote in his preface to *The Union Harmony* (1783), "Fuging music in general is badly calculated for divine worship," and in *Plain Psalmody* (1800), he wrote, "In the general omission of fuges, the Author hopes to meet the approbation and concurrence of the lovers of real devotion." Holden's music generally utilizes slower tempi, continuous texture, and lyric lines. About half of his pieces are in three vocal parts.[45]

These men and most of the other American singing masters who flourished in the last decade of the eighteenth century and the nineteenth moved away from Billings's fuging tunes and rough-hewn native idiom and toward a smoother, more refined, European-based style. But Billings, as well as Read in his earlier years and others less well-known, gave American church music a distinctive voice. Although many of them later turned on that distinctive voice and adopted the smoother, more cultivated idiom of the immigrant European musicians who were arriving in increasing numbers as the century waned, their style of open harmony, modal counterpoint, and folk-like melody would persist in the rural churches of back-country America into the late twentieth century.

---

[45] Daniel, *The Anthem in New England*, 129–32. See also David W. McCormick, "Oliver Holden, Composer and Anthologist" (SMD diss., Union Seminary, 1963); Metcalf, *American Writers and Compilers*, 124–34. On Holyoke, see Metcalf, *American Writers and Compilers*, 114–20.

3

Immigrant Musicians and the First Organs

During the eighteenth century, a number of professional musicians came from England and the continent to ply their trade as professionals. Most turned to church music as one source of income, along with teaching instruments, singing, dancing, swordsmanship, organizing concerts, and importing sheet music and musical instruments. Another group of talented and proficient musicians came not as professionals in search of work, but rather as refugees from war and religious strife, mainly in Germany. Music was integral not only to their worship but to their very culture and way of life as well, and they played and sang with as much zeal as they farmed the rich land of Pennsylvania, where most of them settled.

In general, differences in attitude toward music among various American churches in the eighteenth century reflected ethnic and cultural backgrounds, rather than denominational identities. The Germans who settled in Pennsylvania before 1750 were for the most part either Lutheran or Reformed. The two groups drew on a common musical tradition and body of hymns, or chorales.[1] Nor was

---

[1] John Kelpius and Anthony Aston, *Church Music and Musical Life in Pennsylvania in the Eighteenth Century*, 2 vols. Bound as 4 (Philadelphia: Publications of the Pennsylvania Society of the Colonial Dames of America, 1926-1935; repr., New York: AMS, 1972) 3:261. (Hereafter cited as *CMML.*) See also Theodore G.

this sense of commonality evident only in worship music. Indeed, so closely did the two denominations identify with one another that Reformed congregations often shared buildings and, on occasion, even ministers with their Lutheran neighbors.[2] When the break came in 1793, it was between the German Reformed and their strictly separatist Dutch Reformed co-religionists and only served to ratify the reality that a common culture bound immigrant congregations and churches far more closely than a common theology.

The body of chorales shared by the German Lutheran and Reformed churches derived from several sources. The early reformers, Martin Luther among them, wrote some of the texts and even composed some melodies; however, for the most part they and their successors turned to popular religious songs in the vernacular; to secular songs whose texts they adapted or replaced; and to Latin chants and hymns, which they also translated and adapted for congregational use. Over the years, chorale melodies had come to be associated with particular texts so that a particular melody would be identified by the first few words of its text. Newly written texts might be fitted to older tunes, but each tune was still referred to by the first words of the text originally and traditionally associated with it. The structure of many chorale melodies, four lines of music with the second line a repetition of the first, preserves a vestige of their roots in medieval German song, which was commonly cast in that form.[3]

Religious Communities

If the majority of German immigrants were adherents of the two major denominations, Lutheran and Reformed, the earliest to arrive were communities of smaller radical pietist groups, among them the Hermits or Mystics of Wissahickon led by Jonas Kelpius

Tappert, "The Influence of Pietism in Colonial American Lutheranism," in *Continental Pietism and Early American Christianity*, ed. F. Ernest Stoeffler (Grand Rapids: Eerdmans, 1976) 23–24.

[2] In fact, one can still find such shared buildings in rural Pennsylvania.

[3] The resulting bar form, AAB, is rooted in the art of the medieval *minnesingers*. For a fuller exposition of early Lutheran church music and the chorale, see Friederich Blume, *Protestant Church Music* (New York: W. W. Norton, 1974) 3–113.

(1673–1708), who immigrated in 1694. Kelpius was a graduate of the University of Altdorf who spoke five languages and had interests in science and the occult along with theology and music. Kelpius stopped briefly in Germantown, then he settled his community of forty men, which he called The Contented of the God-loving Soul, in what is now Fairmount Park in Philadelphia, near the Wissahickon Creek, from which they derived their name. The community grew medicinal herbs and observed the heavens with their telescopes, seeking signs of Christ's imminent return.

They were also musicians of some skill, and Kelpius himself compiled a manuscript collection of hymns called *The Lamenting Voice of the Hidden Love at the Time when She Lay in Misery & Forsaken.* This collection contained ten harmonized tunes and both German and English texts. The community made use of musical instruments in worship, and its morning and evening services drew many visitors because of the music.[4]

Kelpius and his Hermits are associated with the first recorded use of an organ in the British colonies. The community furnished music for the ordination of Justus Falckner (1672–1723) to the Lutheran ministry at Gloria Dei Church in Philadelphia on 24 November 1703.[5] Falckner was a graduate of the University of Halle, a center of German pietism. Though he had delayed ordination to

---

[4] The manuscript—in the hand of Kelpius's amanuensis and the last surviving member of the order, the Englishman Christopher Witt (c1675–1765)—is now in the collection of the Historical Society of Pennsylvania. It is reprinted in facsimile with translation on facing pages in *CMML*, 1:21–165; on Kelpius, see *CMML*, 12–17. See also Robert Stevenson, *Protestant Church Music in America* (New York: W. W. Norton, 1966) 32–33.

[5] See *CMML*, 1:197. The Swedish churches ministered to the Lutherans among the early German immigrants, even though the Church of Sweden was orthodox and ceremonial, while most of the Germans were pietists. Kelpius and his Hermits had supplied music for the consecration of Gloria Dei on 2 July 1700. They "furnished not only instrumental music for the occasion, but acted as choristers as well...while the three resident pastors...all robed in surplice and chasuble, conducted the consecration service." Shortly thereafter, Magister Andrew Rudman, the pastor of the church had described the building in a letter to Sweden, "With all this we want some ornaments for our Church...We have also room for a small organ" (*CMML*, 197).

enter business with his brother, Falckner was an active missionary and had a particular interest in music. He had composed a few hymns and two years before had written to Dr. Heinrich Mühlen, an influential church dignitary of Holstein, Germany, asking that an organ be sent because "a well sounding organ would perhaps prove of great profit...even a small organ and music in this place would be acceptable to God."[6] There is no record of any response, and evidence suggests that the organ used at his ordination belonged not to the church but to the Hermits.[7] In any event, the service opened "with a voluntary on the little organ in the gallery by Jonas the organist, supplemented with instrumental music by the Mystics on the viol, hautboy, trumpets and kettle-drums."[8] Kelpius's community, seated on the front benches, then intoned the *Veni Creator* and the *Veni Sancte Spiritus* "to the soft strains of instruments."[9]

Of somewhat problematical musical significance was yet another German community established at Ephrata, near Lancaster, in 1732 by Conrad Beissel (1690/1691–1768). An orphan from his childhood, Beissel had been apprenticed to a baker in Germany who also taught him to play the violin. He immigrated to Germantown via Boston in 1720 and took up a new trade—weaving—under a Baptist missionary. In 1724 Beissel became a Baptist minister. Meanwhile, he had moved to Lancaster County, and after a brief pastorate that ended in a disagreement about Sabbath observance, he established a celibate, seventh-day Baptist community on the banks of the Cocalico, with

---

[6] Falckner to Heinrich Mühlen of Holstein, 1 August 1701, quoted in Orpha Ochse, *The History of the Organ in the United States* (Bloomington: Indiana University Press, 1975) 14–15.

[7] See Julius Sachse, *Justus Falckner* (Philadelphia: printed for the author, 1903) 45–46, 64. See also *CMML*, 1:211 and Raymond J. Brunner, *That Ingenious Business: Pennsylvania German Organ Builders* (Birdsboro: The Pennsylvania German Society, 1990) 46–48, 60.

[8] See Talmage W. Dean, "The Organ in Eighteenth Century Colonial America" (Ph.D. diss., University of Southern California, 1960) 80–88. In context, the Jonas referred to as organist does not appear to have been Kelpius himself. Dean, citing Robert A. Gerson, *Music in Philadelphia* (Philadelphia: Presser, 1940), identifies the organist as one Jonas Auren.

[9] *CMML*, 1:166–76.

thirty-six men and thirty-five women. Beissel took for himself the name Father Friedsam.

By the middle of the eighteenth century, the Ephrata community had grown to about 300 and become a cultural center in Lancaster County. It had its own printing press, and for a time, it produced paper currency for the Continental Congress. Members ran a highly-regarded school to which outsiders sent their children. Women of the community created beautiful manuscript decoration and calligraphy, or *fraktur*. Though the community was pacifist, it tended the wounded for both sides, and its cloister was used as a hospital after the Battle of Brandywine in 1777.

In February 1735, Beissel's community, referred to as the "Solitaries of Cocalico," joined with the "Hermits of the Ridge," remnants of Kelpius's community, to provide music for the funeral of Alexander Moek, leader of the German Baptist or dunker community in Germantown. The two groups chanted the *De Profundis* antiphonally.[10] By that time, however, Kelpius had begun to move from the Lutheran worship forms and music he had apparently been using. The community's earliest manuscript hymnal, *Paradisische Nachts Tropfen* (Divine Showers of the Night), copied during the winter of 1733/1734, included pietistic hymns along with original texts by Beissel.[11]

In fact, Beissel had been gathering and composing hymn texts for some time. Benjamin Franklin printed collections for the community in 1730, 1732, and 1736.[12] The largest collection, comprising some 800 pages and 691 hymn texts, was titled, in

---

[10] E. G. Alderfer, *The Ephrata Commune: An Early American Counterculture* (Pittsburgh: University of Pittsburgh Press, 1985) 54. Sachse's collection of music manuscripts, including some of Beissel's work, is now at the Seventh Day Baptist Historical Society in Plainfield, New Jersey. Other significant holdings are in Butler Library of Columbia University, New York City, and the Historical Society of Pennsylvania, Philadelphia.

[11] The title doubtless alludes to the community's practice, begun in 1735, of holding night-watch services, during which they sang hymns in procession.

[12] Conrad Beissel, *Göttliche Liebes und Lobes Gethöne* (Philadelphia: Franklin, 1730); Beissel *Vorspiel der Neuen Welt* (Philadelphia: Franklin, 1732); Beissel, *Jacobs Kampff- und Ritter Platz* (Philadelphia: B. Franklin, 1736).

Beissel's cryptic style, *Zionitscher Weyrauchs Hügel* (Zion's Fragrant Hill) and printed in Germantown in 1739 by Christopher Saur.[13] Saur, a tailor by trade and a Baptist, had arrived in Germantown in 1724 and set up as a printer in 1731. The various German religious groups, who like Kelpius had either compiled new liturgical books or reprinted the ones they had used in Germany, had heretofore turned to Benjamin Franklin. They welcomed and patronized Saur not only because he was one of their own and did not look down on them, as Franklin seemed to, but also because he owned the gothic German fonts they preferred, whereas Franklin used Roman characters.[14]

By the 1740s, Beissel was composing music and directing the order's choir, displacing a singing master named Ludwig Blum whom he had engaged earlier. He enlarged the original four-part choir of about fifteen women, adding ten men who sang two additional bass parts. Beissel's community apparently made no use of instruments. His compositional output was prodigious. He produced over 1,000

---

[13] Over the next few years, several manuscripts of music for the texts in *Zionitischer Weyrauchs Hügel* were copied by the sisters. Examples survive in the Library of Congress and the Historical Society of Pennsylvania.

[14] Among Saur's imprints were the first American edition of the Mennonite *Ausbund* (Germantown PA: Christoph Saur, 1742)—a collection of religious ballads and hymns containing the names of popular tunes to which the texts were to be sung—and the first type-set music imprint in America, *Kern alter und neuer* (1752), a reprint of a German Reformed hymn collection originally published in Marburg in 1746. A year later the collection was republished by Saur as part of *Neu-vermehrt-und vollständiges Gesang-Buch*, which went through four editions to 1774 (See *CMML*, 2:289–91; Allen Perdue Britton, Irving Lowens, and Richard Crawford, *American Sacred Music Imprints 1698–1810* [Worcester: American Antiquarian Society, 1990] 516–17). (Hereafter cited as *ASMI*.)

Although Saur was a Baptist, his wife Maria was a follower of Beissel from 1726 to the mid-1740s. Saur's relations with Beissel were uneven, not only because of his influence over Maria, but also because Saur took offense at some of Beissel's texts that seemed to him to be glorifying Beissel himself as a religious icon. It was apparently this feud, which seems to have continued until the 1740s, that moved the community to set up its own printing facilities.

Saur was tried by the Colonials for collaboration after the Battle of Germantown in 1777. His property was confiscated, and he died penniless in 1783.

hymns and anthems, as well as settings of whole chapters of the Bible, and two musical renditions of the Song of Songs.[15]

Beissel had definite views regarding the connection between diet and vocal quality. Singers were not to have meat or dairy products, but rather to eat only vegetables and grains. He also insisted on a peculiar mode of posture and vocal production. He directed the group to sing with heads back and lips barely parted. Anglican minister Jacob Duché (1737–1798), an assistant at Christ Church in Philadelphia, heard Beissel's choir in 1771. He was struck with "the peculiarity of their *music*" according to a letter dated October 2 of that year:

> The sisters invited us into their chapel, and, seating themselves in order, began to sing one of their devout hymns. The music had little or no air or melody; but consisted of simple, long notes. The counter, treble, tenor and bass were all sung by women with sweet, shrill and small voices; but with a truth and exactness in the time and intonation.... The performers sat with their heads reclined, their countenances solemn and dejected, their faces pale and emaciated from their manner of living.... I almost began to think of myself in the world of spirits, and that the objects before me were ethereal.[16]

The community's hymnal, bearing the usual mystical title *Das Gesäng der einsamen und verlassenen Turtel-Taube*...(The Song of the Lonely and Forsaken Turtledove...), containing some 800 texts, was compiled in manuscript by about 1746. A version of *Turtel-Taube* was printed on the community's press in 1747 included 277 of them, mostly by Beissel. Subsequent editions and supplements raised the number to 375. The 1200–plus tunes in the manuscript were reduced

---

[15] Alderfer, *The Ephrata Commune*, 108. The author points out that the appearance of a comet in 1743 clearly spurred the production of apocalyptic hymn texts, especially Beissel's own *Cometen-Buch* (Ephrata: The Cloister 1745).

[16] Stevenson, *Protestant Church Music in America*, 34.

to about 500 for use with the printed *Turtel-Taube*. Ephrata's press could accommodate only text; the music was copied by hand. In 1753, the Swedish Provost, Magister Israel Acrelius, wrote: "The younger sisters are mostly employed in drawing. A part of them are now constantly employed in copying musical note books for themselves and the brethren. I saw of these upon which a wonderful amount of work has been expended.... When they sing, each holds a note-book as well as a psalm-book...looking into each alternately."[17] Beissel provided a foreword, prologue, and epilogue to the printed volume, describing *Turtel-Taube* as "a field of flowers, grown forth of many different colors, and of various fragrances as they were produced out of the *Mysterio* of God" and setting forth his theories.[18]

Beissel's musical system was idiosyncratic in its notation, harmony, and melodies, as well as its singing style and theories of vocal production. His hymns and anthems were written in four to eight parts with much doubling at octaves, parallel intervals, crude harmonies, weak progressions, and few dissonances or modulations. The rhythm was free, following the accents of the text, with strong syllables set to longer note values and major triads. Beissel's last collection of hymns, aside from the supplements to *Turtel-Taube*, was issued in 1754. *Paradisisches Wunderspiel* was part print and part

---

[17] *CMML*, 2:39–40. According to *Chronicon Ephratense* (Ephrata: The Cloister, 1786), the tune manuscripts for *Turtel-Taube* were "reverently presented" to Beissel by members of the order. See *CMML*, 3:242.

[18] Conrad Beissel, *Das Gesäng der einsamen und verlassenen Turtel-Taube Nemlich der Christlichen Kirche [The Song of the lonely and abandoned Turtledove, Namely the Christian Church]* (Ephrata: Drucks der Bruederschafft, 1747) and several manuscript tune books, among them those in the New York Public Library and Huntington Library, San Marino, California. See *CMML*, 3:242–46; *CMML*, 2:44; Stevenson, *Protestant Church Music in America*, 34–38; Julius Friederich Sachse, *The Music of the Ephrata Cloister* (Lancaster: printed for the author, 1903; repr., New York: AMS, 1971) 46, 57. The main study of Ephrata's music is Betty Jean Martin, "The Ephrata Cloister and its Music, 1732–1785: The Cultural Religious and Bibliographical Background" (Ph.D. diss, The University of Maryland, 1974). Some of the music is available in Russell P. Getz (ed.) *Ephrata Cloister Chorales...composed by Conrad Beissel* (New York: G. Schirmer, 1971). Alderfer, *The Ephrata Commune*, 130, lists the supplements: *Nachklang* (1755); *Ein Angenehmer Geruch der Rosen und Lilien* (1756) and *Neu-vermehrtes Gesang* (1762).

fraktur and contained both text and music. Apparently as Beissel grew older, he and the community turned to other interests. Hymn production had come to a standstill by 1766.

Although Beissel's music is interesting from a cultural and historical point of view, and the surviving music manuscripts of Ephrata contain surpassingly beautiful *fraktur*, when all is said and done, it was of little or no significance outside the community. One may argue, as does Sachse, that Beissel antedated Billings in establishing a native American idiom,[19] but no case can be made, except superficially, that his idiom anticipated that of Billings in its folk-like character and naiveté. Billings developed a personal style with folk or folk-like elements that influenced his contemporaries and those who followed him, even though that influence eventually took the form of reaction. Beissel's idiosyncratic style was rooted in an equally idiosyncratic and intensely personal mysticism that did not permit of sharing beyond the immediate circle of Ephrata. In the end, even Sachse can only sum up the repertoire thus: "These hymns and tunes were virtually the outpourings of religious enthusiasts, whose nervous systems had been wrought up to a high pitch by incessant vigils, fastings and an abstemious mode of life…. So far as is known, no one connected with the community was a skilled musician."[20]

Organs

Among eighteenth-century immigrants, there were a number of skilled musicians. They tended to cluster in the cities along the East Coast, combining a number of activities such as teaching, instrument repair, and music merchandising to eke out a living. Some churches began to acquire organs during the eighteenth century, providing a steady if not especially generous source of income for musicians with some keyboard skills.

---

[19] Sachse, *The Music of the Ephrata Cloister*, 3–4.
[20] Sachse, *The Music of the Ephrata Cloister*, 49–51.

Most German congregations acquired an instrument as soon as they were financially able.[21] Meanwhile, ensembles of amateur instrumentalists might be drawn from the congregation to provide support for the singing.[22] English churches—even the Anglicans, who had no particular aversion to the use of an organ in worship—were in no particular rush to obtain one.[23] German churches and clergy considered organs and music an indispensable part of the aesthetic and atmosphere of the liturgy. To the pragmatic English clergy and laity, on the other hand, organs were pleasant but by no means indispensable adjuncts to proper worship.

Singing in most English churches was indifferent, and an organ was often the easiest means for improving congregational psalmody. Along with an organ came the need for an organist, and several professional musicians were called from Europe to take charge of newly installed instruments in larger urban churches. As early as 1703, the year of Justus Falckner's ordination to the music of an organ and other instruments at Gloria Dei Church in Philadelphia, Trinity Church in New York established a committee "to confer with and Discourse Mr. Henry Neering, Organ-maker, about making and erecting an organ in Trinity Church in New-York, and if they shall think it meet to agree with him on as easy terms as possible." Apparently nothing came of the affair, for in 1709, William Vesey, rector of Trinity, wrote to the London commissioners, "There is much more wanted, *viz*...a ring of bells and sett of Organs."[24]

---

[21] The exceptions were those groups growing out of the radical reformation Anabaptist sects, who for the most part eschewed organs and choirs.

[22] Brunner, *That Ingenious Business*, 39. Edward C. Wolf, "Music in Old Zion, Philadelphia," *Musical Quarterly* 58/4 (October 1972): 623.

[23] It seems appropriate at this point to observe that Church of England parishes in the colonies are appropriately referred to as Anglican and that it is appropriate to refer to those same parishes as Episcopal only after the War of Independence, and even then, arguably not until 1789.

[24] Arthur Messiter, *A History of the Choir and Music of Trinity Church, New York* (New York: Gorham, 1906; repr., New York: AMS Press, 1970) 290. See also John Ogasapian, *Organ Building in New York City, 1700–1900* (Braintree: Organ Literature Foundation, 1977) 12–13.

Surprisingly enough, the first church to use an organ regularly in its services was located in Puritan Boston, where aversion to the admission of that instrument into worship was most ardent. Thomas Brattle, a prominent Boston citizen, merchant, amateur scientist, and musical dilettante, had procured an English chamber organ for his home well before 1708, for in a diary entry dated 3 September of that year, his friend Samuel Sewall noted, "I used to go to the same room [where he had just attended a funeral] for the sound of Mr. Brattle's Organs." And on 29 May 1711, the Reverend Joseph Green recorded, "I was at Mr. Thomas Brattle's; heard ye organs and saw strange things in a microscope."[25]

Brattle had been a principal founder of the relatively liberal Brattle Square Church in Boston.[26] He died 18 May 1713, and his will stipulated that the instrument should go to the church on the condition that within a year, the congregation had to "procure a sober person that can play skillfully thereon with a loud noise." Liberal though it might have been in comparison to Boston's other Puritan churches, the congregation was not yet ready to admit an organ to its worship. On 24 July, the membership voted to decline the bequest "with all possible respect to the memory of our deceased friend and benefactor."[27]

---

[25] *The Diary of Samuel Sewall, 1674–1729*, 3 vols. (vols. 4–7), Collections of the Massachusetts Historical Society, series 5 (Boston: Massachusetts Historical Society, 1878–1882) 6:235; Samuel P. Fowler, ed., "Diary of Rev. Joseph Green, of Salem Village," *Essex Institute Historical Collections* 10 (1869): 90.

[26] Brattle Street Church was one of the first to abandon the lining out of psalms and preferred the Tate and Brady psalms, used by Boston's Anglican churches, over the congregationalists' own Bay Psalm Book. One contemporary described it as "midway between the Church of England and Dissenters" (Kenneth Silverman, *The Life and Times of Cotton Mather* [New York: Columbia, 1985] 148).

[27] Barbara J. Owen, *The Organs and Music of King's Chapel* 2nd. ed. (Boston: King's Chapel, 1991) 2. In fact, Brattle Street Church would be the first Puritan congregation in Boston to use an organ; however, such would not occur until June 1792. Even then, one prominent member of the congregation offered to reimburse the church the whole cost of the organ and its transportation if the instrument, built by Samuel Green in London, might be thrown overboard before the ship carrying it docked in Boston (see Dean, "The Organ in Eighteenth Century English Colonial America," 11). Seven years later, the centennial sermon commemorating the church's

Brattle had foreseen just such a possibility, and his will directed that should the Brattle Square Church refuse the instrument, it would be offered on the same conditions to King's Chapel, the Anglican parish in the city. On 3 August 1713, King's Chapel accepted the organ, and the next spring it was set up in its new home. A volunteer and amateur from the congregation played it until the following Christmas, when Edward Enstone arrived from England to assume his new duties as organist of King's Chapel.[28] Needless to say, the city's Puritan clergymen were appropriately scandalized. In 1714, Cotton Mather recorded with evident satisfaction that the use of an organ had not increased the membership of King's Chapel.[29]

In New York, South Dutch Reformed Church became the second Colonial church, and the first Calvinist congregation to employ an organ, although not altogether eagerly. The Calvinist reformers of the Netherlands had never destroyed church organs, as had the English during the seventeenth century. Indeed, the period was an especially fruitful one for organ building and literature in the low countries. Although the instruments had no part in Reformed worship, they were played regularly for civic events and concerts. Accordingly, the Dutch burghers of New York had no inherent objection to the presence of an organ in their churches, as did the Puritans of Boston. Moreover, New York was diverse, polyglot, and a relatively tolerant city for its time. Boston still retained the vestiges of its theocratic origins, even though its Puritan ministers and magistrates had long since lost their exclusive hold on the city's legal and political affairs.[30]

---

founding observed of the organ, "That which eighty years ago was rejected when offered freely was then procured at great expense." See Barbara Owen, *The Organ in New England* (Raleigh: Sunbury, 1979) 18.

[28] The instrument served until 1754, when the present stone church was erected and a larger organ was ordered from Richard Bridge in London. Brattle's organ was sold to St. Paul's Church in nearby Newburyport and at some point thereafter resold to St. John's in Portsmouth, New Hampshire, where it still exists.

[29] Kenneth Silverman, *A Cultural History of the American Revolution* (New York: Thomas Y. Crowell, 1976) 40.

[30] Scholes suggests that most Puritans in England had the same view as their Dutch co-religionists; neither group objected particularly to the *presence* of organs in

The organ was presented to South Church in 1727 by the English Colonial governor William Burnet around the time he was departing the city to take up his new duties in Boston. Burnet had grown up in Amsterdam and was therefore familiar with the civic use of organs in that city. He had married the daughter of a prominent New York Dutch family, and her death shortly before his move may have prompted Burnet to present his small residence organ to her church rather than to his own parish, Trinity. Indeed, he may even have had visions of its being put to a similar civic use for all New Yorkers.[31]

The consistory clearly had reservations, but a gift from so distinguished a donor was not something to be refused or disregarded, so on 27 December, the South Church entered into a contract with Hendrick Koek to play the instrument. "Since it has pleased His Excellency, William Burnet, Governor, etc., etc. to present the Low Dutch Reformed Church in New-York with an organ...the same having already been placed in a suitable position...the Rev. ministers...have on the recommendation of His Excellency, Gov. Burnet, appointed Mr. Hendrick Koek as organist." Having engaged an organist, the consistory hedged the prospect of its use with several restrictions. Koek's employment was explicitly limited to "two years and no longer." He would be allowed to play at preaching services but not at communion. He was to admit no one else into the organ loft but the boy who pumped the instrument and whom he would teach to play the organ. In other words, the boy was his apprentice,

---

church buildings—after all, they had no great reverence for a particular building as being "sacred" simply because worship was held there—but only to the instrument's use in worship. See Percy Scholes, *The Puritans and Music in England and New England* (Oxford: Clarendon Press, 1934, 1969) 238–39.

[31] It may also have been Burnet's estrangement from many in New York's English mercantile class, like him communicants at Trinity. As governor, he had restricted their profitable trade with the French in Canada, and the protests that resulted had brought about his removal and transfer to Boston. Although Burnet's father Gilbert was bishop of Winchester, the family had lived in the Netherlands during William's childhood (He was namesake and godchild of William of Orange.). Accordingly Burnet had both an affinity for the Dutch and even for their faith.

and Koek was admonished, "Of the pupil's progress therein the Consistory will expect evidence."[32]

Some thirty years later, the instrument attracted the attention of Ezra Stiles, a Yale-educated Puritan minister, during a visit to the city. As he later wrote, "In the year 1754 I saw in the Dutch calvinist Chh. at New-York a small Organ, which was the first there & had been there I doubt not many years."[33] What became of the organ is not known; it disappeared during the British occupation of New York, between 1776 and 1783.

Around the same time, some Colonial Anglican churches began acquiring organs. In 1728, Christ Church in Philadelphia purchased a small organ, probably of British manufacture, from one of the Wissahickon Mystics, Ludovic Sprogell, for the sum of £200.[34] The same year, St. Philip's Church in Charleston, South Carolina, imported a large organ from England. This instrument, a two-manual with sixteen stops on the main manual and eight in the secondary manual, was probably the first in the British colonies specifically designed and built for a church, and it was certainly the largest organ in North America. Strict Calvinists may well have made something of the fact that the organ was hit by lightning twice in 1744; nevertheless, it remained in St. Philip's until 1833, when it was finally replaced.[35]

On 25 February 1733, five years after St. Philip's received its organ, Trinity Church in Newport, Rhode Island, wrote to Charles Theodore Pachelbel (1690–1750), who had recently arrived in Boston. The philosopher and bishop of Cloyne, George Berkeley, who had been a communicant of Trinity during his residence in the area from 1729 to 1731,[36] had presented the church with a new

---

[32] Ogasapian, *Organ Building in New York City*, 1–2.

[33] Ezra Stiles, *The Literary Diary of Ezra Stiles, D.D., LL.D.*, ed. Franklin Bowditch Dexter, 3 vols. (New York: Scribner's, 1901) 1:58.

[34] See Dean, "The Organ in Eighteenth Century English Colonial America," 89–92.

[35] Ochse, *The History of the Organ in the United States*, 33.

[36] One keyboard, the stop panels, and nameplate still exist in the Newport Historical Society. There seems to be no foundation for the story, retold in Ochse,

organ: a two-manual much like that at St. Philip's. The instrument, built by Richard Bridge in London, had lately arrived from England, and the Vestry of Trinity invited Pachelbel to come to Newport to assist in erecting the instrument and then to assume the duties of organist.[37]

In the decades that followed, still more Colonial Anglican churches acquired organs. Petsworth Church in Virginia had an organ in 1735, although nothing is known about the instrument. The next year, Christ Church in Boston bought an instrument from Newport clockmaker William Claggett. The mechanically adept Claggett may have built the organ; however, it was more likely imported by him for resale.[38]

Trinity Church in New York finally ordered an organ in 1739. It was to be a three-manual instrument, the largest in the colonies and the first known for certain to have been built in North America. The builder was Johann Gottlob Klemm (1690–1762). Klemm, or Clemm as he spelled his name, had apprenticed in Germany, joined Zinzendorf's Moravian settlement at Herrnhut in Saxony in 1726, apparently fallen out with his fellow Moravians, and left for Philadelphia with a group of Schwenkfelders who taken refuge with the Moravians. He arrived in 1733, two years before the first Moravian colonists (with whom the Wesleys traveled) arrived in Georgia and seven years before the first Moravians settled in Nazareth, Pennsylvania.

Klemm finished the Trinity Church organ in July 1741, and the church paid him the £520 contract along with a £40 gratuity. His son,

---

The History of the Organ in the United States, 28–29, that Berkeley had first offered the organ to the Puritan congregation in the town of Berkeley, Massachusetts, named in his honor, and that congregation had turned the instrument down. See Owen, *The Organ in New England*, 6–7. The case of the 1733 instrument may still be seen in the gallery of Trinity Church, though the organ is gone. As for Pachelbel, he moved from Newport to Charleston, South Carolina, in 1740 to become organist of St. Philip's Church.

[37] Pachelbel, son of the great German organist Johann Pachelbel (1653–1706) had arrived in America some three years before.

[38] Ochse, *The History of the Organ in the United States*, 22, 34.

John Jr., became Trinity's organist for one year, but in December 1743, Clement Moore wrote his brother in London on behalf of Trinity's vestry, asking him to "procure for the Church a Good Sober organist; but not to exceed forty pounds Sterling *per annum*, nor to agree for a longer term than three years." John Rice was appointed and remained Trinity's until 1761.[39]

During the 1740s and 1750s, more Anglican churches installed organs. Wealthy urban churches like Trinity in Boston[40] and St. Paul's in Baltimore[41] imported instruments from England. But a growing number of local craftsmen also built organs part-time. In Boston, Thomas Johnston (1701–1767), an engraver and ornamental painter as well as an amateur musician, provided instruments for Christ Church in Boston in 1752, and St. Peter's in Salem in 1754. Bruton Parish Church in Williamsburg, Virginia, had an organ by 1751, though its builder is unknown.[42]

Most of the non-Anglican clergy and congregations resisted the introduction of instruments in worship. Although Edward Bromfield (or Broomfield), Jr. (1723–1746), Harvard-educated and part of a

---

[39] See William H. Armstrong, *Organs for America* (Philadelphia: University of Pennsylvania, 1967) 13–14; Messiter, *A History of the Choir*, 19; and Ogasapian, *Organ Building in New York City*, 3–6. The salary offered by Trinity compared rather poorly with the £100 salary South Church paid Hendrick Koek. Although there seem to have been mechanical problems with it, Klemm's organ served the church for twenty-two years and was sold in 1762 to make way for an instrument by John Snetzler of London. The old instrument disappeared, and the Snetzler was destroyed along with the church in the great fire of 20 September 1776.

[40] Trinity's organ was built by Abraham Jordan of London in 1744 and arrived in Boston on 1 November of that year.

[41] The builder is unknown, but the instrument was installed during late 1748 and early 1749 by Adam Lynne.

[42] All in all, the Great Awakening revivals had minimal effect on Anglican churches, especially those in the cities on the eastern seaboard. The new texts of Watts, still less of Wesley, were not officially accepted by Anglicans, who were, for the most part, using the texts of Tate and Brady's New Version. Metrical psalmody remained the only officially sanctioned congregational music in Anglican parishes until well into the nineteenth century. In fact, as late as 1819, steps were taken against congregational singing of anything other than psalmody. See Stevenson, "John Wesley's First Hymn Book," *Patterns of Protestant Church Music*, 116–17.

prominent Boston Puritan family, had started building an organ "for exercise and recreation...with two rows of keys and many hundred pipes," but it was left incomplete at his death. The instrument was kept in the Old South Church, but almost certainly never used for services.[43]

In some places, the antipathy to organs began to weaken as the years passed. In 1763, the Presbyterian William Dunlap of Philadelphia published a pamphlet recommending the use of an organ to improve congregational psalm singing.[44] Even some New England churches introduced "town viols" as well as wind instruments to support psalm singing. William Billings recommended at least the use of a viol for doubling congregational singing and playing harmonic bass parts.[45]

Apparently, the Congregational Church in tolerant Providence, Rhode Island, was the first New England Calvinist parish in New En-gland to use a small organ, which had been given by a local merchant. Ezra Stiles preached in the church on 22 July 1770 and recorded that "the organ played on in worship." In his itinerary, Stiles made careful notes on its use:

> The course of divine Service in the Congreg. Chh. at Providence under Rev. Mr. Rowland is this.—Congregation rise & the Minister asks a Blessing on the Word & the divine presence in the Solemnities of public Worship—then the people sit, & the Minister reads a Chapter in the Bible—then the bills asking prayers &c are read by the Minister—then the Assembly rise & the Minister prays for a quarter & half an

---

[43] See Ochse, *The History of the Organ in the United States*, 23–28; and especially, Owen, *The Organ in New England*, 22. The instrument was removed when the British commandeered Old South for use as a stable during the occupation of Boston and subsequently was destroyed when the building in which it was stored burned.

[44] James Lyon and Francis Hopkinson, *The Lawfulness, Excellency, and Advantage of Instrumental Music in the Public Worship of God, &c.* (Philadelphia: William Dunlap, 1763). See *CMML*, 1:234.

[45] See Nathaniel Gould, *Church Music in America* (Boston: A. N. Johnson, 1853; repr., New York: AMS Press, 1972) 168–76.

hour—then sing Watts Version of Psalms the People striking in with the Organ & many sing standing, perhaps half the congregation—then Minister takes a Text of Scripture, expounds it & preaches—the people sitting—Sermon being ended, the people rise & the Minister prays a short prayer—then singing & the Organ—then Minister pronounces the Blessing & dismisses the Congregation. But the Organ does not then play.... The Afternoon the same, only in addition, between the last prayer & singing is the Contribution—& the last singing always concludes with the Xtian Doxology, & when it comes to the Doxology the whole Congregation rise & stand with great Solemnity.... The organ is a Chamber organ, as large as a Desk & Book Case, containing about 200 pipes.[46]

St. Michael's Lutheran Church in Germantown, Pennsylvania, had an organ in 1742 that may have been built by Christopher Witt, a member of Kelpius's Hermits. The instrument cost the church only £60, so it must have been small and probably temporary since a new one was acquired in 1751. First Moravian Church in Philadelphia had an instrument by 1743, and an otherwise unknown maker named George Kraft built a small organ for Holy Trinity Lutheran Church in Lancaster, Pennsylvania, sometime before 1744.[47] St. Michael's Lutheran Church in Philadelphia dedicated its new organ, built by Johann Adam Schmahl of Heilbron, Germany, on 12 May 1751. The same year, Augustus Lutheran Church in Trappe, Pennsylvania,

---

[46] Stiles, *Literary Diary*, 1:57–60. Elsewhere in the cited passage, he remarks, "His is the first organ in a dissenting presb. Chh in America except Jersey College [now Princeton].... Perhaps about ten years ago there was an Organ erected in Nassau Hall for the use of the Scholars at public prayers.... I then thought it an Innovation of ill consequence.... The organ has been disused for sundry years & never was much used."

[47] Edward C. Wolf, "Lutheran Church Music in America during the Eighteenth and Early Nineteenth Centuries" (Ph.D. diss., University of Illinois, 1960) 117.

acquired a small organ built by Klemm;[48] and the Moravian Church in New York had an organ before the end of 1754.[49]

Late in 1757, Klemm, who had settled in New York City, rejoined his Moravian co-religionists in Pennsylvania. From his arrival in Bethlehem in late fall 1757 to his death in 1762, he worked with a young cabinetmaker named David Tannenberg (1728–1804). The two built five small organs for Moravian congregations, one of them in North Carolina and the others in Pennsylvania. Tannenberg is now generally considered to be the leading American organ builder of the eighteenth century. Another German émigré, Philip Feyring (1730–1767), was building and repairing keyboard instruments in Philadelphia around 1755, and built large instruments for St. Peter's (1763) and Christ (1766) churches in Philadelphia.[50] Feyring might have presented a formidable rival; however, his premature death in 1767 removed the only potential competition Tannenberg might have had.

Tannenberg was the son of a Moravian shoemaker who had moved to Herrnhut after having been jailed for his faith. The family settled in Bethlehem, Pennsylvania, in 1749. Tannenberg evidently built at least one organ, a small one for Nazareth Hall, before joining forces with Klemm. After the latter's death, he moved to Lititz and proceeded to build forty-one organs for churches as far away as North Carolina. Most of his organs were built for Pennsylvania

---

[48] Brunner, *That Ingenious Business*, 42–54. According to Gottlieb Mittelberger (1715–?), organist of St. Michael's in Philadelphia, there were six organs in Pennsylvania churches in 1751. In addition to the ones mentioned, Mittelberger, who returned to Germany in 1754, lists churches in Providence, New Hanover, and Tulpehocken as owning organs. Brunner dismisses Mittelberger's count as too small a number; indeed, in Philadelphia alone there were at least two other organs in the German Reformed and Moravian churches.

[49] See the account of the 1755 New Year's Eve service in Harry Emelius Stocker, *A History of the Moravian Church in New York* (New York: n.p., 1922) 96.

[50] Brunner, *That Ingenious Business*, 55. Feyring's first organ of record was built in 1762 for St. Paul's Church in Philadelphia. The instrument evoked laudatory notice from Benjamin Franklin in his *Pennsylvania Gazette* of 23 December 1762. Apparently, however, it was owned not by the church but by its minister, and the gentleman took the organ with him when he moved.

German congregations. The majority were quite small and similar to one another. Eight such survive, six of them playable as of this writing. As his reputation grew, the elders of his church evidently became concerned about his frequent absence from the community, for at one point, pressure was brought to bear on him to return to cabinetmaking.[51] He resisted successfully, however, and several of his late organs, among them his largest instruments, were built for non-Moravian churches.[52] Tannenberg was finishing an organ in Christ Lutheran Church, York, Pennsylvania in 1804, when he suffered a stroke from which he died a few days later.[53]

The Moravians

Bethlehem, the city in which John Klemm spent his last years, had been founded in 1741 by the Moravian immigrants with whom the Wesleys had traveled to Savannah, Georgia, in 1735. The group had removed to Pennsylvania in 1740 and established a colony they called Nazareth on land owned by George Whitefield. Within a few months, differences arose with Whitefield over his strict Calvinism, and he evicted the community. The Moravians thereupon bought land of their own nearby and established Bethlehem.[54] By 1757, the city had a sophisticated musical establishment, fully European in its tastes, standards, and repertoire with its centerpiece the famed *collegium musicum*. The same instrumental ensembles and choirs provided music for Moravian worship. Bethlehem's musical activity would reach its height in quality and quantity in the decades between

---

[51] Brunner, *That Ingenious Business*, 70. Tannenberg also came into contact with John Antes, who seems to have taken up building keyboard instruments in addition to his violins. The elders intervened, presumably at Tannenberg's insistence, and Antes was directed to confine himself to making string instruments.

[52] Among his clients was Holy Trinity Lutheran Church in Lancaster, which contracted and built a newer and larger edifice in 1766, as its congregation had grown out of its first building with the small George Kraft organ. Tannenberg's case from his 1773/1774 organ survives in its original location, somewhat enlarged and housing a modern instrument.

[53] The instrument is extant and playable in the York Historical Society.

[54] In 1743, they purchased the site of their previous settlement from Whitefield and reestablished Nazareth.

1780 and 1850. Both George Washington and Benjamin Franklin visited the city and came away impressed with its music.

The community also produced a number of fine, if not outstanding, composers, among them Jeremias Denke (1725–1791), Johannes Herbst (1735–1812), Johann Friederich Peter (1746–1813), and John Antes (1740–1811). Herbst was a pastor of the congregation at Lititz, and almost all his surviving music consists of sacred songs and anthems for Moravian events and occasions. Peter was an organist and violinist whose output includes over a hundred anthems, as well as concert pieces and chamber music. Antes, American-born and a maker of string instruments, traveled to Europe where he met Haydn.

Moravians had a body of hymnody—some of it very old, other hymns relatively recent. Their leader, Count Nicholas von Zinzendorf (1700–1760), had compiled four collections between 1725 and 1731, and these became the basis of the Herrnhut community's 1735 hymnal.[55] These were the hymns, which were sung aboard ship by immigrants, impressed and influenced the Wesleys. Moravian hymnody had roots that antedated Martin Luther and in fact included some of the earliest texts not derived as a whole from psalmody.[56]

Hymn singing was a part not only of the Moravians' worship but of their daily activities. Chorale tunes were often played from the church tower by trombone choirs. Indeed, so important to their life and worship were their hymns that when in 1744, the Lutheran Consistory of Uppsala, Sweden, issued a lengthy letter warning against the Moravians, it cited as evidence of their "gross heresies" the texts of those hymns.[57] As early as 1743, the Moravian church in

---

[55] *Das Gesangbuch der Gemeine in Herrnhuth* (Herrnhuth: n.p., 1735). Tunes were taken largely from Freylinghausen's *Geistreiches Gesangbuch* (Halle: in Verlegung des Wäysenhauses, 1704). In 1714 a second part appeared titled *Neues Geist-reiches Gesang-Bush*. These were the sources of the texts John Wesley had translated and the tunes to which he set those translations, in 1737.

[56] The first collections of Moravian congregational hymn texts were published in 1501 and 1505, more than a decade before Luther nailed his ninety-five theses to the Castle Church door in Wittenberg.

[57] Tappert, "The Influence of Pietism in Colonial American Lutheranism," 16.

Philadelphia had two organs, and its music was attracting attention among the English residents of the city. On 8 June 1744, William Black noted, "We went to the Moravian Meeting, where I had the pleasure to hear an Excellent Comment in Scripture...and after *some very agreeable Church Music*."

As early as 1746, the Moravian church in Bethlehem had an organ, traditionally attributed to Gustave Hesselius. Organs in Moravian churches were generally small and used primarily for accompaniment and with instrumental ensembles. No solo organ literature of any consequence by Moravian composers has come to light, although John Cosens Ogden, an Episcopal clergyman from Portsmouth who visited Bethlehem and Nazareth in 1799, wrote, "According to an universal practice, the organist played a voluntary previous to the arrival of the minister."[58]

But it was the vigorous hymn-singing that played so prominent a role in Moravian worship that attracted the attention of many in the English colonies. The minister generally began, and the congregation and organ joined in as they recognized the hymn. Abraham Ritter, organist of the Moravian Church in Philadelphia for a number of years, described a mid-nineteenth-century evening service as involving fifteen to twenty changes of melody in three-quarters of an hour. The singing alternated among the minister or "liturgicus," the choir, various groups, and the congregation as a whole. Ritter asserted, "The unbroken service requires practical skill in the organist to pass from one melody to another, without change of key, seeing that a succession of modulations would mar the service."[59] Congregational singing was promoted among the

---

The Dutch Reformed Consistory in New York had also condemned the Moravians; however, in 1749 the British Parliament recognized them as an "Ancient Protestant Episcopal Church," thereby conferring a legal protection on them that not even New York's stubborn dominies dared assail. See John R. Weinlick, "Moravianism in the American Colonies" in the same collection: F. Ernest Stoeffler, *Continental Pietism...*, 138.

[58] John Cosens Ogden, *Excursion into Bethlehem and Nazareth, Pennsylvania, in the Year 1799* (Philadelphia: Charles Cist, 1800) quoted in *CMML*, 2:211.

[59] Abraham Ritter, *History of the Moravian Church in Philadelphia* (Philadelphia:

Moravians as a sacred duty. Texts and tunes were matched,[60] and on occasion polyglot congregations sang the same hymn in different languages to its customary tune. At a love feast held in Nazareth in September 1745, a single hymn is recorded as having been sung in thirteen languages simultaneously, including several American Indian dialects.[61]

In the final analysis, though, the Moravian community was self-contained and hermetic. Its worship and music, both the ensemble pieces and the hymnody, stood apart from the rest of Protestant worship music. In the end, elegant though the Moravian musical establishment and tradition were, neither had significant influence on the music of other denominations.

Hayes & Zell, 1857) 113–15. Although the description suggests a Love Feast—a non-sacramental ceremony involving the partaking of a light common meal (often coffee and buns)—Ritter discusses it under the heading "Liturgies and Litanies" and devotes another section (141–44) to the Love Feast. The description also fits a Song Hour: a service of congregational hymns around a single idea or subject. See also Armstrong, *Organs for America*, 77–78.

[60] Ritter, *History*, 149–54. *CMML*, 2:209–19.

[61] Ellinwood, *The History of American Church Music*, 36; Russell N. Squire, *Church Music* (St. Louis: Bethany Press, 1962) 228–29, citing Rufus A. Grider, *Historical Notes on Music in Bethlehem, Pennsylvania from 1741 to 1871* (Philadelphia: John R. Pile, 1873).

4.

Urban Church Music at the Turn of the Century

Boston

Boston's churches resisted the introduction of organs longer than churches in the other large seaboard cities. Other than the Episcopal parishes, only the strikingly progressive Brattle Square Church had an organ by the early nineteenth century, and its introduction had been the occasion of considerable acrimony. Even as it was en route from England, an erstwhile and prosperous member of Brattle Square offered to reimburse the church its costs if the instrument were thrown overboard before the ship docked in Boston. On the other hand, the work of Billings and his colleagues had resulted in a number of flourishing choirs, often supported by *ad hoc* instrumental ensembles. At Park Street Church, for instance, a flute, bassoon, and cello accompanied the fifty-voice chorus.[1] Other churches employed only a cello, commonly referred to as a "church viol," to etch the bass line under the psalm tune, or they simply used a wood pipe to give the pitch.[2]

---

[1] Carol Pemberton, *Lowell Mason: His Life and Work* (Ann Arbor: UMI Research Press, 1985) 7

[2] For nearer a contemporary perspective on the subject of instruments, see

Notwithstanding its dearth of organs, the city was home to at least two prominent English organists in the decades after the Revolutionary War. If William Billings represented the native "tunesmith" tradition in Puritan New England, his contemporary and counterpart in more sophisticated music was the British immigrant William Selby (1738–1798). Rarely have two such dissimilar musicians worked in such close proximity and harmony. Billings taught a singing school at King's Chapel in 1785, and Selby evidently conducted a concert for Billings's benefit on 21 December 1790.[3]

During the 1760s, William Selby served as organist of St. Sepulchre's Church, Holborn, and All Hallows, Bread Street, in London. He was also organist of the Magdalen Hospital chapel and his music appears in that institution's collection.[4] In October 1773, he resigned his London posts and immigrated to Newport, Rhode Island, where he had apparently been called by the vestry. Although Selby's term of service began 20 December 1773, the vestry paid his salary from 1 October as well as his passage from England.[5] His

---

Nathaniel Gould, *Church Music in America* (Boston: A. N. Johnson, 1853; repr., New York: AMS Press, 1972)168–83. Gould's recollections, as distinct from some of his "facts," are valuable and illuminating.

[3] See Kenneth Silverman, *A Cultural History of the American Revolution* (New York: Thomas Y. Crowell, 1976) 473–74; David McKay and Richard Crawford, *William Billings of Boston* (Princeton: Princeton University Press, 1975) 152, 163–64.

[4] Magdalen Hospital Chapel, London, England, *A Second Collection of Psalms and Hymns Us'd at the Magdalen Chapel* (London: Printed for Henry Thorowgood1765?).

[5] Barbara Owen, "The Other Mr. Selby," *American Music* 8/4 (Winter 1980): 477–82 shows from an examination of records in London and Newport that Selby actually remained in London until October 1773, rather than 1771, the date usually given. Owen also found record of a John Selby residing in Boston and of John Selby being paid by King's Chapel on 30 January 1776, around the time it closed during the Revolution. This then is the "Mr. Selby" alluded to in the notice of a benefit concert for Josiah Flagg on 4 October 1771. See also Owen, *The Organs and Music of King's Chapel, 1713–1791*, 2nd ed. (Boston: King's Chapel, 1991) 40–44; and David McKay, "William Selby, Musical Emigré in Colonial Boston," *Musical Quarterly* 57/4 (October 1971): 609–27; and most important, Nicholas Temperley, *Bound for America: Three British Composers* (Urbana: University of Illinois Press, 2003) 12–51.

brother John (1741–1804) was already in New England. He had come to Boston some years earlier to be organist at King's Chapel. John Selby was a loyalist, and when the British soldiers evacuated Boston in March 1776, he left with them. William Selby's sympathies lay with the patriots. By late summer or fall 1776, he had moved to Boston as organist of Trinity Church. When King's Chapel reopened after the Revolution in 1782, William was appointed its organist, and he stayed there until his death in 1798.

William Selby took an active role in the Boston area's musical scene. His small number of surviving compositions are in the usual triadic and homophonic pseudo-Handelian style favored by English musicians of his generation. In addition to an ode composed for George Washington's visit to Boston in 1793, Selby's three known anthems include a setting of Psalm 100 that appeared in a number of collections, a setting of Psalm 117 that Selby published himself, and "Behold He Is My Salvation," also reprinted in several collections, among them Oliver Holden's *Union Harmony* of 1793.[6]

Although they never met, George K. Jackson arrived in America two years before Selby's death. Born in Oxford in 1757, Jackson gained some renown for a book on figured bass he published in London in 1785. He was awarded a doctorate in music by the University of St. Andrew's in 1791. Five years later, he immigrated to America, and over the next few years, he served a succession of churches in the Mid-Atlantic states. In 1801, he presented a recital on a new organ built by John Geib, himself lately arrived from London, in Christ Church in New York,[7] and except for a brief period in Hartford, 1805–1806, he appears to have settled in New York City for the next decade. He was organist of St. George's Chapel from 1802 to 1805 and again from 1806 to 1807.

By 1812, Jackson had moved to Boston as organist of the Brattle Square Church, by that time Boston's largest and most fashionable

---

[6] Ralph T. Daniel, *The Anthem in New England before 1800* (Evanston: Northwestern, 1966; repr., New York: DaCapo, 1979) 85.

[7] John Ogasapian, *Organ Building in New York City, 1700–1900* (Braintree: Organ Literature Foundation, 1977) 25, 187.

congregation. That October, he directed a concert of Handel's music at King's Chapel, including selections from *Messiah* and *Sampson*. The next spring, Jackson, who had failed to register as an alien, was forced to leave Boston and settle temporarily in Northampton. But he clearly gained a following in the Boston musical scene in a relatively short time, for his internal exile provoked a measure of protest in the city. Nevertheless, it was two years before he was permitted to return.

Jackson may have served briefly as organist of King's Chapel after he took up residence again in Boston; however, in April 1815, he became organist of Trinity Church. He remained there for five years. From 1820 until his death in 1822, he was organist of St. Paul's Church. The years after his return from Northampton seem to have soured Jackson as far as American music-making was concerned. According to his contemporary John Rowe Parker, he had become a difficult person, increasingly intolerant of the relaxed standards that so often characterized the predominantly amateur musical performances in his day. He gained a good bit of weight, and his health declined. By 1817, his influence was on the wane and his performances became increasingly infrequent.[8]

Philadelphia

German Lutheran congregations in Pennsylvania had begun to develop musical programs patterned after those of their European counterparts during the second half of the eighteenth century. Choirs had been established to provide special music for the services and to lead the congregational singing. As in Europe, ministers frequently wrote texts for special occasions, which were set to music by their parish organists. Organists played preludes, interludes, and free

---

[8] John Rowe Parker, *Musical Biography, or Sketches of the Lives and Writings of Eminent Musical Characters* (Boston: Stone & Fovill, 1825; repr., Detroit: Information Coordinators, 1975) 129–30. See also Owen, *Organs and Music of King's Chapel,* 47–48; H. Earle Johnson, "George K. Jackson, Doctor of Music (1745–1822)," *Musical Quarterly* 29/1 (January 1943): 113; Charles H. Kaufman, "George K. Jackson: American Musician of the Federal Period," (Ph.D. diss., New York University, 1968); and especially Temperley, *Bound for America,* 123–94.

accompaniments to congregational singing. By the end of the century, music had become as integral a part of the curriculum in Lutheran parish schools in America as it was in Germany. The positions of schoolmaster and parish organist were often combined, and congregations sang numerous hymns they had learned as children, in parts and antiphonally or responsorially with the choir or soloists.[9]

Even earlier, the musical situation in these parishes had been in sharp contrast, not only to that of the English and Dutch-speaking Anglican and Calvinist churches of the middle colonies and New England, but even the non-German Lutheran churches. Henry Melchior Muhlenberg (1711–1787), a practicing musician and clergyman, arrived from Germany in 1741. Muhlenberg had been called as pastor by the Lutherans of Philadelphia, at the time the largest city on the eastern seaboard. He quickly assumed responsibility for other Lutherans in the middle colonies and organized the first synod in 1748.

Muhlenberg's own accounts of preaching in Pennsylvania and New York suggest the contrast. Of one preaching stop in Pennsylvania he reported: "The English were amazed at our singing and almost went into raptures over it, for some of the people had fine voices and knew how to sing in harmony."[10] When he preached to the Lutherans in New York, however, the situation was quite different. There had been only one copy of the hymnbook, and Muhlenberg was forced to resort to the distinctly alien device of lining out the hymns.[11]

---

[9] Edward C. Wolf, "Lutheran Church Music in America during the Eighteenth and Early Nineteenth Centuries" (Ph.D. diss., University of Illinois, 1960) vi–vii. So exhaustive and thorough was Wolf's scholarship that even after thirty-five years, his dissertation, cited in the last chapter, remains a major resource. As will be seen, this chapter relies heavily on it.

[10] E. Clifford Nelson, ed., *The Lutherans in North America* (Philadelphia: Fortress, 1980) 66–67.

[11] John Kelpius and Anthony Aston, *Church Music and Musical Life in Pennsylvania in the Eighteenth Century* 3 vols. bound as 4(Philadelphia: Publications of the Pennsylvania Society of Colonial Dames of America, 1926–1935, 1926; repr., New York: AMS, 1972) 3:298–99. (Hereafter cited as *CMML*.)

The German Lutherans of Pennsylvania imported their first hymnals from Europe. The most common were the Marburg hymnal of 1711 and the Halle hymnal of 1704, enlarged in 1714 to contain 1,500 texts. The Halle hymnal designated well-known chorale melodies for most of the hymns and provided the others with specific tunes and figured basses. The Marburg hymnal had 461 hymn texts, increased to 615 in the 1747 edition, but contained no music. Rather, chorale tunes were assumed for the texts popularly associated with them, and particular ones were suggested for texts lacking traditional tunes of their own. Though the Halle hymnal was influential, it was not reprinted in America. Saur printed six American editions of the Marburg hymnal from 1757 to 1777, and for a time, it became the most widely used German collection. Organists either compiled their own manuscript collections of tunes or used one of the several published chorale books from Germany.[12]

Muhlenberg organized the Lutherans of Philadelphia into a parish in 1742 and oversaw the construction of a new building, St. Michael's, from 1742 to 1748. Three years later, the church dedicated its organ, built by Johann Adam Schmal of Heilbron, Germany. Immigration so increased numbers that a second building was needed, and the cornerstone of Zion Church was laid 16 May 1766. It was the largest church building in the city, yet it had no organ for some years. Two horns supported congregational singing at the dedication services on 25 June 1769.[13]

The year of Zion's dedication, a new pastor arrived from Halle to take charge of the Holy Trinity Lutheran Church in Lancaster,

---

[12] *Das neueste und nunmehre aller-vollständigste Marburger Gesang-buch...* (Hesse: Stocks, 1711); J. A. Freylinghausen, comp., *Geistreiches Gesangbuch* (Halle: in Verlegung des Wäysenhauses, 1704). Among the choral books cited by Wolf are Johann Balthazar König, *Harmonischer Lieder-Schatz oder Allgemeines Evangelisches Choral-Buch* (Frankfurt: Auf Kosten des Autorio, 1738); and Johann Georg Christian Störls, *Neu-bezogenes Davidisches Harpfen und Psalter-spiel...* (Stuttgardt: J. B. Metzler, 1744). See *CMML*, 3:268, 271; Wolf, "Lutheran Church Music in America," 143–48.

[13] Edward C. Wolf, "Music in Old Zion, Philadelphia, 1750–1850," *Musical Quarterly* 58/4 (October 1972): 627. The congregations of St. Michael's and Zion recombined in the late nineteenth century and built a single church. Neither the congregation nor any of the three buildings it occupied is still in existence.

Pennsylvania. Justus Heinrich Christian Helmuth (1745–1825) was a pianist and musical amateur, as well as a poet and composer of hymn texts. Beginning with the publication of his *Empfindungen des Herzens in einigen Lieden,*[14] he produced some sixty collections of poems and hymn and cantata texts until 1817.[15]

In 1779, Helmuth was called as pastor by St. Michael's and Zion. Under his leadership, the combined parish became the largest and most influential German-speaking congregation in the country. Zion, which had Philadelphia's largest auditorium and was within easy walking distance for members of the government, became essentially the national church; the service of thanksgiving for the surrender of Lord Cornwallis was held there on 24 October 1781.

Yet another pastor, John Christopher Kunze (1744–1807), had emigrated from Germany a year later than Helmuth and served St. Michael's and Zion from 1770 to 1784, before going to New York to become pastor of Christ Church there. Kunze published his own 132-page collection of German-language poems and hymns.[16]

In 1782, a committee including Muhlenberg, Helmuth, and Kunze began the planning of a hymnal suitable for use by the German-speaking Lutheran churches of the middle colonies. The resulting collection, *Erbauliche Lieder-Sammlung zum Gottesdienst-lichen Gebrauch,*[17] contained over 700 hymns, many of them from the Marburg hymnal and was used by German Lutheran congregations well into the nineteenth century.[18]

The German Reformed had their own Marburg hymnal, three editions of which had been reprinted by Saur between 1752 and 1772. About a third of the Reformed Marburg's 700 hymn texts were also in the Lutheran Marburg hymnal. After the denomination broke

---

[14] Justus Heinrich Christian Helmuth, *Empfindungen des Herzens in einigen Lieden* (Philadelphia: Melchior Syeiner, 1781),

[15] See Edward C. Wolf, "Justus Henry Christian Helmuth—Hymnodist," *German-American Studies* 5 (1972): 117–47.

[16] John Christopher Kunze, *Einige Gedichte und Lieder* (Philadelphia: Christoph und Peter Saur, 1778).

[17] (Germantown: printed by Leibert & Billmeyer, 1786).

[18] Wolf, "Lutheran Church Music in America," 157–65.

with the Dutch Reformed in 1793, a committee was established to produce an independent hymnal. *Das neue und verbeßte Gesang-Buch*[19] contained some 700 hymn texts and seventy melodies, as well as the 150 psalms and sixty tunes to which they might be sung.[20]

David Tannenberg's only three-manual organ was built between 1786 and 1790 for Zion Church.[21] By that time, the combined parish was building a music program patterned on that of municipal churches in Germany. A special private showing of the organ was given 3 September 1790 for President Washington and other dignitaries of government. So great was interest that three dedication services, on 10, 11, and 17 October were required to accommodate the crowds, even though the building seated 2,500 to 3,000. Pastor Helmuth provided a cantata text for the occasion, set to music by Zion's organist and parish schoolmaster, David Ott.

The Pennsylvania Mercury and Universal Advertiser for 14 October 1790 records: "The excellent instrument of Sacred Musik [*sic*] does great honor to the artist David Tennenberg [*sic*] and to the zeal of the congregation." *The Independent Gazette and Agricultural Repository* for 16 October said of the concert, "The choir sang...[but] the organ chiefly attracted the attendance of the audience, and afforded them the most exquisite delight." *The Federal Gazette and Philadelphia Daily Advertiser* for 11 October commended the congregation: "We sincerely applaud the piety and musical taste, which the congregation has evinced in purchasing at great expense this superb instrument."

That month, Zion engaged John Christopher Moller (1755–1803) to play the organ and to keep it in tune. Moller was born in Germany but had been active in London for at least ten years, publishing a considerable amount of his own music there before he immigrated again in 1790, this time to America. He

---

[19] (Philadelphia: various, 1797–1859).

[20] *CMML*, 3:294–97. The initial printing may have been underwritten privately by the Reverend William Hendel, pastor of the German Reformed Church in Philadelphia and a friend of Helmuth.

[21] Raymond J. Brunner, *That Ingenious Business: Pennsylvania Organ Builders* (Birdsboro: The Pennsylvania German Society, 1990) 9. The instrument cost £1500 (the Pennsylvania pound being worth about $2.67 at the end of the century).

appeared as a harpsichordist in a New York concert and shortly thereafter, in October, presented himself to Zion as a candidate for the post of organist. Like many of his contemporaries, Moller pieced together a living from a variety of musical activities. In Philadelphia, he was active as a composer, teacher, performer and manager of a city concert series, and proprietor of a music store.

But the state of music in the German churches of Philadelphia was now approaching that of city churches in Germany. Moller, along with clergymen Helmuth and Frederick August Muhlenberg (1750–1801), began work on a book of chorale melodies for use, not only with *Erbauliche Lieder-Sammlung*, but also with the German Reformed hymnal then in preparation. The work was announced in late 1795 and early 1796. The project was never completed; evidently, not enough subscriptions were obtained to support it. More to the point, disaster had intervened; Zion and its Tannenberg organ were destroyed by fire 26 December 1794. Moller, having no church position, relocated to New York, where he was appointed organist of Trinity Church and continued with his performing, composing, and publishing.[22]

Nevertheless, this episode of collaboration among Moller and the two ministers highlights a significant difference between German and English parishes in regard to the parish musician. During the latter half of the century, several musicians from England settled in the cities, gleaning a living by combining teaching, theater work, concert management, music merchandising, and playing the organ on Sundays in one or another of the churches. Unlike the Lutherans, Anglican parishes rarely expected extra involvement in parish activities by their organists beyond the Sunday morning duties for

---

[22] Some parts of the ruined Tannenberg organ may have been salvaged and cobbled together into an instrument after the church was rebuilt, or some other temporary organ may have been installed. In any event, it was not until 1811 that the English immigrant builder John Lowe provided Zion with an adequate organ to replace the Tannenberg. On Moller, see Wolf, "Lutheran Church Music in America," 283–85 and "Music in Old Zion, Philadelphia, 1750–1850"; and especially Ronald D. Stetzel, "John Christopher Moller (1755–1803) and His Role in Early American Music" (Ph.D. diss., University of Iowa, 1965).

which they were engaged. Relatively few undertook to train singers or compile collections of music for their parish's use. Those who did teach or compile did so in the hopes of adding to their income. And of course, such general musicians, stitching together what was often a marginal living, had little interest in such things as parish education.

On the other hand, Lutheran parishes like St. Michael's and Zion in Philadelphia replicated a practice in the mother country. Several combined the duties of parish schoolmaster and organist; few English churches maintained parish schools anyway, and rarely if ever would a hireling musician be involved. As a result, German church musicians tended to be involved with their parishes personally as well as professionally, whereas most English church organists considered their Sunday duties nothing more than a professional obligation and had no special interest either in church music or the parish that employed them.

Where music was cultivated in an Anglican parish, it was only because of an interested layman or the rare clergyman who valued music as a part of worship. Standards were not especially high; American churches had no cathedral music establishments as standards or examples. Only at the end of the century, and then only in a few churches, did choirs attempt Anglican chant. Anglican and Episcopal congregations sang metrical psalmody well into the nineteenth century.

In 1761, Christ Church in Philadelphia received a bequest of £100 toward the replacement of the small organ the parish had used since 1728. Philip Feyring completed a three-manual, twenty-seven stop organ with two octaves of pedals for Christ Church in 1766. Meanwhile, James Bremner (d.1780), English by birth, had arrived in Philadelphia in 1763 after a brief stop in New York. A notice in the *Pennsylvania Gazette* for 1 December 1763 announced his readiness to teach "young ladies...the Harpsichord or Guittar" and "young Gentlemen the Violin, German Flute, Harpsichord or Guittar."[23]

---

[23] The two octaves of pedals speak more to Feyring's German orientation—and probably to the example of the German organ recently installed in nearby St. Michael's—than to any progressive musical tendencies on the part of the parish.

In January 1767, Christ Church appointed Bremner organist. Although he would occupy that post off and on until 1774, the guiding spirit behind the music in Christ Church and its companion St. Peter's during those years was Francis Hopkinson (1737–1791), a vestryman of the combined parish.[24] Hopkinson was very much a man of the Enlightenment. He was a lawyer by profession, but his interests ranged far and wide. A patriot and signer of the Declaration of Independence, he was also a poet, essayist, amateur musician, and artist. During the years immediately preceding the Revolution, he was an active presence in the Philadelphia's musical life, joining with local professionals in concerts and even composing music for their performances.

Hopkinson published a volume of sacred music for use in Christ Church and St. Peter's in 1763. The collection contained thirty-seven pieces, for the most part well-known tunes from British sources. It also included two of his anthems for two and three voices and figured bass.[25] At the time, he and William Young were training a group of children from the combined parish as a choir to lead the singing, and their efforts must have borne fruit, for the Vestry of Christ Church and St. Peter's formally recognized the two men's "great and constant pains in teaching and instructing the children" at its meeting of 3 April 1764.[26]

---

[24] *CMML*, 3:240–41. The timing of Bremner's appointment coincides not only with the completion of Feyring's organ but also with Hopkinson's trip to England in 1766–1767. Vestry minutes for 10 December 1770 refer to Bremner as "the late organist," but he was back fulfilling the function in February 1774. See also Oscar G. T. Sonneck, *Francis Hopkinson, the First American Poet-Composer (1737–1791) and James Lyon, Patriot, Preacher, Psalmodist (1735–1794): Two Studies in Early American Music* (Washington: McQueen, 1905; repr., New York: Da Capo, 1967) 29.

[25] Francis Hopkinson, *A Collection of Psalm Tunes, with a Few Anthems and Hymns, Some of Them Entirely New, for the Use of the United Churches of Christ Church and St. Peter's Church in Philadelphia* (Philadelphia: Henry Dunlap, 1763) chapter 3. Allen Perdue Britton, Irving Lowens, and Richard Crawford, *American Sacred Music Imprints 1698–1810* (Worcester MA: American Antiquarian Society, 1990) 333–34. (Hereafter cited as *ASMI*.)

[26] Leonard Ellinwood, *The History of American Church Music* (New York: Morehouse-Gorham, 1953; repr., New York: Da Capo, 1970) 48. At approximately the same time, Hopkinson was engaged in preparing the English-language Psalter for

During the 1780s, Hopkinson's time was taken up by civic duties, and he was forced to give up his work with the children of the combined parish. Nevertheless, he kept up his musical activities as best he could. Late in life, and by now a federal district court judge, Hopkinson proudly claimed to have been "the first Native of the United States who has produced a Musical Composition" in the dedication of his *Seven* [actually, eight] *Songs for Harpsichord*.[27]

William Tuckey (1708–1781) had become clerk of St. Peter's in 1778, and in spite of his advanced age, he may have taken over the work Hopkinson and Young had started. An immigrant from Bristol, Tuckey had had been active in New York since 1753, primarily in the music of Trinity Church, but he was well past his prime by the time he arrived in Philadelphia and made no real mark there in the few years he had left. Tuckey's death on 14 September 1781, along with Hopkinson's decreased involvement in the parish's music, resulted after some delay in the formation of a committee to "regulate the singing at St. Peter's," in December 1782. The committee hired Matthew Whitehead "to instruct twelve persons in singing to accompany the organ," and early the next year, it engaged the highly regarded music master Andrew Law to run a singing school at St. Peter's.[28]

The rector of the combined parish of Christ Church and St. Peter's, and later bishop of Pennsylvania, William White (1748–1836), had little if any interest in music and appears never to have used anything but metrical psalmody in services he led, probably because of associations of hymn texts with "enthusiasm" and such groups as the Methodists, whom he would have considered sectarians. Moreover, White believed that no more than twenty tunes were required by any congregation. "I am convinced," he wrote, "that no circumstance impedes good singing in our churches so much as the great diversity of tunes." Doubtless at his instigation, on 3 April 1785, the Vestry of Christ Church and St. Peter's directed that only

---

the Dutch Reformed churches of New York, which appeared in 1767.

[27] (Philadelphia: J. Aitken, 1788).

[28] *CMML*, 3:243.

familiar tunes be sung and that no new tunes be added, saying that "the singing of other tunes, and frequent changing of the tunes [was]...generally disagreeable and inconvenient."[29]

On the whole, though, White seems to have listened to Hopkinson's advice and even deferred to him on more than one occasion. Busy though he was in the affairs of the new nation by 1785, Hopkinson made time to prepare an eight-page music supplement for American Episcopal Church's proposed *Book of Common Prayer*.[30] White was less than enthusiastic about the inclusion of chants along with the metrical tunes. "Mr. Hopkinson...is desirous of inserting a page of chants; and if I comply with this it will be to gratify him, as he has taken so much trouble in the matter," he wrote to his fellow minister William Smith.[31]

Hopkinson probably first heard Anglican chant, essentially part-singing of non-metrical texts in speech rhythm to a repeated melodic formula, during his visit to England in 1766–1767. Andrew Law, who conducted the singing school at St. Peter's in 1783, included instructions on chanting, along with eight four-voice chant tunes, in a collection he published about that time.[32] Law's model appears to have been the three-voice chants in a collection prepared by James Bremner's brother Robert, and also titled *The Rudiments of Music*.[33]

The proposed prayer book of 1786 contained eighty-four psalms and fifty-one hymn texts; the final version, adopted in 1789 and published October 1790, contained all the psalms in meter, but only

---

[29] *CMML*, 3:245–47.

[30] Episcopal Church, "Tunes Suited to the Psalms and Hymns of the Book of Common Prayer," *The Book of Common Prayer...Revised and Proposed to the Use of the Protestant Episcopal Church* (Philadelphia: Hall and Sellers, 1786).

[31] Horace W. Smith, *Life and Correspondence of the Rev. William Smith, D.D., with Copious Extracts from His Writings*, 2 vols. (Philadelphia: Ferguson Bros., 1880) 2:175; quoted with commentary in Ruth Mack Wilson, *Anglican Chant and Chanting in England, Scotland, and America, 1660–1820* (Oxford: Clarendon Press, 1996) 219. Chapter 8 (217–58) of Wilson's book "Early Episcopal Music in America" constitutes a major resource on the early use of Anglican chant in America.

[32] Andrew Law, *The Rudiments of Music* (Cheshire CT: Law, 1783, 1785).

[33] Robert Bremner, *The Rudiments of Music* (London: printed for the author, 1762); Wilson, *Anglican Chant and Chanting*, 222.

twenty-seven hymns. More hymn texts would be added in 1808 and 1826, to make a total of 212 hymns, many of them from non-Episcopal sources; however, there was no real effort to follow up on Hopkinson's work by producing an official collection of tunes comparable to those published by the Lutherans. Instead (with one minor and unsuccessful exception), unofficial tune collections were issued by individuals and parishes, right through the nineteenth century.[34]

Sometime before 1787, Hopkinson drafted a lengthy and informative letter to White regarding the use of an organ in church. Hopkinson prefaced his remarks by emphasizing the subordinate role of music in general and the instrument in particular to the spoken word. He described the purpose of church music as "adoration," taking David as his example and psalmody as the proper vehicle. Hopkinson advocated the use of an organ to enhance musical praise, but only within strict limitations. The organist should not attempt to show off his skill or to entertain the congregation with the solo piece or voluntary, which was commonly played at the time between the psalm and the lessons. Rather, this voluntary should last no more than five minutes and maintain the spirit of the season, psalm, or scripture readings that followed it. As for chant, Hopkinson saw no reason for it not to be "pleasing and animating," so long as it was treated as "a species of *recitative*, which is no more than speaking musically." Unison congregational chanting was to be supported with

---

[34] For example, Israel Terril, *The Episcopal Harmony* (New Haven: West Society, 1802); John Cole, *The Beauties of Psalmody* (Baltimore: Cole & Hewes, 1805) and *Episcopal Harmony* (Baltimore: G. Dobbin ad Murphy, 1811); Trinity Church, Boston MA, *Hymns for Trinity Church* (Boston: Munroe, Francis & Parker, 1808). Cole was the clerk of St. Paul's in Baltimore, and his 1805 collection contained seven chants for morning and evening canticles with text underlaid to quarter notes, suggesting a rigid manner of performance. See Wilson, *Anglican Chant and Chanting*, 239, 266. The first and only official sanctioned collection of music prior to the Civil War was the *Tune Book*, prepared for the House of Bishops and issued in 1858. The volume met with little success; indeed, plans for an authorized Episcopal hymnal would not get underway until 1865, in the wake of the appearance of the authorized English hymnal *Hymns Ancient and Modern*. The first official Episcopal collection with music was the 1916 hymnal.

harmony played on the organ and sung by a choir of "at least a half dozen voices in the organ gallery."

Metrical psalm tunes, wrote Hopkinson, should be introduced clearly on the organ "with only a few chaste and expressive decorations." The purpose of organ interludes between verses was to give the congregation a chance to take a breath while reflecting on what they had just sung; accordingly, the organist should make every effort to maintain the spirit of the text. Hopkinson advised that such interludes not exceed sixteen measures in triple meter, ten or twelve in duple—about a stanza's length of text. The closing voluntary, Hopkinson advised, should have "some analogy with the discourse delivered from the pulpit." It should be consistent with the spirit of the sermon, whether thoughtful or joyous. In general, Hopkinson concluded, the organ should always be dignified, and the organist should never attempt to entertain with tuneful "airs, lilts and jiggs."[35]

In 1793, two years after Hopkinson's death, Benjamin Carr (1768–1831) arrived in Philadelphia. Carr probably studied in London with Charles Wesley, the son of the great hymn writer and, like his more talented if somewhat erratic brother Samuel, a recognized composer. Benjamin emigrated along with his brother Thomas and their father, Joseph Carr. Thomas and Joseph settled in Baltimore and opened a music dealership and publishing concern. Benjamin started a similar business in Philadelphia and shortly thereafter opened a branch in New York. He sold the New York store to James Hewitt in 1797. Like other expatriate English musicians, Carr became involved in several aspects of musical life. He taught and took part in concerts, but his primary interest, both in

---

[35] Francis Hopkinson, "A Letter to the Rev. Doctor White, Rector of Christ Church and St. Peter's, on the Conduct of Church Organs," in *The Miscellaneous Essays and Occasional Writings of Francis Hopkinson, Esq.* 3 vols. (Philadelphia: T. Dobson, 1792) 2:119–26. The full text is given in Orpha Ochse, *The History of the Organ in the United States* (Bloomington: Indiana University Press, 1975) 427–30. The actual date of the letter is uncertain. White was elected bishop of Pennsylvania in 1787, and although he remained as rector of the combined Philadelphia parish, it seems likely that the heading would make some allusion to the title of bishop, had it been written after his elevation.

England and America, was clearly the stage. Most of his compositions consisted of popular songs, keyboard music, and stage works.

Though he remained an Anglican, Carr spent his career as organist of two Catholic churches. Shortly after his arrival in Philadelphia, he was appointed by St. Joseph's. St. Augustine's was completed in 1801, and that June, Carr became its organist. He stayed at St. Augustine's for the next thirty years until his death. During those years, he gave performances of Handel's *Messiah* and Haydn's *Creation*, both in abbreviated versions.

Like their Protestant neighbors, Philadelphia's Catholics, many of them German, had maintained the continental European custom of fine music as best they could in their new land. As far back as Christmas Day 1749, Lutheran Pastor Peter Kalm recorded in his diary having attended Catholic worship at St. Joseph's in Philadelphia, which, according to Kalm, had the only functioning organ in the city. "Three sermons were preached there, and that which contributed most to the splendor of the ceremony was the beautiful music heard today. It was this music which attracted so many people.... The officiating priest was a Jesuit, who also played the violin, and he had collected a few others who played the same instrument. So there was good instrumental music, with singing from the organ-gallery besides."[36]

St. Mary's, a much larger church than St. Joseph's, was completed in 1763, and its trustees hastened to establish a singing school for the choir by the very next year. By 1779, the church's music was in a fine state. The *Pennsylvania Packet* dated 10 July of that year described how members of the Continental Congress and other distinguished personages attended St. Mary's on 4 July as

---

[36] Wolf, "Lutheran Church Music in America," 30. The account gains in view of the relatively small number of Catholics resident in Philadelphia. In 1732 when St. Joseph's opened as a mission chapel staffed by the Jesuits, there were about forty, mostly Germans. Nearly the decade after Kalm's visit, the 1757 militia census still showed only 378 adult Catholics living in the city. See Edwin Scott Gaustad, *Historical Atlas of Religion in America*, rev. ed. (New York: Harper & Row, 1976) 35.

guests of the French minister to listen to "a *Te Deum* solemnly sung by a number of good voices accompanied by the organ."[37]

In 1787, the Protestant silversmith and music publisher John Aitken issued his *Compilation of Litanies and Vesper Hymns and Anthems as They Are Sung in the Catholic Church*, following it up with a second edition in 1791. The collection included mass settings, a requiem, litanies, and English- and Latin-language choir "anthems" for voices with keyboard accompaniment. As might be expected, most of the pieces were by European composers.[38]

Carr compiled and edited his own collection of music for Catholic worship, although most of the pieces were by Anglican composers and Carr had borrowed a good bit from similar publications for Protestant worship. Unlike Aitken's book, half of the pieces were by Americans and the other half by foreign composers. The fifty-eight pieces in Carr's *Masses, Vespers, Litanies, Hymns & Psalms, Anthems & Motets* included eight anthems, two masses, vespers, and responses. Settings were for two trebles and bass, and the keyboard accompaniment was to be read from an unfigured bass line. Among the anthems is a Christmas pastiche, pasted together from fragments of Handel, Haydn, and Corelli. The introduction acknowledges Bishop John Carroll of Baltimore, where the collection was published, and the "managers" of St. Mary's Church in Philadelphia. The reasons for the latter remain unclear since the music was apparently intended for Carr's choir at St. Augustine's.[39]

---

[37] *CMML*, 3:304, 326–29.

[38] *ASMI*, 90–91. Beginning somewhat later, early in the nineteenth century, compilers came to draw increasingly upon continental-European composers, adapting various genres of their music to church use. Such might reasonably be expected among the ethnic Catholic parishes; however, as will be seen it also became more and more the practice among "cultivated" Protestant church musicians during the mid-nineteenth century.

[39] Benjamin Carr, *Masses, Vespers, Litanies, Hymns, & Psalms, Anthems & Motetts...for the Use of the Catholic Churches in...United States of America* (Baltimore: privately printed, 1805). Carr's introduction is dated Philadelphia, 1 August 1805. See *ASMI*, 215–16; Frank J. Metcalf, *American Writers and Compilers of Sacred Music* (New York: Abingdon, 1925; repr., New York: Russell & Russell, 1967) 139–40; Elwyn A. Weinandt and Robert H. Young, *The Anthem in England and America* (New

Along with Carr's own music, his collection included a number of pieces by his fellow English immigrant in Philadelphia Rayner Taylor (c. 1747–1825). As a boy, Taylor had sung in the choir of the Chapel Royal in London. He went on to a modestly successful career composing for the London stage. Taylor landed in Baltimore in October 1792, served briefly as organist of St. Anne's Church in Annapolis, and then settled in Philadelphia. From 1795 to 1813, he was organist of St. Peter's Church and thereafter of St. Paul's Church. Taylor was probably the best composer of his era in America, and he could certainly have done quite well writing for the theater in America; yet, he did little stage work, concentrating instead on teaching and church music. William Smith's *The Churchman's Choral Companion to His Prayer Book* contains eleven pieces by Taylor, and his music continued to be reprinted in similar publications up through the mid-nineteenth century.[40]

New York

During its years as the nation's capital and until the second decade of the nineteenth century, Philadelphia was also its largest city. In the mid-eighteenth century, New York was essentially a cosmopolitan commercial town with clearly discernable, if intertwined, Dutch and English roots.

Although they were of more diverse backgrounds by the eighteenth century, the earliest Lutherans in New York had been Dutch for the most part, grudgingly tolerated at best by their

---

York: Free Press, 1970) 224–25. On Carr as a church musician, see Ronnie L. Smith, "The Church Music of Benjamin Carr" (DMA diss., Southwestern Baptist Theological Seminary, 1969); *CMML*, 3:255; Ellinwood, *The History of American Church Music*, 106–107. On Carr's theatrical activities, see Stephen Siek, "Benjamin Carr's Theatrical Career," *American Music* 11/2 (Summer 1993): 158–84.

[40] Wilson, *Anglican Chant and Chanting*, 234. See also *ASMI*, 576; *CMML*, 3:254. On Taylor, see John Rowe Parker, *Musical Biography* (Boston: Stone and Fovill, 1825) 179–82. See also John A. Cuthbert, "Rayner Taylor and Anglo-American Musical Life" (Ph.D. diss., West Virginia University, 1980); Victor Fell Yellin, "Rayner Taylor," *American Music* 1/3 (Fall 1983): 48–71; especially Temperley, *Bound for America*, 52–122; and William Smith, *The Churchman's Choral Companion to His Prayer Book* (New York: printed for the author, 1809)

Reformed neighbors, even though the two groups bore a greater resemblance to one another than the Lutherans did to their German and Swedish fellow Lutherans in Pennsylvania and the Delaware Valley. Moreover, the New York congregation, being a branch of a minority denomination both in Amsterdam and New York, lacked the organized support that the established Church of Sweden gave to its daughter parishes and even to the German churches in the middle states.

Hymnals and service books were difficult to procure, and the primarily Dutch Lutherans of New York had nothing like the singing tradition of their German co-religionists. It will be recalled that Muhlenberg was forced to resort to lining out hymns at the New York church when he preached there. A letter from Pastor Wilhelm Christoph Beckenmeyer to the Amsterdam Consistory, dated 21 October 1725, put the musical situation in New York's Lutheran church bluntly: "The people are not capable of singing a hymn properly, and upon several occasions they have stuck in the middle of a hymn."[41]

The situation was somewhat better among the Anglicans at nearby Trinity Church.[42] The vestry had adopted Tate and Brady's Psalter in 1707, and a clerk led the congregation in the few tunes necessary to accommodate its limited number of meters. Trinity followed the pattern of a number of urban churches in England. The vestry had established a charity school in 1709, and in April 1739, anticipating the arrival of an organ for which it had contracted a year earlier, the parish began to use children to lead the congregational singing. The organ was installed in 1741, and some months later John Rice arrived from London to become organist. At the same time, a Joseph Hildreth was engaged to train about fifty boys from the charity school as a choir. This arrangement apparently proved satisfactory, for it lasted well over a decade until Hildreth resigned

---

[41] Wolf, "Lutheran Church Music in America," 41.

[42] Interestingly, the two churches were named Trinity and located across Rector Street from one another on the west side of Broadway. Of course, the Anglican (later Episcopal) Trinity Church, now in its third building, still occupies that original site at the head of Wall Street.

and left the city in 1753 under suspicion of arson, of having had something to do with the fire that destroyed Trinity Church's two-year-old school building in February 1750.

In October 1753, William Tuckey (1708–1781)[43] arrived from Bristol, lately a vicar-choral of Bristol Cathedral and clerk of the parish church of St. Mary-le-Port on the Bristol waterfront. Like the other British émigré musicians who would follow shortly, Tuckey hoped to combine a number of musical activities, among them church music, into a relatively comfortable living. In advertising his professional skills in March 1754, he warned clearly that he was prepared to leave the city if the patronage for his talents that he anticipated and deserved was not prompt in coming.[44]

The previous January, Tuckey had been appointed clerk of Trinity Church at a salary of £25 *per annum*, sharing the position with a Mr. Eldridge. Evidently, Tuckey's responsibility was to be mainly musical. In addition to his work with Trinity's charity school choir to which he added some adults, he also established his own singing school using the parish's facilities two nights a week.

Evidently, Tuckey's outside engagements interfered with his duties as parish clerk. The next November, the vestry dismissed him from that office; however, they must have valued his musical talents, for he continued training Trinity's charity school children and had charge of music for the dedication of St. Paul's Chapel in November 1766.

Tuckey maintained an active presence on New York's musical stage. On New Year's Day 1769, he sang the role of Mr. Peachum in John Gay's popular *Beggar's Opera*. He organized and conducted several concerts of vocal and instrumental music, including the first American performance of a sizable portion of Handel's *Messiah*, "the Overture and sixteen other Pieces," in a private concert hall on 3

---

[43] On Tuckey, see Amy Aaron, "William Tuckey, A Choirmaster in Colonial New York," *Musical Quarterly* 64/1 (January 1978): 79–97; and Arthur Messiter, *A History of the Choir and Music of Trinity Church, New York* (New York: Gorham, 1906; repr., New York: AMS, 1970) 19–31.

[44] William Tuckey, advertisement titled "*William Tuckey*," *New York Mercury*, 11 March 1754, 3.

October 1770 and again at Trinity Church in April 1772. Tuckey was also a respected composer. His music was included in numerous collections, from James Lyon's *Urania* to the first and second editions of Oliver Holden's *The Union Harmony*.[45]

Like most English church musicians of the era, Tuckey's music is typically in four vocal parts, melody over harmony, with quasi-contrapuntal motion and brief passages for one or two voices. His melodies make frequent use of dotted rhythms, especially lombardic figures, often characterized as the "Scotch snap." His harmonies are invariably uncomplicated tonic/dominant. Like his contemporaries, Tuckey was heavily influenced by Handel and given to imitating such Handelian gestures as repeated words and phrases.[46]

In 1773, Tuckey tried to publish a complete setting of Anglican service music by advance subscription, including *Te Deum, Jubilate*, and burial music. The project was apparently abandoned because of insufficient interest among possible subscribers. That year, James Rice is recorded as taking over training the charity school choir. He may, in fact, have been related somehow to John Rice, who had served as Trinity's organist years before. In any event, there is no further mention of Tuckey in connection with Trinity's music. In any case, Trinity was destroyed by fire 20 September 1776, and two years later, Tuckey was appointed clerk of St. Peter's in Philadelphia. He died 14 September 1781 and was buried in the churchyard of Christ Church, Philadelphia.

As for Trinity, the British occupation of New York intervened, and the church was not rebuilt until 1789/1790. In 1791, Trinity took delivery of a new organ by Henry Holland of London, and in 1795, John Christopher Moller removed to New York from Philadelphia to become organist of Trinity Church. All available evidence suggests that the Holland organ was nowhere near as fine

---

[45] John Lyon, *Urania* (Philadelphia: William Bradford, 1761); Oliver Holden, *The Union Harmony* (Bost: Thomas and Andrews, 1793, 1796).

[46] For a complete example of Tuckey's work, see KNIGHTON, to the text of Tate & Brady's Psalm 100, from Simeon Jocelin, *The Chorister's Companion* (New Haven: T & S Green, 1782) in W. Thomas Marrocco and Harold Gleason, *Music in America* (New York: W. W. Norton, 1964) 181–82.

an instrument as either the Snetzler that Trinity had lost in the fire or the Tannenberg that Moller had played in Philadelphia.[47]

By the 1750s, the musical situation had changed somewhat among New York's Lutherans. During the previous decade, Dutch immigration had ceased while German migration into the city had increased, and for a time, services were conducted in three languages. Muhlenberg's leadership had brought the New York church into the orbit of the Pennsylvania Lutherans, and he himself was in New York during 1751/1752. A more-or-less uniform liturgy replaced independent parish usage.[48]

An unofficial English-language Lutheran hymnal appeared in 1765. *Psalmodia Germanica*[49] was a reprinting of a London hymnal of the same name, itself a combination of two earlier collections printed in 1722 and 1725, combined in 1732 and then reprinted again in 1756. No music was included, but appropriate tunes were indicated. The collection and a supplement totaled some 279 pages and contained 120 texts. Although it lacked the official approval of the New York Lutheran Ministerium, the book nevertheless enjoyed wide use in English-speaking congregations for some forty years. The official English-language Lutheran hymnal was published in 1795, mainly through the efforts of John Christopher Kunze, who had left Philadelphia in 1784 to become pastor of Christ Church in New York. Like Helmuth in Philadelphia, Kunze spoke German; unlike Helmuth, however, he not only did not resist the introduction of English into worship but encouraged it. Kunze had tried to preach in English, but finally had to give up and engage George Strebeck, an English-speaking assistant in 1794. Strebeck assisted Kunze in the preparation of the hymnal.[50]

---

[47] On that instrument, see Ogasapian, *Organ Building in New York City, 1700–1900*, 13–15.

[48] Wolf, "Lutheran Church Music in America," 37–46.

[49] Johann Christian Jacobi, *Psalmodia Germanica: or, the German Psalmody: Translated from the High Dutch. Together with Their Proper Tunes and Thorough Bass* (New York: H. Gaine, 1756 misprinted; *recte* 1765). As noted in the text, there was no music in the New York publication, the title notwithstanding.

[50] Harry J. Kreider, *History of the United Lutheran Synod of New York and New*

Titled *A Hymn and Prayer-Book for the Use of Such Lutheran Churches as Use the English Language,*[51] the book contained 240 hymns. Over half of them were translated from the German, and many had previously appeared in *Psalmodia Germanica*; the remainder were English Moravian texts from that denomination's 1789 hymnal. There is no music; however, each text is referenced by means of a number to one of sixty chorale tunes listed at the end of the volume.[52]

Kunze's perspective was distinctively orthodox; however, Strebeck's was not. Although he had been confirmed a Lutheran, he had strong Methodist leanings and had for a time been an itinerant preacher in the latter denomination. Before being ordained by the Lutheran Ministerium in 1796, he had agreed not to give any kind of support to those who wished to break away from Kunze's Christ Church to form their own English-language parish; less than a year later in June 1797, Strebeck did precisely that. The same year he published his own English-language Lutheran hymnal for the congregation of Zion Church, *A Collection of Evangelical Hymns Made from Different Authors and Collections for the English Lutherans.*[53] The contents consisted of English-style texts with neither tunes nor tune references, drawn from such writers as Cowper, Newton, and Watts.

The New York Ministerium, understandably outraged at Strebeck, moved to expel him in September 1797. Kunze intervened, and the younger minister was suspended instead, contingent on his repenting his act of schism. The ministerium also adopted a resolution refusing recognition to any English-language Lutheran congregation formed where there was a nearby Episcopal church, on the grounds that German and English theologians had agreed on the occasion of the accession of George I, first of the Hanoverian English kings, that the Anglican thirty-nine articles represented a satisfactory theological equivalent to the Augsburg Confession.

England (Philadelphia: Muhlenberg Press, 1954) 1:30–41.

[51] John C. Kunze, *A Hymn and Prayer-Book for the Use of Such Lutheran Churches as Use the English Language* (New York: Hurton and Commardinger, 1795),

[52] Wolf, "Lutheran Church Music in America," 53–57, includes a list of the tunes.

[53] (New York: John Tiebout, 1797).

By 1799, the Lutheran ministers had run out of patience with Strebeck and the decree of expulsion was voted. A year later he declared his repentance and was reinstated. At the same time, the ministerium retreated from its 1797 resolution and accepted his English-speaking congregation, now named Zion Church, into fellowship. The group managed to build its own church on Mott Street in 1802, and Kunze, ever the conciliator, preached the sermon at the consecration service. Two years later, Strebeck bolted to the Episcopal Church, attempting unsuccessfully to take his congregation with him.

The ministerium asked Zion Church's new pastor, the Reverend Ralph Williston, to compile another collection of hymns for English-language worship. Williston's *A Choice Selection of Evangelical Hymns* included texts by Wesley, Watts, and other English writers, but relatively few traditional Lutheran chorale texts.[54] The arrangement of the 437 hymns did not follow the liturgical year, and the collection in general was clearly not keyed to traditional Lutheran practice. Rather, it represented a pronounced tendency toward emulating general Protestant worship, even though the liturgy included in the book was essentially a translation of the Pennsylvania Ministerium's liturgy as adopted by the New York ministers in 1796. In 1810, Williston also defected to the Episcopal Church, and this time the Zion Church congregation followed him.

The next year, the ministerium ordered the compilation of still a third English hymnal. F. H. Quitman's *A Collection of Hymns and a Liturgy for the Use of Evangelical Lutheran Churches*[55] was no more distinctively Lutheran in character than Strebeck's compilation or Williston's. Once again, its contents consisted largely of English metrical hymns, and the liturgy allowed great freedom for adaptation to any degree of liturgical usage by individual congregations. The English metrical texts necessitated the adoption of the tunes used by other English speaking denominations. Indeed, few, if any, English translations of German chorale texts were made that fit their traditional chorale melodies until much later in the nineteenth

---

[54] R. Williston, *A Choice Selection of Evangelical Hymns* (J. C. Totten, 1806).

[55] (Philadelphia: G. & D. Billmeyer, 1814).

century. Nevertheless, the collection was widely adopted by English-speaking churches and went through several printings over the next twenty years.[56]

These goings-on in New York can only have confirmed Helmuth's resolution to bar the use of English in his Philadelphia parish. He had already seen, certainly with alarm, how his Swedish co-religionists, cut off from further immigration and from their old-country sources of new pastors while at the same time being pressured by their younger members to adopt worship in English, had engaged Episcopal ministers as "assistants," and eventually followed these young ministers into the Episcopal Church.[57]

For Helmuth, the key to preventing such from happening in his own parish was to hold rigorously and exclusively to German as the language of worship. His stubbornness brought about a split in his Philadelphia congregation, led by none other than Gen. Peter Muhlenberg, the son of the parish's founding pastor Henry Melchior Muhlenberg. Muhlenberg's group left St. Michael's and Zion to form their own English-speaking church, St. John's, in 1806.[58]

Still, Helmuth did not yield. He played a significant role in the production of a volume of music for use with the Lutheran hymnal,

---

[56] Wolf, "Lutheran Church Music in America," 57–67; see also Wolf, "Peter Erben and America's First Lutheran Tunebook in English," in *American Musical Life in Context and Practice*, ed. James R. Heintze (New York: Garland, 1994) 51–54. Zion Episcopal Church no longer exists, having been absorbed over several mergers into what is now the Church of St. Matthew and St. Timothy. On Williston and Zion, see David Clarkson, *History of the Church of Zion and St. Timothy of New York 1797–1804* (New York: G. P. Putnam, 1894) 1–14. On Strebeck, see J. Newton Perkins, *History of St. Stephen's Parish in the City of New York, 1805–1905* (New York: Edwin S. Gorham, 1906) 11–27. On the issue of English Lutheran Churches in America, Kunze, Strebeck, and Williston, see H. George Anderson, "The Early National Period," in *The Lutherans in North America*, ed. E. Clifford Nelson, rev. ed. (Philadelphia: Fortress, 1980) and especially Kreider, *History of the United Lutheran Synod of New York and New England*, 30–37.

[57] Especially bitter for Helmuth must have been the loss in 1789 of Philadelphia's Gloria Dei (Old Swedes') Church, less than a century after Justus Falckner had been ordained there.

[58] See Alvin W. Skardon, *Church Leader in the Cities: William Augustus Muhlenberg* (Philadelphia: University of Pennsylvania, 1971) 2–5.

published in 1813. *Choral-Buch für die Erbauliche Lieder-Sammlung* had 266 chorale melodies with figured bass, about half of them dating from before 1700.[59] By that time, however, Helmuth was carrying through an even more ambitious project in conjunction with other German-speaking Protestant groups in the middle colonies.

No better example can be found of ethnicity and culture transcending denominational boundaries among Pennsylvania Germans than the combined Lutheran and Reformed hymnal. The collection grew out of a determination by both groups that German be preserved as the language of worship in their churches, even though many younger members wanted services in English. *Das Gemeinschaftliche Gesangbuch* was second in popularity only to *Erbauliche Lieder-Sammlung* among German Lutheran congregations.[60] It contained nearly 500 hymns, with chorale melodies indicated for those texts not traditionally associated with a particular tune. The collection of melodies in *Choral-Buch für die Erbauliche Lieder-Sammlung* was, of course, also usable with the newer collection.[61]

Some musicians of German extraction also played an active role in Episcopal Church music. Charles Theodore Pachelbel (1690–1750), born in Nuremburg and son of Johann Pachelbel, had arrived in Boston around 1732, one of the first immigrant musicians in America. After two years as organist of Trinity Church, Newport, he left for Charleston, giving a concert in New York on the way. He was appointed organist of St. Philip's in 1740, and he remained there until 1748 when his health, and probably his playing as well, began to deteriorate. He spent the last two years of his life as an independent singing master.

Among Pachelbel's students in Charleston was Peter Pelham, born in London in 1721, but a resident in Boston from early childhood. Pelham was twelve or thirteen in 1734, when he arrived in Charleston to begin his study with Pachelbel. In 1743, Pelham returned to Boston and became organist of Trinity Church. In 1750,

---

[59] See Wolf, "Music in Old Zion," 622–52.

[60] (Baltimore: various, 1817–1850).

[61] Wolf, "Lutheran Church Music in America," 67–69.

he moved again, this time to Williamsburg, Virginia. In 1755, he installed the organ in the Burton Parish Church and became its organist, clerk of the House of Burgesses, and town jailer.[62]

John Christopher Moller, who had relocated to New York early in 1795 to become organist of Trinity Church after the 26 December 1794 fire had destroyed the organ he played at Zion Church in Philadelphia, made little if any mark on Trinity's music in the eight or nine years left to him. But another musician who moved from Philadelphia to New York at about the same time Moller did was to play a prominent role in New York church music for the next four decades. Peter Erben (1770/1771–1861), American-born but culturally and ethnically German, first appears in New York business directories for 1795. From then until 1800, he was listed as a grocer or tanner.

In 1800, Erben founded a Society for Cultivating Church Music, essentially a singing school, sponsored at first by Trinity Parish. From 1800 until 1850, when he moved to Brooklyn to spend his last years, the city directories carried Erben as a music teacher or "professor,'" and for one year, 1843, as an organ builder, the craft of his more famous son Henry Erben.[63] In 1800, Peter was organist of Christ Church (Episcopal); in 1806, he succeeded James Hewitt as organist of the Middle Dutch Reformed Church.

By 1807, Erben's singing school was being sponsored by the Episcopal clergy and churches of the city, and he began a thirty-two-year tenure as organist in Trinity Parish—beginning at St. George's Chapel until 1813, then at St. John's Chapel, and finally at Trinity Church itself from 1820 to 1839. Erben reached the height of his musical activity from 1815 through 1817. Newspaper notices for those years announced special musical programs at St. John's under his leadership. A letter from him to Bishop John Henry Hobart, dated 21 February 1816 and clearly prepared in response to Hobart's

---

[62] The *South Carolina Gazette* for 5 March 1749 contains notice of a singing school led by Pachelbel, meeting twice a week. See Byron Wolverton, "Keyboard Music and Musicians in the Colonies and United States of America before 1830" (Ph.D. diss., Indiana University, 1966) 146–55.

[63] In addition to Wolf, "Peter Erben," see J. Ogasapian, *Henry Erben: Portrait of a Nineteenth Century Organ Builder* (Braintree: Organ Literature Found-ation, 1980).

request for advice, discusses the propriety of organ voluntaries during Lent and provides a list of pieces with comments.[64]

In January 1817, sessions of Erben's singing school, renamed the Association for Improvement in Sacred Music, were scheduled for Monday and Thursday evenings. That same month, he advertised himself as an organ builder, announcing the completion of an instrument for a church in Richmond and soliciting new contracts. The following May, Erben gave notice of three organs for sale; at the same time, he proposed to compile and publish by subscription a 116-page volume of psalm and hymn tunes and a sixty-four page collection of anthems.[65]

Although it is not clear that Erben ever published the proposed collections, he did issue some twenty items, including pieces by Clementi and Hook, his own music, and five collections of sacred music. The first of these, *A Collection of Tunes, for the Use of the Dutch Reformed Churches in the City of New York*, appeared in 1806 and contained 85 tunes, one anthem, and one set-piece, for two, three, and four voices. The next two appeared in 1808: *Sacred Music in Two Three and Four Parts, selected from European & American Publications* and *Sacred Music Being a Collection of Anthems in Score...Suitable for Singing Societies and Private Families.*

The former collection bore the endorsement of Bishop Benjamin Moore of New York and included sixty-five tunes, along

---

[64] Reproduced in Morgan Dix, *A History of the Parish of Trinity Church in the City of New York*, 7 vols. (New York: G. P. Putnam's Sons, 1898–1905) 5:124–25.

[65] See Erben's advertisements in editions of *New-York Evening Post* dated 4 January, 6 January and 21 May 1817. See also Wolf, "Peter Erben," 58–60. Albert Stoutamire, *Music of the Old South: Colony to Confederacy* (Rutherford NJ: Fairleigh Dickinson University Press, 1972) 127, quotes confirmation from the "Record Book of St. John's Parish," 17 May 1816 [n.p.] that a representative of the parish was commissioned to acquire an organ from a New York builder (in context certainly Peter Erben) valued at $1,000. The allusion in one of the cited advertisements to organs on hand suggests that Erben might have been an agent for another builder, possibly British; or even that he subcontracted or imported organs and then attached his name to them. At one time, his heirs possessed a small square piano from approximately this period, obviously of English manufacture but bearing his label. See Ogasapian, *Henry Erben*, 1.

with an introduction, wherein Erben wrote, "Of right, the treble part [to which Erben had given the melody or 'air'] belongs exclusively to the female voice.... The TENOR and Counter [alto] parts are mere accompaniments to the TREBLE and BASS, calculated only to fill up the harmony." As was the usual practice of the time, the treble staff with the air was printed immediately above the bass staff. The latter collection contained thirteen anthems and set pieces for two to four voices and keyboard by such long-forgotten English composers of the period as Kent, Leach, and Peene.[66] Sometime between 1807 and 1810, Erben issued another collection of English anthems. *Sacred Music for the Use of Singing Societies and Private Families Selected and Adapted to the Piano Forte* contained seventeen pieces, including a work by Handel.[67]

His activities among the Anglicans at Trinity notwithstanding, Erben maintained his ethnic and religious ties. On the morning of 31 October 1817, he had charge of the music for the German-language service at Christ Lutheran Church in New York, celebrating the tercentennial of the Reformation.[68] That year, certainly one of the most active of his career, he compiled his largest tune book, *A Collection of Church Tunes Composed and Arranged to the Different Metres in the English Lutheran Hymn Book, Now in Use throughout the United States of America*,[69] to accompany the New York Ministerium's *A Collection of Hymns and a Liturgy for the Use of Evangelical Lutheran Churches* of 1814.

The 104 pages of music, along with a title page and index immediately following it, contain 109 tunes, only eleven of them

---

[66] *ASMI*, 258–61 describes the 1806 and two 1808 collections.

[67] Peter Erben, *Sacred Music: for the Use of Singing Schools, Societies, and Private Families* (New York: Published for the Compiler & Sold at J. Hewitt's Musical Repository, Maiden Lane, n.d.). Only one copy has come to light as of this writing, discovered by Edward C. Wolf at the Cooper Hewitt Museum in New York. See Wolf, "Peter Erben," 62, from which the passage is quoted.

[68] Wolf, "Lutheran Church Music," 81. S. P. Taylor had charge of the music for the English-language service that afternoon in St. Paul's Chapel.

[69] Wolf, "Peter Erben," 64–70, discusses this in some depth, and provides a list of its 109 tunes. Professor Wolf was able to date the collection based on the address of the engraver. Thomas Birch worked at 38 Vesey Street only during 1817.

German in origin. Most of the music represents typical Anglo-American repertoire. Even though much reuse of tunes was to be expected with 520 hymn texts, Erben carefully suggested particular tunes for each text from the New York collection, giving a single stanza of that text as an example, along with its meter. The majority of tunes appear in four voices, although some are in three voices and a few in two. The arrangement is in open score with the melody and bass in the two lowest staves, an archaic arrangement.

Some years earlier, and under circumstances not difficult to imagine even if not clearly documented, Erben had formed a friendship with the Reverend William Smith. Smith had been born in Scotland around 1754, graduated from King's College, Aberdeen in 1774, and ordained in the Scottish Episcopal Church. Such a background may well account for his subsequent efforts to introduce ceremonial in the American Episcopal churches, for the Scottish church maintained a measure of the seventeenth-century ritual practices that had largely disappeared from the English church during the eighteenth century.

Smith immigrated to America in late summer or autumn 1784. Over the next three years, he served parishes in Maryland and Pennsylvania. In 1787, he became rector of St. Paul's Church, Narragansett, Rhode Island, where Ezra Stiles recorded in his diary having heard Smith preach on the subject of "vanity."[70] More to the point, Smith introduced the regular use of Anglican chant at Narragansett.

St. Paul's was not the first American church to employ chant. As already noted, Francis Hopkinson had attempted to interest his rector at Christ Church in Philadelphia, the Reverend (later bishop) William White, in adopting the practice and certainly tried chanting with the choir there as early as 1783. Tuckey may have tried chanting on occasion at Trinity Church in New York. Be that as it may, the earliest documented use of chant in America occurred on Christmas Eve 1787 in St. Michael's Church, Marblehead, Massachusetts.

---

[70] Ezra Stiles, *The Literary Diary of Ezra Stiles, D.D., LL.D.*, ed. Franklin Bowditch Dexter, 3 vols. (New York: Scribner's, 1901) 3:330.

There is evidence that St. Michael's adopted the regular use of chant for morning and evening services during the next year.[71]

But it was Smith who became the most prominent advocate of chant in the late eighteenth and early nineteenth century. He went on to serve parishes in Newport and Norwalk, Connecticut. In 1800, he opened a school on Gold Street in New York City. From that year until his death in 1821, he spent most of his time in the city, except for four years between 1802 and 1806, when he headed a small seminary in Cheshire, Connecticut.

During his years in New York, Smith acquired an interest in organ building and actually made a few small organs, including one for Zion Church. But his main interest was in restoring the liturgy and especially Anglican chant. He probably had some influence on Israel Terril's *The Episcopal Harmony*, with its four chants;[72] and Smith himself edited *The Churchman's Choral Companion to His Prayer Book*, intended to provide for "services in prose" and accordingly, containing no metrical psalm tunes but rather four anthems, thirty-five chant settings for Morning and Evening Prayer, and six chants for the Communion service.[73]

Smith's school was near St. George's, and he became a communicant there. Given his interest in music and organs, it is scarcely surprising that he and Erben struck up a friendship. Around 1811, certainly at Smith's urging, Erben tried to introduce chanting at St. George's. The results were discouraging. Members of the congregation, including a warden, walked out in anger, and the experiment was dropped immediately. The event must have been fresh in his memory when a frustrated Smith wrote to Bishop Hobart 8 August 1811 on the subject of his *Companion*: "I am truly sick of defending a work which I am confident stands in no need of defense, but there is no withstanding prejudice and private conception."[74]

---

[71] Wilson, *Anglican Chant and Chanting*, 225.

[72] Israel Terril, *The Episcopal Harmony* (New Haven: West Society, 1802); *ASMI*, 577–78.

[73] William Smith, ed., *The Churchman's Choral Companion to His Prayer Book* (New York: printed for the author, 1809); *AMSI*, 560–62.

[74] Anstice, *A History of St. George's Church in the City of New York*, 58.

In the last decade of his life, Smith continued his advocacy for chant with a polemic text against metrical psalmody called *The Reasonableness of Setting Forth the Most Worthy Praise of Almighty God* and a guide for congregations, *An Assistant to the Evangelical Psalmodist.*[75] He died at Erben's home on 6 April 1821.[76]

For all his frustrations, Smith was ahead of his time. Even before he died, chant had gained a firm foothold in the Episcopal Church. Many clergymen favored chant as a means of singing accurate prose translations of the psalms rather than the metrical quasi-paraphrases of the Tate and Brady New Version. Smith's efforts to restore liturgical integrity and distinctiveness to Episcopal worship would be vindicated in the decades after his death, as the effects of the Oxford movement in England were felt in America: a new interest in history, ceremonial, and church architecture. Indeed, the century would bring a renewed sense of formality in all aspects of life, religion not excepted, and a new—if romanticized—interest on the part both of Lutherans and Episcopalians in their distinctive traditions.

In one sense, Peter Erben became a victim of Smith's efforts. He was retired from Trinity in 1839 in favor of Edward Hodges, lately arrived from Bristol via Toronto. Like other musicians of his generation, Erben's competent and practical, but generally undistinguished and undifferentiated, approach to church music had run its course and gone out of style. By mid-century Erben, along with such lesser contemporaries as Peter K. Moran (d.1831) of Grace Church, would be counted as hopelessly amateurish. Not quite fifty years after Erben's death, his successor at Trinity, Arthur Messiter, dismissed his work out of hand: "Eighteen years of his incumbency have left no mark upon musical history.... As an instance of stagnation and neglect, it is stated that Jackson's Te Deum in F had been sung at Trinity Church on *every Sunday for nearly twenty years.*"[77]

---

[75] William Smith, *The Reasonableness of Setting Forth the Most Worthy Praise of Almighty God* (New York: printed and sold by T. and J. Swords, 1814) and *An Assistant to the Evangelical Psalmodist* (New Haven CT: *Connecticut Herald*, 1816).

[76] Jacob F. Howe, "Chanting in the Protestant Episcopal Church and Its Author," *American Historical Record* 3/25 (January 1874): 19–20.

[77] Messiter, *A History of the Choir and Music of Trinity Church*, 37–38.

Charleston

Charleston, though by no means as large as New York, Boston, or Philadelphia, was probably the most culturally advanced city in America in the eighteenth century. It had the best harbor in North America between New York and New Orleans, and its coastal climate attracted, not only merchants, but also wealthy planters who with their families abandoned the sultry heat of their tidewater plantations for the gracious life of their townhouses in Charleston, leaving their slaves and overseers to cultivate the rice crop that financed their elegant lifestyle. The city had America's first permanent orchestra, and its concentration of wealth supported theaters and balls. Charleston suffered a lengthy occupation by the British during the Revolution; however, the city recovered its grace and elegance after the war.

In the years following the Revolution, St. Michael's Church had an extraordinarily musical rector in the Reverend Henry Purcell (1742–1803). A native of Hereford and graduate of Oxford, he had been assistant minister at St. Philip's and chaplain to the Second South Carolina Regiment. Unlike most Anglican clergymen, he took the patriot side during the Revolution and had to flee the city. On his return to the city after its evacuation by the British in 1782, he was made rector of St. Michael's Church, Charleston's second Anglican parish, founded in 1761. Its vestry had quickly appointed a clerk to read the responses in the service and to lead the congregation in singing the psalms. Two temporary organs supported the singing, and in 1764, the parish had engaged Benjamin Yarnold, formerly organist of St. Philip's, who had emigrated from London in 1753. In 1768, an organ by the great London builder John Snetzler was set up in the new church. Yarnold returned to England, and by the time of Purcell's arrival, the organist at St. Michael's was Peter Valton (1740?–1784), who had earlier replaced Yarnold at St. Philip's.

Like Yarnold, Valton was British and had served as deputy organist of the Chapel Royal, Westminster Abbey, and Handel's own parish church, St. George's in Hanover Square. He had served St. Philip's from 1764 to 1780, and he began his duties at St. Michael's in 1781. Unfortunately, he had but a year at St. Michael's and approximately two years of life left by the time Purcell arrived. One year after Valton's death, Yarnold returned from England and resumed his old position at St. Michael's. But his tenure too was brief; he died in June 1787.[78] Neither Valton nor Yarnold was an especially gifted musician. Purcell, on the other hand, was an amateur musician of some accomplishment, a composer, and an advocate for good church music. He and Valton composed new tunes for the congregation's psalmody,[79] and by 1786, records mention a male choir.[80]

Purcell responded to the reduced number of hymn texts from the fifty-one in the annex of the 1785 *Book of Common Prayer* to twenty-seven in the 1789 edition, by issuing a hymnal with tunes[81] in collaboration with the Reverend Robert Smith of St. Philip's.[82] At the same time, Purcell trained a choir of boys from the parish's orphanage. As a result, not only St. Michael's but also St. Philip's had a functioning choir, and in 1793, there is record of the boys being engaged to sing at a local theater.[83]

The use of boys from St. Michael's orphanage ended in 1801 probably because the orphanage now had its own chapel, and consequently the mandatory attendance by the children at St. Michael's had ended. But Purcell, by now in his sixtieth year and nearing the end of his life, may well have lacked the strength to keep up with rehearsing the boys. The musical situation at St. Michael's had clearly changed by 1803. A set of instructions to the organist, dated 27 February, directs him to chant the *Venite* and *Te Deum* along with

---

[78] See Wolverton, "Keyboard Music and Musicians," 146–60.

[79] For an example of Purcell's own "cultivated" style, see Robert Stevenson, *Protestant Church Music in America*, (New York: W. W. Norton, 1966) 55–56.

[80] G. W. Williams, *St. Michael's, Charleston, 1751–1951* (Columbia: University of South Carolina Press, 1951) 205–206. See Williams, "Charleston Church Music 1562–1833," *Journal of the American Musicological Society* 7/1 (Spring 1954) 38.

[81] Henry Purcell and Robert Smith, *A Selection of Psalms with Occasional Hymns* (Charleston: W. P. Young, 1792, repr., Charleston: E. Morford, 1809).

[82] Among American denominations, the Episcopal Church (along with the Dutch Reformed) was especially diffident about the adoption of hymn texts.

[83] Williams, *St. Michael's, Charleston*, 207. In London, the practice of renting out the services of choirboys, even those from the Chapel Royal, to theaters was relatively common.

the clerk, presumably in the absence of a choir. The organist was also to choose appropriate tunes for the psalm texts and to "play a solemn & well adapted Voluntary preceding the first Lesson."[84]

By 1805, efforts were under way to form another choir of boys, this time from within the parish, rather than from the orphanage. Shortly thereafter, St. Michael's began another period of musical growth under the leadership of Jacob Eckhard (1757–1833); like Pachelbel, Moller, and Erben, he was a musician of German Lutheran rather than English extraction. At the same time Peter Erben was becoming active in New York, Eckhard, some fourteen years older, was making his mark in Charleston. Born in Hesse-Kassel, he had come to America in 1776 as a band musician in the Hessian army. He remained after the war, settling briefly in Richmond before moving to Charleston in 1786.[85] On 15 April of that year, he was appointed organist, clerk, and schoolmaster by the German-speaking congregation of St. John's Lutheran Church. Eckhard quickly became a leading figure in Charleston's musical life. In 1809, he was appointed organist of St. Michael's, where he remained until his death in November 1833.[86]

Eckhard's rector at St. Michael's was the Reverend Theodore Dehon, shortly to become bishop of South Carolina. Like his Philadelphia colleague William White, Dehon eschewed hymn texts as too suggestive of Methodist "enthusiasm," instead preferring metrical psalms "that all the congregation should be able to unite their voices in the praise of God.... Tunes should be few, plain and calculated to move them to devotion."[87]

---

[84]Williams, *St. Michael's, Charleston*, 208.

[85] George W. Williams, "Jacob Eckhard and His Choirmaster's Book," *Journal of the American Musicological Society* 7/1 (Spring 1954): 41–47. Williams's assertion that he served as organist of St. John's in Richmond during that time is doubtful; indeed, there is no record of an organ in St. John's before the Peter Erben's organ arrived in 1817 (Stoutamire, *Music in the Old South*, 127).

[86] Eckhard continued an active member of the Lutheran congregation. His successor at St. John's, after a two year hiatus, was his son Jacob Jr., who predeceased his father by eleven months and was succeeded by another son, George.

[87] Rev. Theodore Dehon, "On Psalmody," *Sermons I* (Charleston: n.p., 1820) 211, quoted in Williams, "Jacob Eckhard," 42.

St. Michael's had continued to use the hymnal prepared years earlier by Purcell and Smith for Charleston's two Episcopal churches. Shortly after taking up his duties, Eckhard assembled a volume of music to go with that hymnal. The collection contained a section of 110 psalm and hymn tunes, among them pieces taken from American and English collections, tunes by local composers including Valton and Purcell, and ten German chorale melodies. Some of the latter had new Anglo-American names: "Herr Jesu Christ dich zu uns wend" became "Tradd Street," "Christus der ist mein Leben" was retitled "Granby," "Wenn wir in höchsten Noten sind" renamed "St. Philip's New," and so on. The second section contained an assortment of single and double chant tunes for the morning office, but only one, the *Gloria in Excelsis*, for the communion service. The third and final section of Eckhard's manuscript contained five anthems, two by Eckhard himself, two Christmas pieces by the English composers Francis Linley the younger and Capel Bond, and one anthem for Independence Day by an unnamed composer.[88]

---

[88] In addition to Williams, "Jacob Eckhard," and *St. Michael's, Charleston*, see Ellinwood, *History of American Church Music*, 89–91. One copy of the manuscript book is known to be extant, held by St. Michael's Church. It bears Eckhard's signature and contains a copy of the vestry's listing of the organist's "duties," alluded to above. Parts of the compilation were published years later under the title *Choral-Book* (Boston: J. Loring, n.d.) It was issued around 20 May 1816. See *Jacob Eckhard's Choirmaster's Book*, ed. Notes by George W. Williams (Columbia: University of South Carolina Press, 1971).

5.

The Revival Era

In a very real sense, the religious ferment of the Second Great Awakening during the early nineteenth century defined the nature and place of religion in the United States. Having thrown off the rule of what they saw as a capricious earthly despot, Americans in their new democracy seemed just as eager to dethrone their perceived image of a similarly capricious heavenly one.[1]

The Episcopal churches in Virginia and the Congregational and Presbyterian churches in New England were disestablished. The intellectual influence of New England's educated ministers declined almost to irrelevance, although they strived vainly to resuscitate

---

[1] There is a quantity of literature on the nineteenth-century American revivals, some of it cited at appropriate points in the course of this and subsequent chapters, for instance Nathan O. Hatch, *The Democratization of American Christianity* (New Haven: Yale University Press, 1989). Perhaps the classic general study is William G. McLoughlin, *Revivals, Awakenings and Reform: An Essay on Religion and Social Change in America, 1607–1977* (Chicago: University of Chicago Press, 1978). Readable and popular, but somewhat outdated, is Bernard A. Weisberger, *They Gathered at the River* (Boston: Little Brown, 1958). For valuable background and societal insights on the period of disestablishment and pre-Civil War religion, see Paul K. Conkin, *The Uneasy Center: Reformed Christianity in Antebellum America* (Chapel Hill: University of North Carolina Press, 1995); Ann Douglas, *The Feminization of American Culture* (New York: Knopf, 1977); and Timothy L. Smith, *Revivalism and Social Reform* (New York: Abingdon Press, 1957; repr., Baltimore: Johns Hopkins University Press, 1980).

elements of the defunct Puritan theocracy buttressed by a pallid version of Puritan theology. Congregationalism underwent a theological split that resulted in the loss of several venerable churches to the Unitarian liberalism.

Less formal, vernacular groups, such as the Baptists and especially the Methodists, experienced large-scale conversions, particularly in camp meetings on the western frontier that were held over periods of several days. In essence, Americans embraced individualism and egalitarianism in religion as well as in politics and law. The effects of the revivals were felt by the German Reformed churches and to a lesser degree the German Lutheran churches of Pennsylvania. Rural Presbyterian and Congregational churches underwent revivals that also lasted several days or even weeks. Many of these churches adopted revival practices as a permanent part of their regular worship.

The liberal Unitarian parishes remained aloof from the revivals. And although the Episcopal Church officially ignored them, the pietistic rhetoric of personal religion found its way into the writings and sermons of the leader of the high church wing Bishop John Henry Hobart of New York. The low church evangelical wing found much in common with the revivals' emphasis on personal faith over apostolic authority, historical doctrine and tradition, and doctrinal discipline. Some revival practices may be seen in the extra "meetings" favored by these low church evangelicals; however, the music and aesthetic of the revivals exerted relatively little effect on the regular worship ritual and music of the Episcopal Church. In fact, official distaste for any hint of revivalist "enthusiasm" kept the Episcopal Church from officially sanctioning any significant body of congregational hymnody in place of, or in addition to, metrical psalmody until after the Civil War.

In city churches, the singing masters of the eighteenth century had for the most part been displaced by trained musicians and a more cultivated church music, although most hymn texts were still metrical psalms, usually Tate and Brady or Watts.[2] The music of the

---

[2] While the old "Scots'" Presbyterian churches still used Rouse's 1649 metrical

tunesmiths moved south and west with the singing masters themselves. Itinerant masters and their singing schools persisted in the east through the first quarter of the century and as late as mid-century in such urban centers of the Midwest as Cincinnati; however, their work was steadily relegated to rural parishes where it eventually joined with folk hymns and spirituals that had grown up in small rural Baptist churches, which were often pastored by unlettered farmer-preachers. Eventually, the songs and choruses were used in camp meetings as well.[3]

Folk Hymnody

The beginnings of the American folk hymn are found in the late eighteenth and early nineteenth century, when several collections of more personal, emotional hymn texts were printed for use in private devotions (as opposed to public worship, where anything more extreme than Watts was frowned upon) and for recreation. These texts found favor in the less formal evangelical churches. Ministers lined them out to congregations, who sang them to well-known British folk and secular tunes.[4]

Indeed, some irregular metrical patterns in the texts betray the secular songs with whose melodies they were matched. The classic example is the early-eighteenth-century English broadside "Ballad of Captain Kidd":

Psalter, the Presbyterian General Assembly had officially approved Watts's "psalms" for general use. Thus, by this time, most Protestant churches, with the exception of Episcopal and Lutheran parishes, were singing Watts texts.

[3] Interestingly, the music of Billings and his fellow singing masters underwent revival in the Boston area, in concerts by groups in period costume and using old-fashioned pitch pipes, as early as the 1850s. See Judith T. Steinberg, "Old Folks Concerts and the Revival of New England Psalmody," *Musical Quarterly* 59/4 (October 1973): 602–19.

[4] Of course, the practice of fitting sacred texts to well-known secular melodies, *contrafactum*, antedates the Reformation. Over the years, it was adopted by Luther, used for metrical psalmody and then Wesleyan hymnody as we have seen, and even extends into church music of our own time.

My name was Robert Kidd when I sailed, when I sailed.
My name was Robert Kidd when I sailed.
My name was Robert Kidd, God's laws I did forbid,
So wickedly I did when I sailed, when I sailed,
So wickedly I did when I sailed.

Its distinctive meter matches a number of hymn texts, for instance the following two:

What wondrous love is this, O my soul, O my soul.
What wondrous love is this, O my soul.
What wondrous love is this that caused the God of bliss
To bear the dreadful curse for my soul, for my soul,
To bear the dreadful curse for my soul.

and

Our bondage it shall end, by and by, by and by.
Our bondage it shall end, by and by.
From Egypt's yoke set free; Hail the glorious jubilee,
And to Canaan we'll return by and by, by and by,
And to Canaan we'll return by and by.[5]

The Christian Harmony; or, Songster's Companion was compiled by Jeremiah Ingalls (1764–1838) of Newbury, Vermont, a tavern-keeper, Congregational deacon, and singing master.[6] Its 144 pages

---

[5] The two texts appear in editions of B. F. White and E. J. King, *The Sacred Harp*, 3rd ed. (Philadelphia: S. C. Collins, 1859) 159 and 224. The connection between the ballad and hymn texts, by no means undisputed over the years, was put forth by George Pullen Jackson in his pamphlet prepared for the centennial observance of that collection, *The Story of the Sacred Harp, 1844–1944* (Nashville: Vanderbilt University, 1944). Jackson later expanded the thesis in "The 400–Year Odyssey of the 'Captain Kidd' Song Family—Notably Its Religious Branch," *Southern Folklore Quarterly* 15/4 (December 1951): 239–48.

[6] Jeremiah Ingalls, comp., *The Christian Harmony; or, Songster's Companion* (Exeter: Henry Ranlet, 1805).

contained 137 hymns and four choir set pieces. About half were typical New England tunesmith fare, for example the fuging tune "Northfield." The other half were folk hymns of the type used in the rural Baptist and evangelical churches of the area. Some are apparently Ingalls's own pairings of sacred texts with dance and folk tunes, which he then surrounded with second and third voices in harmony. Still other melodies may well be originals cast in the folk-song style of the British Isles—structured with gapped scales or modes—but not actual borrowings of existing folk tunes.[7]

Camp Meeting Choruses

A second source of popular vernacular hymnody was the camp meeting. Camp meetings were held on the frontier from the late eighteenth century on. They provided the settlers, whose farms were at a considerable distance from one another and from the nearest church, with a social outlet as well as a religious one. Shortly after the turn of the nineteenth century, the momentum picked up dramatically; by 1811, some 400 camp meetings had been held, and by 1820, there were over 1,000.[8]

The atmosphere at a camp meeting was highly emotional, and spontaneous outbursts and physical movement were the order of the day. These—together with the size of the crowd that gathered, the number of preachers exhorting separate groups at the same time, and the limited number of hymnals available—called forth a different

---

[7] Allen Perdue Britton, Irving Lowens, and Richard Crawford, *American Sacred Music Imprints 1698–1810* (Worcester MA: American Antiquarian Society, 1991) 346–47. (Hereafter cited as *ASMI.*) See David G. Klocko, "Jeremiah Ingalls *The Christian Harmony; or, Songster's Companion* (1805)" (Ph.D. diss., University of Michigan, 1978). A facsimile has been published with introduction by Klocko (New York: DaCapo, 1980).

[8] Two definitive studies on the subject provide background. See Paul Keith Conkin, *Cane Ridge: America's Pentecost* (Madison: University of Wisconsin, 1990); and Hatch, *The Democratization of American Christianity*, which addresses hymnody in context. On the roots and background of the camp meeting movement, see Leigh Eric Smith, *Holy Fairs: Scottish Communions and American Revivals in the Early Modern Period* (Princeton: Princeton University Press, 1989). Still valuable also is John Boles, *The Great Revival, 1787–1805* (Lexington: University Press of Kentucky, 1972).

kind of music: one that was itself (or at least seemed to be) spontaneous, that would sweep the crowd along, be picked up quickly, and sung by all. It would reinforce the shouting exuberance and sense of excitement. In short, it was a kind of music that would not only underscore the content of the message but also match the spirit of the plain-spoken, emotionally charged preaching.

The basic element in a camp meeting song was the chorus. A chorus usually consisted of a short, repetitious text, sometimes of two lines, set to a simple, catchy melody with strong rhythm. Choruses could be attached to the end of a pre-existing hymn, sung alone, or interspersed between lines of a hymn text that was known to all or that was lined out by the preacher or leader in the manner of a call-and-response, as in the following hymn:

O who will come and go with me?
I am bound for the land of Canaan.
I'm bound fair Canaan's land to see,
I am bound for the land of Canaan.
O Canaan, bright Canaan, I'm bound for the land of Canaan,
O Canaan it is my happy home,
I am bound for the land of Canaan.

There were also repetitive texts in which single phrases or words changed with each stanza, with potential for further improvisation. Such repetitious chorus hymns could be learned quickly, sung on the spot, and easily remembered for future use. The tunes were simple, of limited range and vocal demands, and often with strong and marked rhythm to which the crowd could clap hands or march. The net effect of camp meeting singing was hypnotic. Even Frances Trollope, who reacted with deep distaste and pungent comment to the camp meeting she witnessed in Indiana during summer 1829, found herself caught up by the drama of the singing:

The preachers came down from their stand...beginning to sing a hymn, calling upon the penitents to come forth. As they sung [sic] they kept turning themselves round to every part of the crowd, and, by degrees, the voices of the whole multitude joined in the chorus. This was the only moment at which I perceived anything like the solemn and beautiful effect I had heard ascribed to this woodland worship. It is certain that the combined voices of such a multitude, heard at dead of night, from the depths of their eternal forests, the many fair young faces turned upward, and looking paler and lovelier as they met the moon-beams, the dark officials in the middle of the circle, the lurid glare thrown by the altar-fires on the woods beyond, did altogether produce a fine and solemn effect, that I shall not easily forget.[9]

Shape-Note Collections

The hymns and their tunes were passed on orally at first; however, the popularity of camp meetings quickly caused collections to be printed. Such collections contained, not only camp meeting choruses and folk hymns, but also the repertoire of the American singing masters that was being supplanted in the more settled East Coast areas by the cultivated European and European-style of church music. In general, the hymns were in three voices: melody in the tenor, bass below, and treble above. Alto voices, if any, doubled the bass at the octave, and since women's voices commonly doubled the

---

[9] The full account appears in Frances Trollope, *Domestic Manners of the Americans*, ed. Donald Smalley (New York: Knopf, 1949) 167–78. On the music of the camp meetings, see Ellen Jane Lorenz, *Glory, Hallelujah!: The Story of the Campmeeting Spiritual* (Nashville: Abington, 1980). The figures on the number of camp meetings by 1811 and 1820 are taken from Lorenz, *Glory, Hallelujah!*, 22. A basic study, albeit one to be approached with care, is George Pullen Jackson, *The White Spiritual in the Southern Uplands* (Chapel Hill: University of North Carolina, 1933; repr. New York: Dover, 1965). Also basic is Buell Cobb, *The Sacred Harp: A Tradition and Its Music* (Athens: University of Georgia Press, 1978). Annabel Morris Buchanan's *Folk Hymns of America* (New York: J. Fischer & Bro., 1938) and is also valuable, but difficult to locate.

Although their number and frequency began to taper off by the 1830s, camp meetings retained their popularity through the Civil War and beyond. Indeed, the political rallies and torch-light parades of the nineteenth and early twentieth centuries partook heavily of the camp meeting tradition.

melody in the tenor and men's voices, the texture was six voices, occasionally seven or even eight if there happened to be an independent alto or "counter" as became more frequent in later editions and publications. The melodies were generally modal and the perfect intervals, open fifths and octaves, predominated in the harmony.

The prototype for the collections that appeared during the first third of the century was John Wyeth's *Repository of Sacred Music, Part Second*.[10] Wyeth (1770–1858) was a Cambridge-born Unitarian who had traveled as far away as the Caribbean island of Santo Domingo before settling in Harrisburg, Pennsylvania, in 1792 as postmaster and editor of a local newspaper. In 1810, probably as a business venture, he compiled and published his first collection, which he named *Repository of Sacred Music*. It contained standard pieces that were culled from earlier collections. The book apparently found a ready market in the number of immigrants passing through Harrisburg on their way west; by 1834, it had gone through six editions.[11]

In 1813, Wyeth issued *Repository of Sacred Music, Part Second*, unrelated to the former volume, but evidently titled so as to capitalize on its success. This latter volume consisted mainly of camp meeting and folk hymns and singing school music. Some fifty-eight of its 149 pieces had not been published before, and of the fifty-eight, forty-four were folk hymns. This volume was also well received; some 25,000 copies were sold.[12]

Both of Wyeth's collections and the folk-hymn compilations that followed his *Part Second* utilized a shape-note system for the reading of music. As was noted previously, John Playford's *Brief Introduction to the Skill of Musicke* used the solfege letters, F[a], S[ol], L[a] and M[i], as did John Tufts's *An Introduction to the Singing of*

---

[10] John Wyeth, *Repository of Sacred Music, Part Second* (Harrisburg: John Wyeth, 1813)

[11] *ASMI*, 629.

[12] Irving Lowens, "John Wyeth's *Repository of Sacred Music, Part Second* (1813): A Northern Precursor of Southern Folk-Hymnody," *Music and Musicians in Early America* (New York: Norton, 1964) 138–55.

Psalm-Tunes.[13] Combined, the four syllables produced the requisite intervals for a complete major scale. In 1803, Andrew Law coupled the syllables with a system of shaped note heads, each shape indicating one of the four syllables.

Law did not place his shape-notes on a staff with lines and spaces. That had been done two years earlier by William Little and William Smith, whose *Easy Instructor, or a New Method of Teaching Sacred Harmony* was published in Philadelphia in 1801 and went through eight editions to 1810 and a total of thirty-four printings to 1820. Little and Smith's repertoire was standard fare.[14] What set the book apart, however, was its system of notation: shape notes on a traditional staff. The shape-note system was (and still is) simple enough so that musically untutored people could be taught quickly to sing diatonic lines with an amazing level of dexterity, using Fa, Sol, and La plus Mi for the leading tone (hence the term "fasola-ing" for reading from shape-notes). Moreover, placing shape notes on a staff meant that the collection could be used by those who could read music in the traditional manner as well as those who solfeged by means of the note shapes. Wyeth, and those who followed him, made Little and Smith's system common in folk-hymn collections.[15]

---

[13] John Playford, *An Introduction to the Skill of Musicke*, 7th ed. (London: W. Godbid, 1674); John Tufts, *An Introduction to the Singing of Psalm-Tunes* (Boston: S. Gerrish, 1726).

[14] Of the 156 pieces in Wyeth's 1810 *Repository of Sacred Music*, half had been published earlier in Little and Smith's *Easy Instructor*.

[15] *ASMI*, 437–44. See also Jackson, *White Spirituals in the Southern Uplands* (Chapel Hill: University of North Carolina Press, 1933; repr., New York: Dover, 1965) 13. A full historical and bibliographic study may be found in Irving Lowens, "*The Easy Instructor* (1798–1831): A History and Bibliography of the First Shape Note Tune Book," *Music and Musicians in Early America*, 115–37. There is some question as to whether Law had conceived the idea of shape-notes as early as 1795. Law later maintained that ill health and problems with printing had prevented him from publishing with the new system until 1803. See Irving Lowens, "Andrew Law and the Pirates," *Music and Musicians in Early America*, 82–83. Actually, William Little applied for a copyright in 1798, along with Edward Stammers of the Urania Society in Philadelphia, so Little probably deserves the credit as inventor of the system combining shape-notes with the staff: a triangular notehead for Fa, round for Sol, square for La, and diamond for Mi.

Ananias Davisson's (1750–1857) *Kentucky Harmony* contained a rudimentary introduction on singing (including directions on improvising a pendulum metronome) and 143 pages of music in shape notes grouped in three sections.[16] The first section consisted of hymns in four voices. The melody was in the tenor, as usual, with the text printed over it; the bass below; a "counter" above; and treble topmost. All parts, save the bass, were intended to be sung by a mix of men and women. A second section contained "more lengthy and elegant pieces, commonly used in concert or singing societies," and the third consisted of "several anthems and odes of the first eminence, together with a few pieces never before published," among them works by Billings, French, and other native singing masters.

Davisson included seventeen new tunes, thirty-two folk hymns, and the pieces by Billings and his fellow tunesmiths. A large proportion of the material was taken from Little and Smith, and some were culled from Wyeth's collection also. The tunes carried a meter (for example, L.M., C.M.) and an indication of tonic and modality. Major and minor were termed "sharp key" and "flat key," respectively, so E-minor was "flat key on E," and A major was "sharp key on A."[17] *Kentucky Harmony* was followed quickly by a number of similar collections, among them Allen D. Carden's *Missouri Harmony*.[18]

Benjamin Franklin White (1800–1872) probably had a hand in the preparation of William Walker's *Southern Harmony*.[19] Nine years later, along with E. J. King, White issued the first edition of the best-

---

[16] Ananias Davisson, *Kentucky Harmony* (Harrisonburg VA: Davisson, 1816–1826).

[17] A facsimile has been issued, with introduction by Irving Lowens (Minneapolis: Augsburg, 1976). See also Jackson, *White Spirituals*, 26.

[18] For a general list, see Jackson, *White Spirituals*, 25. More authoritative and exhaustive is Richard Stanislaw, *A Checklist of Four-Shape Shape-Note Tunebooks* (Brooklyn: I.S.A.M., 1978). See also Marion J. Hatchett, "Early East Tennessee Shape-Note Tune Books," *The Hymn* 46/3 (July 1995): 28–47. Allen D. Carden, *Missouri Harmony* (St. Louis: Carden, 1820).

[19] This is according to Jackson, *The Sacred Harp*, ix-x. White and Walker were brothers-in-law; they were married to sisters. William Walker, Southern Harmony (Spartansburg SC: W. W. Walker, 1835).

known and longest-lived collection, *The Sacred Harp*. White went on
to establish the Southern Music Convention in 1845, and other
similar organizations grew up over next decades, resulting in a
tradition of Sacred Harp singing for both worship and recreation that
continues to the present in the South, from northern Florida to
Texas and Oklahoma. By 1960, *The Sacred Harp* had gone through a
dozen editions and is still in print (although revisions from 1902 on
made significant changes).[20]

Over its first four editions—1844 to 1869—the volume of the
collection nearly doubled, from 263 pages to 477.[21] *The Sacred Harp*
was arranged in the usual three sections. Part 1, "consisting of pieces
used by worshipping assemblies,"contained hymns, most of them in
three voices with the air in the middle voice or tenor, underlaid with
the text. Most of the tunes were modal, but a number were clearly
tonal and diatonic. Similarly, most of the tunes have obscure,
apparently folk, origins; others, like Oliver Holden's "Coronation,"
are clearly traceable.

Part 2, "consisting principally of pieces used in singing schools
and societies," contained longer pieces, many of them fuging tunes,
with more varied rhythmic patterns and difficulties requiring some
measure of rehearsal. Part 3, "consisting of odes and anthems,"
contained longer and more difficult works. In the third edition

---

[20] Singing schools and the cultivation of folk hymnody for worship and
recreation are still found in rural Southern churches. See Buell Cobb, *The Sacred
Harp*, 64; Paul Gillespie, ed., *Foxfire* 7 (Garden City: Doubleday, 1982) 280–346
provides first-hand data. In addition to Sacred Harp singing, there are active, albeit
smaller, groups in the South that maintain a tradition of singing from other
collections for worship and recreation, among them William Walker's later, seven-
shape shape-note collection, *Christian Harmony* (Philadelphia: E. W. Miller and W.
Walker, 1867) and William H. and Marcus L. Swan's *The Harp of Columbia*
(Knoxville: published by the authors, 1849–1855) and its seven-shape shape-note
successor, *The New Harp of Columbia* (Nashville: W. T. Berry, 1867) used by the Old
Harp Singers of Tennessee. Even where the books themselves are not used, they
contribute in part to an oral tradition of melodies, for instance among some
Appalachian Primitive Baptist congregations. See Beverly Bush Patterson, *The Sound
of the Dove: Singing in Appalachian Primitive Baptist Churches* (Urbana: University of
Illinois Press, 1995). See also Jackson, *White Spirituals*, 324–37.

[21] Cobb, *The Sacred Harp*, 85–89.

(1859), for example, there are twelve works, half of them for four voices. Three of the anthems are by Billings: his Easter Anthem, "I Am the Rose of Sharon," and "David's Lamentation."

Urban Revivals

The early nineteenth-century camp meetings were essentially a rural phenomenon. Among urban congregations and clergymen, the concept was still the Puritans' view of the service as "God's Schoolhouse." There was not any sort of liturgical formality. As Alexis de Tocqueville observed, "There is no country in which Christianity is less clothed in forms, symbols and observances…or where mind is fed with clearer, simpler or more comprehensive conceptions."[22] The hour-long sermon that interpreted a particular passage of scripture in a formal and systematic manner was still central. It was preceded by scripture reading, psalms (read and sung), and a lengthy prayer. City clergy and congregations remained suspicious of camp-meeting-style "enthusiasm."

Nevertheless, these settled churches in towns and cities were also experiencing revival. Indeed, by 1810, the leading ministers of New England looked to revivals as an adjunct to private worship and as the means by which the elect came under conviction and were converted. As such, they linked private devotion and public worship. Here too, Calvinism would be replaced with evangelical piety in many town and city churches. Doctrine would be supplanted by individual experience and predestination by free grace for all. But in the first decades of the century, while rural crowds listened to the emotional exhortations of unlettered preachers, urban congregations listened to sermons by educated and ordained visiting evangelists like Asahel Nettleton (1783–1844).

Nettleton graduated from Yale in 1809. He did not settle in a parish, but rather he worked as a traveling evangelist in eastern Connecticut. Nettleton's technique was intellectual, in the tradition of Jonathan Edwards. He worked closely with the orthodox pastors of

---

[22] Alexis de Tocqueville, *Democracy in America*, trans. G. Lawrence, ed. J. P. Payer (Garden City: Doubleday, 1975) 448.

churches in which he preached and subscribed to the Calvinist view that revivals were sent by God, not as dispensations of free grace to all, but rather to winnow out the elect.

Nettleton's opposite among revival evangelists was Charles Grandison Finney (1792–1875). Finney was trained as a lawyer in upstate New York, but he underwent a conversion in 1821 and devoted the remainder of his life to preaching revival, borrowing many of his techniques from the camp meetings. Finney saw revivals as a series of manmade techniques aimed at winning any and all possible souls. While Nettleton sought to confine passion to private devotions and to maintain decorum in public worship, Finney used his lawyerly skills to plead to the emotions of his listeners. He prayed for the conversion of some (including ministers) by name, issued altar calls, placed those "under conviction" on an "anxious bench" near his preaching platform where he could exhort them even more forcefully, and ran "protracted meetings"—revivals that lasted days or weeks, like camp meetings. Eventually, Finney came to believe that all worship should aim at revival, and, indeed, many of his techniques became an integral part of regular evangelical worship long after the 1830s had passed and the "seasons of refreshing" had faded from popular memory.

Nettleton's evangelistic activities came to an end in 1822 when he was stricken with typhus. During a lengthy convalescence, he occupied himself by compiling a collection of hymn texts by Watts, Wesley, Newton, and others. As might be expected of a strict Calvinist, he included no popular revival hymns or camp meeting choruses. Nettleton's *Village Hymns* appeared along with a companion volume of tunes, Nathaniel and S. S. Jocelyn's *Zion's Harp* and went through seven editions over the next three years.[23]

---

[23] Sandra Sizer, *Gospel Hymns and Social Religion: The Rhetoric of Nineteenth-Century Revivalism* (Philadelphia: Temple University Press, 1978) 66–67. Paul Garnett Hammond, "Music in Urban Revivalism in the Northern United States, 1800–1835" (DMA diss., Southern Baptist Theological Seminary, 1974) 114–17. Hammond's remains the major study of the period, dovetailing with Paul Gaarder Kaatrud, "Revivalism and the Popular Spiritual Song in Mid-Nineteenth-Century America, 1830–1870" (Ph.D. diss, University of Minnesota, 1977). See Asahel

Finney, on the other hand, made little or no use of music's emotional power in spite of his practice of appealing directly to his listeners' emotions through speech. Finney himself enjoyed music. He played the cello, sang reasonably well, and had directed a children's choir as a young man. But he distrusted music's efficacy and considered it both frivolous and a distraction from the sinner's duty to agonize over his soul. "A *great deal of singing* often injures a prayer meeting.... Common singing dissipates feeling," he later wrote.[24] He was especially wary of popular hymnody.

Thomas Hastings

The musician most closely associated with Finney was Thomas Hastings (1784–1872). His family had moved from his native Connecticut to Clinton, New York, when young Thomas was twelve. By 1800, he was leading his own singing schools; and in 1815, he published his first collection, a compilation made for the Oneida County Musical Society. The book continued in print, albeit with a new title and occasional minor revisions, until 1836.[25]

Hastings's *Dissertation on Musical Taste* was the first critical essay on music to appear in America. Although its scope was general, Hastings's main objective was clearly to improve church music and to increase interest in it among professional musicians and intelligent amateurs. He spoke out especially against ineptness and inappropriateness. For Hastings, music was the expression of "sentimental feelings," and its quality was in direct proportion to its effect on the listener. Church music was to be "chaste and simple," "moderate in its pretensions," and "decent [insofar as it fulfills] the express purpose of assisting the devotions of the pious." Accordingly, there was to be no tolerance in churches for "frivolous trash or unmeaning jargon."

Nettleton, *Village Hymns for Social Worship* (New Haven: Goodwin, 1824) and Asabel Nettleton, *Zion's Harp* (New Haven: N. and S. S. Jocelyn, 1824).

[24] Charles Grandison Finney, *Lectures on Revivals of Religion* (New York: Fleming Revell, 1868) 130–31; see also *Memoirs of Rev. Charles G. Finney* (New York: Fleming Revell, 1876) 101.

[25] Thomas Hastings, *The Utica Collection* (Utica: n.p., 1815) becoming *Musica Sacra* in later editions.

Hastings considered congregational singing without the support of a "well-disciplined choir" or organ to be "radically defective." Musical taste and skill could only be gained through experience and training, not only in rhythm, intonation, diction, and other aspects of musical technique, but also in the cultivation of "appropriate emotions." Accordingly, Hastings warned against engaging an incompetent and irreligious singing master.

Hastings strongly advocated the disciplined European style—"scientific" and "cultivated" were the terms frequently used at the time—in the composition of church music. "Until very lately, a correct and effective piece of harmony was scarcely to be found among our compilations in any of this class of composition." Among the faults he found were "strong predilections for concords...rude attempts at fugue and imitation...[and a] general fondness for rhythm and the imitative [pieces suggesting dances and marches]."[26]

In 1823, Hastings moved to Utica as editor of the pro-revival Presbyterian weekly, the *Western Recorder*. It was there that he met Finney, who came to Utica to conduct a revival during the winter of 1825–1826 at the church Hastings attended and of which he was an elder. Finney went on to other revivals in New York and New England, attained national fame with his Rochester revivals of 1830 and 1831, and then took a pastorate at the Chatham Street Chapel in New York City.

Hastings stayed in Utica until 1832. The year before, a congregational minister named Joshua Leavitt (1794–1873) published a compilation titled *The Christian Lyre* containing 203 hymns intended expressly for congregational singing.[27] For the most part they were in the folk style with many texts set to secular tunes. Leavitt intended that all should sing the melody; he provided only melody and bass for all but two three-voice and three unison pieces. The hymn text and tunes were arranged on facing pages with first

---

[26] Thomas Hastings, *Dissertation on Musical Taste* (Albany: Websters & Skinners, 1822; repr., New York: Da Capo, 1974) 15, 30, 64–69, 73–75, 202–204.

[27] Joshua Leavitt, *The Christian Lyre* (New York: J. Leavitt, 1831).

stanzas printed between the treble and bass staves. *The Christian Lyre* was very popular, going through twenty-six editions until 1846.[28]

Leavitt had tried unsuccessfully to interest Finney in adopting the collection for his church and revivals. Indeed, as far as is known, Finney never even replied to Leavitt. Nevertheless, as if in response, Hastings and Lowell Mason (1792–1872) collaborated to produce a competing collection, *Spiritual Songs for Social Worship* in 1832. The book contained 233 texts and eighty-three tunes. Of the settings, 128 were for three voices and twenty-six for two. The remainder of the settings were divided between unison and four-parts. Texts and tunes were arranged on facing pages, as Leavitt had done. As might be expected, Hastings and Mason included no secular tunes. Indeed, in the introduction to the collection, the compilers decried the presence in revival music of "insipid, frivolous, vulgar and profane melodies."[29]

In 1832, the year *Spiritual Songs* appeared, Hastings withdrew from editing the *Western Recorder* and moved to New York City to take charge of the music for twelve churches, including Finney's Chatham Street Chapel. He remained in New York for the rest of his life. From 1835 to 1837, he edited a monthly called *Musical Magazine*. Insufficient subscribers, and possibly the collapsing economy, doomed the publication. In total, Hastings produced thirty-four collections, some in collaboration with contemporary church musicians, among them Lowell Mason, William B. Bradbury, Isaac Woodbury, and George Root. He composed about 1,000 pieces of sacred music. Among his published writings was an informative set

---

[28] Hammond, "Music in Urban Revivalism," 124. The collection also introduced James Waddell Alexander's translation, "O Sacred Head Now Wounded" to the Passion Chorale tune. More typical, however, were pairings like the text "Jesus! Thy love" with the tune associated nowadays with Robert Burns's "Auld Lang Syne," a coupling that also appeared in *The Sacred Harp*.

[29] Lowell Mason and Thomas Hastings, *Spiritual Songs for Social Worship. Adapted to the Use of Families and Private Circles in Seasons of Revivals...* (Utica: Hastings & Tracy & W. Williams, 1832) 3. See Carol A. Pemberton, *Lowell Mason, A Bio-Bibliography* (New York: Greenwood, 1988) 51.

of "sketches" (as he called them) based on actual experiences and constituting a casebook of examples for ministers and musicians.[30]

Lowell Mason

The main figure in urban revivals was Lyman Beecher (1775–1863). Beecher began as a conservative, like Asahel Nettleton; in fact, Nettleton was ordained in Litchfield, Connecticut, during Beecher's pastorate there. Beecher had moved to Boston by 1827, and that year the two men joined in an attempt to restrain Finney's attempts to bring his revival techniques into churches, in effect bridging the gap between public worship and the camp meeting. As it turned out, Beecher and Finney were subsequently reconciled, and Finney even conducted a lengthy revival at Beecher's Bowdoin Street Church in Boston in 1830 and 1831.

Although Beecher came to adopt many of Finney's techniques in his own revivals, he did not share Finney's antipathy toward music. On the other hand, although Beecher was fond of scratching out dance tunes on an old violin when the mood struck him, neither he, his fellow urban clergy, nor their cultivated congregations had much sympathy for the native art of the tunesmiths, the naiveté of folk hymns, or the emotionalism of camp meeting choruses. In their view, the "devotional" music of regular worship sufficed for revival. Thus, Beecher joined with other Boston clergymen to persuade Lowell Mason—who, although he earned his living as a banker, had achieved a good bit of note in the musical life of Savannah, Georgia—to return to Boston and take charge of the music in their churches.

Mason (1792–1872) had removed from his native Medfield, Massachusetts, to Savannah during the winter of 1812/1813, to work in the dry goods business of Edward Stebbins, chairman of the board of the Independent Presbyterian Church. In 1815, Mason became choir director at the church and five years later its organist. He was

---

[30] Thomas Hastings, *The History of Forty Choirs* (New York: Mason Brothers, 1853). In addition to Hammond, "Music in Urban Revivalism,'" 62–65, see also James E. Dooley, "Thomas Hastings, American Church Musician" (Ph.D. diss., Florida State University, 1963).

also the superintendent of the church's Sunday school from 1815 to 1827. While in Savannah, Mason studied with the German immigrant musician F. L. Abel (1794–1820) and composed some anthems and hymn tunes. He also compiled a collection of church music for use with his choir, and around 1820, he began to cast about for a publisher. On 20 June 1821, he wrote back to Boston, to the editor of *The Euterpeiad*, John Rowe Parker:

> For several years past I have been constantly importing from Europe the best publications of Sacred Music...I have selected many pieces from Haydn, Mozart, Beethoven and other celebrated German composers.... Two things I principally fear—1st—that my collection will be too classical...[that] musical taste is not sufficiently advanced to appreciate these authors—2nd—I fear that there will be objection to the harmonizing of the old established church tunes—as Old Hundred, Angel's Hymn, St. Ann's.[31]

Probably under Abel's influence, Mason had developed a preference for German composers, as well as a style of church music that he (and Parker) would term "correct" and "scientific." His explicit model and, indeed, his source for some pieces was William Gardiner's *Sacred Melodies from Haydn, Mozart and Beethoven*, which had gained a measure of popularity in America and been reprinted here in 1818.[32] Around the same time, Mason made contact with Thomas Hastings, who had already built his reputation as a church musician in New York. During 1824, Hastings's church music column in the *Western Recorder* alluded to Mason as "the distinguished musician from Savannah."[33] Mason knew Hastings's

---

[31] Carol A. Pemberton, *Lowell Mason, His Life and Work* (Ann Arbor: UMI Research Press, 1985) 32. Pemberton's is the definitive biographical study of Mason.

[32] William Gardener, *Sacred Melodies from Haydn, Mozart and Beethoven* (London: printed for the author, 1812, 1815).

[33] Michael Broyles, *Music of the Highest Class: Elitism and Populism in Ante-Bellum Boston* (New Haven, Yale University Press, 1992) 77. Broyles's critical insights in his chapters on sacred music reform and on Mason (33–91) are especially

Dissertation on Musical Taste and agreed with his positions on church music. Indeed, he would put into practice Hastings's principles—church music should be simple, unaffected, and devotional as distinct from concert music; congregation and choir should be backed by an organ, notwithstanding the denomination's aversion to the instrument; and the only real way to improve church music was by teaching children from an early age.[34]

Unable to find a publisher for his collection in Savannah or Philadelphia, Mason visited Boston in 1821 and solicited the support of the corpulent, prickly, and fading but still influential George K. Jackson for his project. With Jackson's endorsement—doubtless gained at least in part by Mason's inclusion of some of his music in the compilation—the *Boston Handel and Haydn Society Collection of Church Music* appeared the next spring.[35]

Parker announced the collection's impending release: "The Handel and Haydn Society's collection of Church Psalmody is nearly completed, and will be ready for public sale next week.... It is next to impossible not to regard this production with the highest approbation...we hope [it] will be received, as a standard for all tastes."[36]

Jackson received the dedication in recognition of his "exquisite taste, profound knowledge and unrivalled skill" and returned the compliment on the page opposite: "It is much the best book of the kind I have seen published in this country, and I do not hesitate to give it my most decided approval." Abel's posthumously published testimonial shared the page with Jackson's encomium: "HAVING

---

perceptive and illuminating.

[34] Pemberton, *Lowell Mason, His Life and Work*, 29.

[35] Lowell Mason and H. Wiley Hitchcock, *The Boston Handel and Haydn Society Collection of Church Music; Being a Selection of the Most Approved Psalm and Hymn Tunes; Together with Many Beautiful Extracts from the Works of Haydn, Mozart and Beethoven, and Other Eminent Modern Composers* (Boston: Richardson & Lord, 1822; repr., New York: Da Capo, 1973). Mason's collection is not to be confused with the earlier Handel and Haydn Society, *Boston Handel and Haydn Collection of Sacred Music* (Boston: Thomas Badger, 1821) which contained oratorio excerpts for concert use.

[36] John R. Parker, "Metrical Psalmody," *The Euterpeiad* 3/1 (30 March 1822): 5; John R. Parker, "Handel and Haydn Society Collection of Church Music—continued," *The Euterpeiad* 3/3 (27 April 1822): 22.

critically examined the manuscript copy of 'THE HANDEL AND HAYDN SOCIETY COLLECTION OF CHURCH MUSIC'...I cheerfully recommend it as a work in which taste, science and judgment are happily combined."[37] Mason's name did not appear in this first edition. As he later wrote, "I was then a bank officer in Savannah and did not wish to be known as a musical man, and I had not the least thought of making music my profession."[38]

The collection, patterned after Gardiner's, contained the sort of "cultivated" European repertoire that had superseded the work of even such living native composers as Read, Holden, and Swan. The few American pieces it contained had been reharmonized in a "scientific," manner by Jackson. Of course, neither Mason nor his Boston colleagues would tolerate shape notes; the notation in his collection was the usual round heads on staves, and the arrangement was similarly as usual for the period: four voices, the bass with figures for keyboard accompaniment, melody in the tenor with text laid in over it, and two upper voices—counter and treble.

The book opened with Old Hundredth, attributed, as it would regularly be during the first half of the nineteenth century, to Martin Luther. Another piece would engender great public awe and favor during the same period: the so-called "Luther's Judgment Hymn." Mason used the text "In robes of judgment, lo he comes," rather than the later and far more frequent "Great God, what do I see and hear." The tune is that of the German chorale, *Nun freut euch, lieben Christen g'mein*, rechristened "Monmouth."

Mason's usual practice, however, was to adapt hymn tunes from works by major European composers. The opening motif of Handel's aria from *Messiah*, "I know that my Redeemer liveth," for instance, is compressed into a common meter tune and then fit with a doggerel text, "I know that my Redeemer lives, And ever prays for me./

---

[37] Throughout his career Mason would show an uncanny knack for cultivating friendships that would assist him in promoting himself and his work.

[38] Frank J. Metcalf, *American Writers and Compilers of Sacred Music* (New York: Abingdon, 1925; repr., New York: Russell & Russell, 1967) 212. Mason's name would not appear on the title page of the collection until the ninth edition, some ten years later.

Salvation to his saints he gives, And life and liberty." Other psalm and hymn tunes were similarly adapted from secular pieces, operatic and instrumental, by such composers as Beethoven, Vogler, Pleyel, Corelli, Viotti, Haydn, and Mozart, along with English pieces by Burney, Tans'ur, Croft, Blow, and others. The anthems and set pieces were mostly English, the work of such figures as Madan and Jackson.[39]

The *Boston Handel and Haydn Society Collection of Church Music* received an enthusiastic reception. A letter in *The Euterpeiad* headed "Psalmody" and signed "Middlesex" described how the writer had "perused with much satisfaction, a late Book of Psalmody, published by the Handel and Haydn Society of Boston, with the harmonies revised and corrected by Dr. G. K. Jackson." The paper continued "Mr. Lowell Mason, now resident in Savannah, Georgia, was several years engaged in collecting this truly erudite epitome of refined and tasteful melodies." Under the title "The Progress of Sacred Music," Parker wrote:

> We would wish to call the attention of all classes to the late Book of Psalmody published by an institution, of which as a member, we feel a degree of pride in belonging.
>
> The rehearsal on Tuesday evening last, from the new collection, at Boylston Hallo, was fraught with many of the most chaste and sublime specimens ever composed.
>
> The performance of the several pieces gave us a most striking illustration of the effects produced by a correct arrangement, particularly in the inner parts; and while the ear was delighted with a concord of harmonies, the mind realized

---

[39] See Elwyn A. Weinandt and Robert H. Young, *The Anthem in England and America* (New York: Free Press, 1970) 232f. In point of fact, Boston church music tastes had for some time been veering toward "correct" English composers and away from the rough-cut tunesmiths. In addition to trends described in the last chapter, note should be taken of James Hewitt's (1770–1827) *Harmonia Sacra* (Boston: Joseph T. Buckingham, 1812), which included works by Croft and Boyce. Hewitt was organist of Trinity Church; however, his main musical interest was secular.

a conviction of the great affinity displayed between sense and sound.[40]

The collection went through numerous editions and remained in print until after 1858. It influenced a number of other compilations, among the earliest Nathaniel D. Gould's (1781–1864) *Social Harmony*.[41] *Social Harmony* contained seventy-six tunes, eight of them by Handel, three by Haydn, four by Mozart, and one "Russian," explicitly intended for "those who prefer devotional music, to the giddy song." Gould had been a member of the Handel and Haydn Society since October 1820, and he would certainly have been among the first to acquire a copy of Mason's publication.[42] In retrospect, the contents and even the influence of *The Boston Handel and Haydn Collection of Church Music* were of far less significance than its effect. It served to draw public attention and to launch the professional career of arguably the single most influential man—for better or for worse—in the history of American church music and music education.

On 7 October 1826, Mason spoke by invitation on the subject of church music at Beecher's Hanover Street Church in Boston. The speech was well received, and he was asked to repeat it two days later at the Third Baptist Church. On 11 October, at the request of a delegation headed by Beecher, he provided a copy for publication.[43]

Mason's main thesis regarding church music was that worship and not musicianship was the primary concern, or as Mason himself

---

[40] John Rowe Parker, "The Progress of Sacred Music," *The Euterpeiad* 3/4 (11 May 1822): 29–30.

[41] Nathaniel D. Gould, *Social Harmony* (Boston: Thomas Badger, 1823).

[42] Janyce G. Ingalls, "Nathaniel Duren Gould (1781–1864)" (MM thesis, University of Massachusetts, Lowell, 1979) 22. Gould was an active singing master throughout his life; however, his significance in music history rests more on his later *Church Music in America* (Boston: A. N. Johnson, 1853).

[43] Lowell Mason, *Address on Church Music: Delivered by Request, on the Evening of Saturday, October 7, 1826, in the Vestry of Hanover Church, and on the Evening of Monday, Following in the Third Baptist Church, Boston* (Boston: Hilliard, Gray & Co., 1826). Pemberton, *Lowell Mason: His Life and Work*, 40–42, and *Lowell Mason: A Bio-Bibliography*, 96.

put it, "Singing [in worship] shall be considered as much of a devotional exercise as prayer." To that end, he delineated a few precepts: church music should be simple, "correct," unostentatious, and singable; the text set carefully so that it is carried well by the music and the two complement each other; and singing should be by the congregation, supported by a capable choir of devout singers and a judicious choice of instruments. An organ was preferred, cello was acceptable in the absence of an organ, but the violin was to be avoided because of its secular connotations as a popular dance instrument. Both choir and organ were to be for support only and not for display or solo; and finally, congregational singing would be improved most in the long run if children were taught music from an early age.[44]

Mason's music and arrangements supported his philosophy. Throughout his career, his pieces were characterized by simple intervals, regular rhythm, conservative ranges that seldom exceeded an octave, and harmonies that were unadventurous to say the least. Though he might adopt German chorale tunes without change, he would never be so venturesome as to employ a Bach harmonization. On the other hand, his avoidance of the open consonant harmonies and fuging tunes of earlier generations in America certainly correlated with his advocacy for a smoother, more European, "scientific," and cultivated way of singing. He was not the first to make such a connection. Andrew Law had noted before that the earlier untutored tone, harsh and grating, went hand-in-hand with such unremittingly consonant and parallel harmonies, whereas smooth, trained voices singing such pieces would "cloy, sicken and disgust."[45]

Mason's ideas were well calculated to appeal to the clergy and laymen he was addressing. The printed speech went through two editions, and the Boston clergy were resolved to have Mason in charge of their churches' music. Between December 1826 and April

---

[44] Broyles, *Music of the Highest Class*, 74–75.

[45] *ASMI*, 421. Michael Broyles, "Lowell Mason on European Church Music and Transatlantic Cultural Identification: A Reconstruction," *Journal of the American Musicological Society* 3S8/2 (Summer 1985): 336.

1827, they made him three offers, all of which Mason refused. Then, in late summer 1827, he changed his mind, probably because of the prospect, if not the certainty, that he would also become president, and therefore conductor, of the Handel and Haydn Society, recently fallen on bad days. Indeed, in September 1827, he was elected president of the society.

Mason thus became conductor of an amateur chorus numbering 100, made up for the most part of men. The relatively small number of women all sang the soprano part; doubled at the octave by several tenors, called "soprano leaders." Men, rather than women, sang the alto part. Even by the end of Mason's Handel and Haydn Society years, the alto section remained overwhelmingly male with no more than two or three women able to hold their own on the part alongside the men.[46]

Mason was to be paid $2,000 for serving three prominent Boston churches in six-month rotation: Beecher's Hanover Street Church, his son Edward's Park Street Church, and the Essex Street Church. He took up his duties with energy, forming and drilling choirs and compiling collections. He turned the Handel and Haydn Society's fortunes around with performances of such works as *Messiah* and *Creation*. When he left the presidency of the society in 1832, an arrangement for splitting royalties on the extremely profitable *Collection of Church Music* had been worked out such as to secure the society's fortunes and to leave Mason well enough off financially so that he could undertake music in the Boston public schools without remuneration.

By the time Mason rotated back to Lyman Beecher's parish in 1831, its Hanover Street building had been destroyed by fire (fed by barrels of spirits stored in its cellar by a merchant who had rented the space). A new building in the fashionable "gothick" style was built on Bowdoin Street, in which a three-manual organ was installed by the

---

[46] Stanley R McDaniel, "Church Song and the Cultivated Tradition in New England and New York" (DMA diss., University of Southern California, 1983) 75–76.

finest builder in Boston Thomas Appleton. Here Mason stayed for the next fourteen years, leading a choir of some seventy voices.[47]

Mason's music education activities in Boston are well documented elsewhere, and in any case, they lie outside the scope of this book. Suffice it to say, however, that the ostensible (and in Mason's mind, probably real) excuse for introducing music in Boston's schools was explicitly to promote psalmody in the churches in the years to come. His first compilation expressly for children was the *Juvenile Psalmist* of 1829, followed by the *Juvenile Lyre* the next year. He taught classes for children in 1832–1833 at the Bowdoin Street Church, and in 1833, he founded the Boston Academy. From 1837, he was in charge of music in the city's public schools and ran training sessions in music for teachers.[48]

During the same period, Mason published a number of compilations, among them *Spiritual Songs for Social Worship* and *The Choir or Union Collection*, both of 1832; *The Boston Collection of Anthems* (1834); *The Boston Anthem Book* (1839); and the immensely popular *Carmina Sacra* of 1841, which, with its sequel *The New Carmina Sacra* of 1850, sold around a half-million copies, making Mason financially secure.[49]

He even entered into the competition among the extremely popular shape-note books. His *Ohio Sacred Harp* contained a twenty-

---

[47]The building subsequently became the Church of the Advent and then St. John the Evangelist, where Everett Titcomb served as organist and choirmaster for several years in the early and mid-twentieth century. The Church of St. John the Evangelist still occupies that old Bowdoin Street Church, and on visiting it, one is surprised at the comparatively modest dimensions, especially considering the size of the organ Appleton installed and the choir Mason directed there.

[48] See for example Pemberton, *Lowell Mason, His Life and Work*, 61–139 *passim*; and James A. Keene, *A History of Music Education in the United States* (Hanover: University Press of New England, 1965) 96–126 *passim*.

[49] His worth, late in life, was estimated at about $100,000. Although the sum seems modest by today's standards or the fortunes amassed by the post-Civil War "robber barons," its purchasing power at the time was equivalent to the not inconsiderable sum of $1.34 million today. And judging by contemporary accounts of his generosity, Mason would probably have been worth a good deal more had he not been as generous as he was to religious and musical causes of his time, to say nothing of individuals such as the Beethoven biographer, Alexander Wheelock Thayer.

page introduction advocating a seven-note solmization system and providing shape-notes for that number of scale degrees.[50] Mason by no means approved of shape-note reading, however, and published a somewhat patronizing disclaimer in the 1840 edition: "*The Sacred Harp* is printed in patent notes (contrary to the wishes of the authors) under the belief that it will prove much more acceptable to a majority of singers in the West and South."[51]

In late April 1837, Mason departed on his first trip to Europe. Although his visit seems ostensibly to have been for the purposes of learning Pestalozzian educational methods, his journal records at least as much about his impressions of European church music. He met Vincent Novello, publisher and organist, and heard a Haydn Mass at his Portuguese Chapel in London. He went to Westminster Abbey and the chapel where Isaac Watts had been pastor years before, observing with surprise that the psalms and hymns were still lined out. He said, "Singing was wretched…the chapel was a mean place."

The service at St. Paul's Cathedral, with its choir of charity children, did not accord with his Congregational inclinations. He said, "There are many customs strange to one accustomed like myself to the plain and simple manner of doing things in America—the pomp, splendor and parade—even servants and those who perform the office of sexton—door keeper, etc. [that is, probably the vergers] are dressed in such a style that a simple American might take them for the Lords and great ones." And so it went in England. In May, he met William Gardiner at Novello's in London. The two discussed church music, but Mason was not at all taken with the man who had been his model. Indeed, he disapproved of Gardiner's "profane expressions."

On the other hand, German singing impressed Mason. At the Jacobikirche in Hamburg, the service was long, but the singing of chorales was "very solemn and devotional." Similarly, the congre-

---

[50] Lowell Mason, *The Sacred Harp* (Cincinnati: Truman & Smith, 1834, 1840; Boston: Shepley & Wright, 1836).

[51] Jackson, *White Spirituals*, 17–18.

gational singing of chorales at the Sophienkirche in Dresden, led by a choir of eight or ten boys and the same number of men, was "sublime and devotional.... But it is power that produces the whole musical effect, as there is no *variety*."

If nothing else, his season of visiting Europe's churches had taken a few of the rough corners off Mason's aversion to ceremonial, expressed after his visit to St. Paul's months earlier. Back in London in September, he attended worship at the Moravian Chapel on Fleet Street and remarked in his journal, "I like liturgy to some extent, and should be glad to attend church where one is used."[52]

All in all, Mason seems to have had a measure of ambivalence about European church music. As Thomas Hastings wrote his brother in Detroit on 1 November 1837, "Europe has no style *strictly devotional* that compares at all with what we are cultivating in this country. Mr. Mason says the same."[53]

Still, Mason's European experiences may have prompted at least one of his publications, his *Book of Chants* (1842), with a preface advocating chant as simple and manifestly non-secular and as providing the appropriate emphasis for text. Mason seems always to have had a partiality for chant; however, he was never able to affect a transfer of its popularity from the Episcopal Church, part of whose tradition it was but with which he had no substantive contact, to the evangelical churches with which he was associated.[54]

Mason continued in charge of the music at Bowdoin Street; however, by this time much had changed. On the one hand, financial panic had set in; on the other, Mason's own Presbyterian Church was splitting into Old Style and New Style, ostensibly over the issue of revival, but actually over the far deeper issue of the morality of slavery. In any case, the fires of the Second Great Awakening were burning low, and the giants of revival were settled into academic positions. Beecher had left Boston to head the Lane Seminary in

[52] Michael Broyles, ed., *A Yankee Musician in Europe: The 1837 Journals of Lowell Mason* (Ann Arbor: UMI Research Press, 1990) 29–33, 35, 43, 59–60, 64, 124.

[53] Robert Stevenson, *Protestant Church Music in America* (New York: W. W. Norton, 1966) 81.

[54] See Broyles, *Music of the Highest Class*, 87.

Cincinnati. Nettleton, never quite recovered from his bout with typhus, was at the Hartford Seminary in Connecticut and approaching the end of his days. Finney had departed his pulpit in New York after a brief season for a professorship at Oberlin, from which he would issue, from time to time, to conduct revivals that were coming to seem more and more irrelevant.

In 1844, Mason left Bowdoin Street Church to direct the music at Central Congregational Church, a new and fashionable edifice that had been built on Winter Street in 1841. By 1843, Central Church was drawing members away from other churches in the city. Mason settled in with a new organ and choir of 100 voices, many of whom had moved with him from Bowdoin Street. At Central Church, Mason went so far as to introduce Anglican chant, with at least a measure of congregational approval. He also evidenced increased interest in choral repertoire. His compilation with George James Webb, *The Psaltery*, contained Zingarelli's "Go Not Far from Me, O Lord" and the motet traditionally, but inaccurately, attributed to Richard Farrant, "Lord, For Thy Tender Mercies' Sake."[55]

But Mason's days in Boston were numbered. He was clearly contemplating retirement, for his agreement with Central Church allowed him an escape should he decide to retire or leave the city. Indeed, in 1845, political machinations brought an end to his work in Boston's public schools. To what degree Mason himself was responsible for this is not clear. At least in some quarters, he appeared to have become imperious. On 4 July 1848, Hastings waspishly wrote his brother: "Deliver me from such teaching as I heard him put forth in all the vehemence of up and down dogmatism.... A multitude of Mason's old adherents have become our patrons.... Friend Lowell will use every exertion to establish himself in the west, and will in his own opinion do good much in proportion as he can multiply and sell books."[56]

---

[55] Lowell Mason and George James Webb, *The Psaltery* (Boston: Wilkins & Carter, 1845).

[56] Stevenson, *Protestant Church Music in America*, 81.

Finally, in 1851, Mason resigned his position in Boston and moved to New York, where his sons Daniel and Lowell had business interests. It is not clear if Mason intended to resume musical activity in New York. On the other hand, the city was the nation's cultural center, or fast becoming that center. Several friends and former associates were active in New York. Thomas Hastings (who had evidently kept his opinions of Mason between himself and his brother) was there, although he too was entering the twilight of his career. William B. Bradbury (1816–1868), who sang in Mason's choir and had succeeded him as organist at Bowdoin Street Church, was now director of music at the Broadway Tabernacle. George F. Root (1820–1895), who had been in New York since 1844, had visited Mason shortly after his arrival and evidently persuaded him to collaborate in a series of teachers' institutes.

On the evidence, New York's evangelical churches were certainly in need of someone like Mason. One may take with a grain of salt the impressions recorded in his journal by a visiting Scottish clergyman in 1844: "The music of the churches where I officiated was sweet and tasteful; but I was sorry to observe that...it was handed over almost entirely to the choir which sat in the gallery, aided by an organ and other musical instruments. The congregation...appeared to listen as to a performance."[57]

However, at approximately the same time, one of the city's own music journals was decrying the "neglect and indifference" on the part of both clergy and congregations, fostering the use of "music which is anything rather than devotional."[58] Around the same time, Professor Erickson wrote back to a friend in Norway, complaining of the poor church music in New York in similar terms: congregations that listened silently to choirs rather than joining in the singing; poor choirs whose members had no interest in improving; organists who

---

[57] George Lewis of Ormiston, *Impressions of America and the American Churches* (Edinburgh: W. P. Kennedy, 1848; repr., New York: Negro Universities Press, 1968) 38–39.

[58] "Church Music," *The Message Bird* 1/14 (15 February 1850): 234.

played popular tunes; and numerous collections of poor music, poorly harmonized.[59]

Clearly there was work for Mason, but that work would have to wait. In December 1851, Mason and his wife set sail for Europe. They landed on New Year's Day, and for the next fourteen months, through March 1853, they visited churches in several countries. Toward the end of his stay, Mason taught in London and compiled his *Handbook of Psalmody*. He also sent back a steady stream of letters, published as a book on his return.[60]

Mason was, if anything, more impressed with the congregational singing he heard on his second trip: the chanting and Watts' hymns at W. H. Havergal's St. Nicholas Church, Worcester; the 3,000 singers at the Nikolaikirche in Leipzig; and the congregation at the Kreuzkirche in Dresden. On 7 June, he visited Calvinist Zurich and listened to the precentor-led congregational singing without organ support. The experience confirmed for him that such was a failure. Organs and choirs were required to support the congregation. Indeed, Mason concluded that the organist need pay no heed to the text and expression, but rather concern himself solely with playing loudly and firmly, supporting the singing of the large group.

In his letter of 29 March 1852, Mason reformulated his philosophy of congregational singing: there need be no concern for listeners because there were to be no listeners. All present were to be singers, so quality, enunciation, articulation, and so on were of no importance. The only important thing was the mass of tone. He wrote:

> Is congregational singing desirable? Go with me to the Nicolai Church in Leipzig. Mark the movings of your own spirit, and you will not need the answer to the question from

---

[59] Unsigned, "Church Music," *Dwight's Journal of Music* 1/24 (18 September 1852): 189–90. The letter had been sent to the *New York Musical World and Times*, according to *Dwight's*.

[60] Lowell Mason, *Musical Letters from Abroad* (New York: Mason Brothers, 1854; repr. with an introduction by Elwyn A. Weinandt, New York: Da Capo Press, 1967).

another.... The *plain song of all the people* above science, above art, above everything save Him into whose presence it hastens one...I came away wishing that the people of America [would] hasten to take appropriate preparatory measures for its introduction.... Music is regarded as one thing, and the singing of hymns quite another. In the singing of the *chorale* by the people, good music is not looked for or expected.[61]

Even as he wrote, New York's Fifth Avenue Presbyterian Church was completing its new edifice at Nineteenth Street, a large auditorium with 200 pews and open rafters to add resonance to the singing. The pastor, James Waddell Alexander, was more than sympathetic; he had translated the German chorale "O Sacred Head Now Wounded" for congregational singing. Mason could not have asked for a more kindred spirit. He was appointed music director at the Fifth Avenue Church in May 1853 and promptly dismissed the choir and orchestra. A small organ was rented and the process began. Alexander wrote, "Lowell Mason is our leader, but since his return from Europe, he is so bent on severe tunes and congregational singing...that while I am tickled immensely, the people are disappointed."[62]

With the installation of a large organ—the first in the church— by George Jardine, in 1855, Mason seems to have realized his objective. *Dwight's Journal* recorded, "The whole people join in, supported by the stronger voices which are placed to the front side seats."[63] Alexander himself wrote a month later, "If univocality were all, we have, I think, fully attained the end of making our people sing. I have never heard a louder chorus out of a German church. As for

---

[61] Mason, *Musical Letters*, 66–68, 88; See also John Ogasapian "Lowell Mason as a Church Musician," *Journal of Church Music* 21/7 (September 1979): 6–10.

[62] Fifth Avenue Presbyterian Church, New York, NY, *A Noble Landmark of New York. The Fifth Avenue Presbyterian Church: 1808–1958* (New York: Fifth Avenue Church, 1960) 33.

[63] N.A., "Musical Chit-Chat," *Dwight's Journal of Music* 8/4 (27 October 1855): 29.

melody and harmony, your deponent saith not."[64] Mason led the congregation while his son William played the organ. A "choir" of uncertain size was spread through the room. Mason's success was described as "marvelous...and there is no church in the city where so many join in the singing."[65]

The most tangible result of Mason's experiences with congregational singing in Europe and in New York was probably the congregational hymnal he edited with Edwards A. Park and Austin Phelps in 1859, some time after his retirement from Fifth Avenue Church. *The Sabbath Hymn and Tune Book*—published simultaneously that year by Mason Brothers in New York, Crosby, Nichols Lee & Co. in Boston, and Root & Cady in Chicago—was small octavo, rather than oblong, and printed the tune in four parts, close score, bass and soprano in large notes and the middle two voices in smaller ones at the top of each page. Three or four texts, which could be sung to that tune, were printed below on the same page. The 1,200 hymn texts, 411 tunes, thirty-nine chants, and twenty-two short anthems made for one of the first comprehensive congregational hymnals in the modern sense.[66]

It is difficult to assess fairly Mason's legacy to American church music. On one hand, he provided a measure of professionalism and dedication; on the other, he was ever open to the entrepreneurial opportunity. There is no doubt that he was sincere in pursuing his

---

[64] Quoted in Elfrieda Kraege, "The Organs of the Fifth Avenue Presbyterian Church," *The Tracker* 18/2 (Winter 1974): 3.

[65] Fifth Avenue Presbyterian, *A Noble Landmark*, 33–34.

[66] It is worth noting that while Mason included chorale texts in *The Sabbath Hymn and Tune Book*, he was inconsistent in regard to their tunes. So Alexander's translation, "O Sacred Head," (356) is set to the bland and dull "Canonbury"; whereas Jane Borthwick's 1846 translation of the Moravian hymn "Jesus, Still Lead On," (350) uses the traditional 1698 tune by Adam Drese, albeit renamed LEWIN. Note in context the not entirely disingenuous word of approval in Austin Phelps, Edwards A. Park and Daniel Furber, *Hymns and Choirs: or, The Matter and Manner of the Service of Song in the House of the Lord* (Andover: Warren F. Draper, 1860; repr., New York: AMS Press, 1971) 401: "The tunes in the Sabbath Hymn and Tune Book, appear to have been prepared with a steady eye toward the principles which we have laid down."

goal of what he viewed as good church music—simple, singable, and "refined." At the same time, he was singularly insensitive to what we recognize in retrospect to have been a folk tradition in hymnody; then again, it was already in the process of being relegated to the backwaters of rural America. That insensitivity and relegation might well have been played a role in preserving the tradition by isolating it in the protective pocket of the southern uplands.

Moreover, in the urban northeast, where Mason had spent his most productive years and his strongest efforts toward cultivating what he considered to be good church music, the effect of his work was fading even as he passed from the scene. A New Englander who signed him- or herself as "X" wrote *Dwight's Journal* complaining of the:

> Trashy flood of new singing books.... New abominations are daily added, partly *original compositions*, so called, defying all known laws of composition, partly arrangements from secular music...introduced, like wolves in sheep's clothing, into the service of the sanctuary, [for example] *Batti batti...*, hearing Zerlina sing to that tune "Gently Lord, O Gently Lead us"...I cannot help thinking that if our choirs would take the old "Handel and Haydn Collection," published many years ago, and discard all the rest, they would find there all that is really needed for their part of the musical service.[67]

Dwight himself editorialized, "Every one complains of the unsatisfactory condition of church music all around." He went on to blame the popular lack of taste and affinity for the cheap and vulgar—asking why the Catholic Church had been able to maintain art when Protestants could not—as well as commercialism, sectarianism, and above all, the lack of faith in and respect for music.[68]

---

[67] Unsigned, "Church Music," *Dwight's Journal of Music* 1/24 (18 September 1852): 186–87, 189-90.

[68] Unsigned, "Church Music," *Dwight's Journal of Music* 3/11 (18 June 1853): 84–85.

In retrospect, Mason's musical legacy is a mixed one; it is difficult to separate his sincere faith and dedication to providing music for the revivalist Protestantism of his time from his keen business instinct as to what and how much the church choir market would embrace and absorb. The main accusation against Mason—and there is justice in raising it—is that he rifled the European repertoire for attractive morsels that he could pulp down into grist for his musical mill, thereby vitiating the church (and school) music tastes of Americans for generations to come.

But by the same token, tangential though it may be to church music as such, he and those who followed him (in school music up through the middle of the present century) also made available and accessible to millions of children and adults, especially those at a distance from an increasingly sophisticated urban culture, melodies they might not otherwise have heard (diluted though the music may have been) from masterpieces they might not otherwise have known existed.

Mormons

New sects, distinctively American in character, grew up in the heat of the Second Great Awakening. Probably the most successful such group, the Latter Day Saints or Mormons, was born in 1830 in Western New York, an area so evangelized as to be called the "burned-over district." Hymnody played a major role in Mormon culture from its beginnings. Joseph Smith, the church's founder, directed his wife Emma Smith to select hymns for church use. By 1832, the texts, drawn from evangelical writers like Watts and Wesley, were being printed in the church's newspaper, *The Evening and Morning Star*. The organization's first hymnal, *A Collection of Hymns*, was printed in 1836. Of its 127 hymn texts, slightly over fifty were out of other denominations with some alterations to fit Mormon beliefs; the remainder were by Mormon authors.

By the 1840s, evolving theology, a tightly controlled organizational leadership, a steady infusion of European immigrants, and tensions with non-Mormons culminating in the migration and settlement in the Great Basin during 1846–1847, combined to create a new outlook and discourse among the Mormons. This, in turn, was reflected in the development of a new and distinctive hymnody focused on doctrine and on the image of a "Zion," which the faithful found in their new city by the Great Salt Lake.

The European immigrants brought with them a love of music—in particular, a group of Welsh converts who arrived in 1849, whose singing tradition brought a new energy to the chorus that had existed since the 1830s. As early as 1876, the choir performed Handel's *Messiah*. By that time, the ensemble had become known as the Tabernacle Choir, and in years to come, it would become a major element in the Mormon image and in American Music.[69]

---

[69] Michael Hicks, *Mormonism and Music: A History* (Urbana: University of Illinois Press, 1989) 9–45. Hicks is the standard and authoritative history of Mormon music and includes a detailed discussion of early hymnody. David W. Stowe, *How Sweet the Sound: Music in the Spiritual Lives of Americans* (Cambridge: Harvard University Press, 2004) 77–90, including an illuminating juxtaposition of Shaker and Mormon hymnody; Stephen Marini, *Sacred Song in America: Religion, Music, and Public Culture* (Urbana: University of Illinois Press, 2003) 223.

6.

Outside the Revival Sphere

For nineteenth-century American religion in general and the major denominations in particular, disestablishment resulted in something akin to a market-driven competition. Freedom of religions worship and association weakened denominational loyalties, and the proverbial melting pot was heated by the fires of the camp meetings and revivals of the Second Great Awakening. By the 1830s, most churches that could afford them were buying organs not only to support and improve congregational singing but also to enhance their worship. The few holdouts were predominantly conservative Calvinists; for instance, many Scottish Presbyterian churches held strictly to their old Psalters. A thriving organ-building industry was centered in the northeast: Thomas Hall and Henry Erben in New York and Thomas Appleton, William Goodrich, and the Hooks in Boston were beginning to find a national clientele.[1]

---

[1] The history of organs and organ building in America is beyond the scope of this book; however, there is a fairly ample bibliography on the subject, some of it already cited herein. The definitive general study is Orpha Ochse, *The History of the Organ in the United States* (Bloomington: Indiana University Press, 1975). Like any pathbreaking work, Ochse's sowed the seeds of new research that would ultimately outdate its information, and it is now, some twenty years after its publication, in some need of revision in the light of the very books it inspired: among them, John Ogasapian, *Organ Building in New York City, 1700–1900* (Braintree MA: Organ Literature Foundation, 1977) also in need of revision; Barbara Owen, *The Organ in New England* (Raleigh: Sunbury Press, 1979); and Raymond J. Brunner, *That*

Some urban churches cultivated music as an attraction. Skilled musicians were more likely to be available in cities. Moreover, there were at least a minority of people who were resistant to the blandishments of the revivalists and fashionably taken with the romantic attitude toward the arts. Naturally, the denominations with the greatest potential to capitalize on these trends were those with aesthetic and historical traditions: the Roman Catholic, Lutheran, and Episcopal churches.

On the other hand, these denominations' worship rituals and tradition of educated, ordained, and settled clergy made it difficult for them to compete against the Methodist circuit-riders and Baptist farmer-preachers for the American frontier folk, who were proudly self-reliant, constantly on the move, and contemptuous both of formal religion and of formal education. Much of their strength (even that of the Lutherans) was concentrated in eastern cities, the very places of their greatest potential appeal.

Of the three, the Roman Catholic Church bore the greatest burden. Outside the cities on the eastern seaboard, Catholics and the log chapels that served as their churches were few and scattered. Priests were scarce, sacraments were administered infrequently, and many Catholics on the frontier simply lost touch with their religion. Even in the cities, the Catholic Church was weak in comparison to other denominations, at least until the great immigrations beginning in the 1830s. In many cases Catholics could not afford to build their own churches, but were forced to worship, often with surprising informality, in buildings abandoned by Protestant congregations. Only in Baltimore, with its five churches and magnificent cathedral designed by Benjamin Latrobe and completed in 1818, did the Catholic Church show a mature presence. New York, by contrast, had but four churches (including old St. Patrick's Cathedral) for its 35,000 Catholics in 1830,[2] and Boston but one, a modest structure that served as the first Holy Cross Cathedral.

Ingenious Business (Birdsboro: Pennsylvania German Society, 1990).

[2] Jay P. Dolan, *Catholic Revivalism: The American Experience* (Notre Dame: University of Notre Dame Press, 1978) 3–9 and *The Immigrant Church: New York's*

The Lutherans were still dealing with issues of language and differences among themselves. The English-speaking Lutherans were divided regarding deism and pietistic revivalism. The German-speaking Lutherans were sorting out their relations with their fellow Germans in the Reformed Church. Most English-speaking congregations in New York, New Jersey, and Pennsylvania had adopted F. H. Quitman's *A Collection of Hymns and Liturgy*, known as "The New York Synod's Hymn Book."[3]

Quitman's collection had little of the traditional Lutheran hymnody, but rather it consisted of English texts by such writers as Isaac Watts and Anne Steele, a Baptist poet. The general tenor was rationalist rather than pietist or orthodox. The 1834 edition, responding to the revivalist spirit of the previous decades, added 180 hymns, among them texts by such English evangelicals as James Montgomery and John Bowring.[4]

The General Synod in Gettysburg, Pennsylvania, also published an English-language collection, *Hymns Selected and Original, for Public and Private Worship*.[5] Like the New York Synod hymnal, the 766 texts[6] were generic English rather than distinctively Lutheran, following the influence of the synod's ecumenical and liberal polemicist Samuel Schmucker. The Lutherans probably came close to being assimilated by the general Protestant ethos. While some pastors were influenced by fashionable liberal deism, others adopted populist Finneyite devices, utilizing the anxious bench and organizing protracted meetings of their own in spite of the official disapproval of the Pennsylvania Ministerium.

Irish and German Catholics, 1815–1865 (Baltimore: Johns Hopkins University Press, 1975) 13.

[3] F. H. Quitman, *A Collection of Hymns, and a Liturgy* (Philadelphia: G. & D. Billmeyer, 1814).

[4] Carl F. Schalk, *God's Song in a New Land: Lutheran Hymnals in America* (St. Louis: Concordia, 1995) 67–75.

[5] General Synod of the Evangelical Lutheran Church in the United States, *Hymns Selected and Original, for Public and Private Worship* (Gettysburg: General Synod of the Evangelical Lutheran Church in the United States, 1828).

[6] This number increased to 965 in 1841 and then to 1,024 in 1852.

As it turned out, the first decades of the nineteenth century marked a liturgical low point for Lutherans in North America. Until the immigrations of the 1830s revitalized and reoriented it toward its historical roots, eventually resulting in a restored liturgy in 1847, Lutheran worship lacked a real sense of liturgical tradition. Instead, its worship was, for the most part, like that of many other groups: alternating scripture (although not necessarily that prescribed for the particular Sunday) and prayers around a forty-five minute sermon, bracketed by a couple of hymns.[7]

All in all, the greatest advantage fell to the Episcopal Church. Indeed, perceived as the "only socially and theologically acceptable alternative to antebellum evangelicalism," a "refuge of peace and order" against the excesses of revivalism, and moderate in its view of temperance and abolitionism, it claimed many converts from other denominations.[8]

Unlike the Lutherans, Episcopalians—whether high- or low-church—did not deviate from the order set forth in the Book of Common Prayer. The evangelical, low-church faction placed emphasis on personal experience, scripture, and sermon, whereas the high churchmen concentrated instead on doctrine, authority, and tradition. For the low churchmen, the farthest departure from the Book of Common Prayer order during regular worship was scarcely more than an extemporaneous prayer before the sermon and possibly an exhortation. Their evangelical bent manifested itself in their informal Sunday evening "lectures" and weekday services. They avoided the trappings of revivalism—such as the anxious bench—and in general, they steered clear of cooperation with other churches in community revivals.[9]

---

[7] Schalk, *God's Song in a New Land*, 80–89; E. Clifford Nelson, ed., *The Lutherans in North America* (Philadelphia: Fortress, 1980) 95, 100, 107–108, 124–25, 206.

[8] Robert Bruce Mullin, *Episcopal Vision/American Reality* (New Haven: Yale University Press, 1986) 96, 117–24.

[9] Ralph Gerald Gay, "A Study of the American Liturgical Revival, 1825–1860" (Ph.D. diss., Emory University, 1977) 139–47. On Episcopal evangelicals, see Diana H. Butler, *Standing against the Whirlwind: Evangelical Episcopalians in Nineteenth-*

Although there were exceptions—for instance, the 1826 revival at West Point led by chaplain (later bishop of Ohio) Charles Pettit McIlvaine that converted the future Louisiana bishop and Confederate general, Leonidas Polk—for Episcopalians, even evangelicals, the revival was not significant. In the words of the evangelical bishop of Virginia, Richard Channing Moore, it was no more, than "a season of more than usual interest in the subject of religion, produced by the special influence of the Holy Spirit"— words that could well have been uttered by Jonathan Edwards a century before.[10]

Yet, in spite of their faithful adherence to the Book of Common Prayer, and for all the Anglican traditions to which they were heir, the musical and ceremonial level in most Episcopal churches was undistinguished. The usual service was Morning Prayer, followed immediately by the litany and ante-communion, all leading to the sermon. Congregations sat mute or murmured, while clerks made their responses for them and choirs did their singing, even when the setting was a Tate and Brady metrical psalm to a familiar congregational tune. By the 1830s, the quartet choir had made its appearance, especially in cities, and the psalmody sung in many churches borrowed its musical style and content from popular ballads and the stage.[11]

If there was consistency in following the order in the Book of Common Prayer, there was not necessarily uniformity in how it was followed. Some congregations stood during the singing of psalms; others sat. Many clergymen read or talked to one another while the congregation stood or sat silently (many of its members believing that singing was vulgar) as the clerk and the choir sang. Organists accompanied the psalmody with interludes between verses and sometimes even between lines. Sometimes an organ voluntary was

---

Century America (New York: Oxford University Press, 1994); and Allen C. Guelzo, *For the Union of Evangelical Christendom: The Irony of Reformed Episcopalians* (University Park: Penn State University Press, 1994) especially chapters 1–3.

[10] Jane E. Rasmussen, *Musical Taste as a Religious Question in Nineteenth-Century America* (Lewiston NY: Edwin Mellen Press, 1986) 15–18.

[11] Rasmussen, *Musical Taste*, 37–56.

played before the service as a prelude or at the beginning of it as the minister entered, or a psalm—often the Genevan Psalter's "Old Hundredth" Doxology—might be sung at that point. The postlude—"playing the congregation out," it was often termed—was becoming more common, although it was by no means universal. A so-called "middle voluntary" was often played after the reading of the psalms in Morning Prayer before the first lesson. As Edward Hodges recalled years later, near the end of his career:

> It was a critical thing for an inexperienced or inexpert organist to sit down to perform such a voluntary, in the presence of a large, attentive, and possibly classical congregation. It constituted, as it were, a musical discourse; and it was delivered, in many a church, as regularly as the sermon. But there can be no doubt, that, unless the organists were far superior to their successors of the present day, the discourse was frequently any thing but profitable to the hearers.[12]

If the flame of Anglican musical tradition was also guttering in England during that era, it was tended in some small fashion by the cathedral establishments.[13] America had no such models to look to for musical leadership and no "medieval" Gothic-style churches as yet (and certainly no ruins, which were so beloved of the period) to excite the romantic soul. As Frances Trollope described them in 1832, "The churches [of New York] are plain, but very neat, and kept in perfect repair within and without; but I saw none which had the

---

[12] Edward Hodges, "Voluntaries," *New York Musical World* 17/320 (16 May 1857): 307.

[13] There is a small but growing bibliography on nineteenth-century English church and cathedral music. See, for example, Bernarr Rainbow, *The Choral Revival in the Anglican Church* (New York: Oxford University Press, 1970); Nicholas Temperley, *The Music of the English Parish Church* (New York: Cambridge, 1979); William Gatens, *Victorian Cathedral Music in Theory and Practice* (Cambridge: Cambridge University Press, 1986); and John Ogasapian, *English Cathedral Music in New York: Edward Hodges of Trinity Church* (Richmond: Organ Historical Society, 1994).

least pretensions to splendor; the Catholic Cathedral in Baltimore is the only church in America that has."[14] In 1848, Alexis de Tocqueville made a more general observation: "I have seen no country in which Christianity is less clothed in forms, symbols and observances than it is in the United States, or where the mind is fed with clearer, simpler or more comprehensive conceptions."[15]

On an evening ten years before Tocqueville penned his observations, a teen-age youth recorded his own impressions in what would become one of the period's monumental diaries. George Templeton Strong, raised a strict Presbyterian but now about to join New York's oldest Episcopal parish, had attended the consecration of St. Peter's Roman Catholic Church on Barclay Street on 15 February 1838, and was drawn back by the music he heard, chiefly the ersatz Mozart "Twelfth Mass." Careful to profess a good Protestant's distaste for the ritual, he nevertheless averred, "The music was such as I never heard before. No wonder the Catholic faith has so many votaries and so devoted."[16]

Strong attended St. Paul's Chapel most Sundays. Its organist was Samuel Priestley Taylor (1779?–1875), who had emigrated from England around 1806 and enjoyed a measure of respect in the city's musical circles. Until his experience at St. Peter's, Strong had been satisfied enough with Taylor and even awestruck by his "playing" of Old Hundredth: "[21 May 1837] Except for some anthems, that's the

---

[14] Frances Trollope, *Domestic Manners of the Americans* [1832], ed. Donald Smalley (New York: Knopf, 1949) 342. Benjamin Latrobe's Baltimore Cathedral (still standing, but now the Basilica of the Assumption) had been completed less than a decade before.

[15] Alexis de Tocqueville, *Democracy in America*, trans. G. Lawrence, ed. J. P. Mayer (Garden City: Doubleday, 1975) 448. By this time, of course, two New York Episcopal congregations, Trinity and Grace, were worshiping in large gothic structures, the former by Richard Upjohn and the latter by James Renwick, Jr.

[16] Vera Brodsky Lawrence, *Strong on Music: I. Resonances, 1836–1850* (New York: Oxford University Press, 1988) 8–9. The entry is dated 25 February 1838. Strong's father and half-sister went to the "Scotch" Presbyterian Church on Cedar Street, pastored by the Reverend Joseph McElroy. At the time, Strong was attending St. Paul's on Broadway Sunday mornings and joining his family at the Presbyterian church for the evening service.

finest piece of church music I ever heard: noble, plain, simple and majestic. Well played, with a good many voices (and it wants a good many to give it effect) it strikes my ear more than anything." Now a regular visitor to St. Peter's for its music, he was impatient with the music at St. Paul's: "[8 April 1838] [St. Paul's] ought to give us all the music possible—much more than they do. Why don't they chant the *Te Deum*? And the *Gloria in Excelsis*? And I think it would be a good plan to imitate the Catholic service and chant most of the responses."

Music was an important element among the primarily German Catholic population in Philadelphia. St. Joseph's seems to have had an organ as early as 1749, and the Lutheran pastor Kalm remarked on the quality of music there. St. Mary's, built in 1763, had appointed Benjamin Carr organist shortly after his arrival from England. From 1801 on, he served as organist of St. Augustine's in that city, among other things performing abbreviated versions of Handel's *Messiah* and Haydn's *Creation* over his thirty-year tenure. Carr's successor, Benjamin Cross, introduced Haydn and Mozart masses so that the music program at St. Augustine's resembled closely that of St. Peter's in New York. Similarly, the choir of Baltimore's Cathedral of the Assumption gave the city its first performances of the Rossini *Stabat Mater* and *Haydn's Creation*.[17]

This handful of prominent city churches maintained the quality, prestige, and visibility of their programs. Protestant visitors were welcomed; indeed, St. Peter's was well aware of the admiration for its music and carefully burnished its reputation by employing well-known musicians and integrating repertoire like the "Twelfth Mass" and Mozart's *Requiem* into the regular liturgy, in addition to presenting concert performances of pieces like Rossini's *Stabat Mater*.

It must be borne in mind that even the larger cities had no real concert halls, and proper ladies, and even many gentlemen, were

---

[17] Robert R. Grimes, "How Shall We Sing in a Foreign Land: Music of Irish-Catholic Immigrants in the Antebellum United States" (Ph.D. diss., University of Pittsburgh, 1992) 189; Grimes's superb dissertation, revised and published under the same title in 1996 by the University of Notre Dame Press, is the definitive work in an all-too-sparse bibliography on the subject to date. As will be seen, much of this chapter relies on its findings.

reluctant to be seen entering a theater, even for a serious concert. Churches were, therefore, the only places where music could be performed or heard, either occasionally as when one or more musicians organized an "oratorio," or on a regular basis as at St. Peter's in New York.[18] Nevertheless, many Catholics in the congregation quite properly resented the presence of Protestants; for having come only for the music, they ignored the liturgy. As they would at any concert or the theater, they thought nothing of conversing among themselves during lulls between pieces or of standing on the kneelers for a better view. Indeed, in 1837, the Bishops' Synod in Baltimore warned against the liturgy becoming a vehicle for musical entertainment.[19]

From the perspective of the Protestant attendees, Catholic church music—at its best composed by recognized masters, often performed unapologetically with instruments in addition to the organ, and acknowledged to be the most refined (to use the favored expression of the period)—could often be heard only during Catholic worship. Music-loving Protestants were obliged to attend mass (or vespers) on occasion, but some clearly felt called upon to disassociate themselves and their love for the music from the "superstitions" of the ritual in progress by action and conversation during non-musical moments. As it turned out, however, others—and Strong was to become one of these—came to take an aesthetic interest in the liturgy itself as an art form, even as they denied any religious interest in it.[20]

---

[18] The earliest concert halls to be built were usually termed "academies," thus suggesting an educational purpose for them and distancing them from the slighted suspicion that they might somehow be related to theaters. In all fairness, theaters of the time were major places of solicitation by prostitutes. In many cases, the topmost balcony was set aside for them to entertain their clients. Accordingly, rare indeed was the woman who dared hazard her reputation by attending the theater, even with an escort.

[19] Grimes, "How Shall We Sing," 157, 181–87. Grimes's source for the abuses is a letter in the *New York Fireman's Journal* 9 (3 March 1849): 4. As late as 1862, unsigned, "St. Peter's Church," *Dwight's Journal of Music* 21/13 (28 June 1862): 100 characterized high mass at St. Peter's as a "grand carnival."

[20] Grimes, "How Shall We Sing," 124 aptly characterizes this as "tension between romantic interest in the medieval period and the Protestant rejection of such

Over the following years, Strong went often to St. Peter's, both for services and concerts of sacred music ("oratorios" in the parlance of the time), and recorded approbation of the music in terms such as "most beautiful" and "truly glorious." He noted with approval the use of professional singers from the theatrical and concert stage, a position that was not shared by contemporary Protestant clergy and laity or for that matter by any but a few church musicians.[21]

But churches like St. Peter's, St. Augustine's in Philadelphia, and Baltimore's cathedral were rare musical exceptions among Catholic churches. Benedict J. Fenwick, bishop of Boston at about the time Strong was making those entries in his diary and an amateur singer and pianist himself, estimated that some two-thirds of all Roman Catholic churches had no singing at all. The fastest growing immigrant Catholic groups, the Irish, had been so harassed in their homeland over the centuries and their religion suppressed as idolatrous that their liturgical and musical tradition had been lost to them, and they had virtually to develop a new one in America.[22]

Fenwick's predecessor in Boston, Bishop John Cheverus, had published a collection of texts sung at his cathedral.[23] The volumes included English versions of such hymns as *Conditor alme* ("Bright Maker of the starry poles") and *Ave Maris Stella* ("Hail, Thou resplendent star"). However, the first collections of music for Catholic worship in America were prepared by Protestants, and much, if not most, of it was repertoire drawn from contemporary Protestant worship.[24]

---

ritual and its music."

[21] Lawrence, *Resonances*, 6, 10–13.

[22] See Richard D. Wetzel, "Catholic Church Music in the Midwest before the Civil War: The firm of W. C. Peters & Sons," in *American Musical Life in Context and Practice to 1865*, ed. James R. Heintze (New York: Garland, 1994) 204–205. For a readable and trenchant, albeit informal, analysis of the problem, up to the present, see also Thomas Day, *Why Catholics Can't Sing* (New York: Crossroad, 1990).

[23] John Cheverus, *Anthems, Hymns, etc. Usually Sung at the Catholick Church in Boston* (Boston: n.p., 1800).

[24] John Aitken, *A Compilation of Litanies and Vespers, Hymns, and Anthems, as They Were Sung in the Catholic Church* (Philadelphia: Thomas Dobson, 1787) (2nd ed. 1791); and Benjamin Carr, *Masses, Vespers and Litanies...* (Philadelphia: n.p., 1805)

Thus, between the two extremes—the handful of city churches that maintained elaborate music programs and the two-thirds or more of the Catholic churches that had no music at all—there were number of parishes that sang English-language hymns like their Protestant neighbors. Not until the 1840s and 1850s was there significant effort on the part of the hierarchy to impose some degree of standardization after the Roman model. Even at that, two books of chant that were published, *Kyriale; or Ordinary of the Mass* and the *Roman Vesperal*, saw use in seminary and college chapels, rather than parish churches.[25]

Fenwick himself took one of the first steps toward standardization and Romanization by sponsoring the publication of *The Catholic Church Service Book* in 1833.[26] With a few exceptions, all texts were Latin; indeed, the volume consisted, as one notice put it, "almost entirely, that is, with very few exceptions, of GREGORIAN Music, harmonized and arranged for the Organ or Piano."[27] Accidentals were added to chant melodies making them closer to

---

and *A New Edition of Masses, Vespers and Litanies...* (Philadelphia: n.p., 1811). They were followed by Charles Tawes, *A Compilation of Litanies, Vespers, Chants, Hymns, and Anthems* (Philadelphia: n.p., 1814), and John David, *Collection of Sacred Hymns for the Use of Catholic Churches in Kentucky* (Bardstown: Bard and Edrington, 1815); Grimes, "How Shall We Sing," 36–38, 74–78. David, whose personal preferences ran to plainchant, was bishop of Bardstown from 1811, and something of a musician himself. He led a singing class in Bardstown. His cathedral replaced its piano with an organ in 1817, and the bishop himself became organist.

[25] *Kyriale; or Ordinary of the Mass* (Baltimore: John Murphy, 1857) and the *Roman Vesperal* (Baltimore: John Murphy, 1857); Grimes, "How Shall We Sing," 225–28. On the tension between American Catholic laity and the hierarchy in New York and Philadelphia, see among several items: Dolan, *The Immigrant Church*; and Richard Shaw, *Dagger John: The Unquiet Life and Times of Archbishop John Hughes of New York* (New York: Paulist Press, 1977).

[26] Composed, selected, and arranged by the first masters...., *The Catholic Church Service Book* (Published at the request of the present bishop of Boston for the use of his Diocese) (Boston: S. H. Parker, 1833).

[27] *The Jesuit* 4 (1833): 84 as cited in Grimes, "How Shall We Sing," 139. The book's introduction advised that the Gregorian be sung "slowly and solemnly; taking care that every word and every syllable be distinctly pronounced." See Grimes, "How Shall We Sing," 156.

diatonic, and figured basses were provided for keyboard accompaniment. The volume also contained choral repertoire (including Allegri's *Miserere*), two masses (one of them actually chant) and a requiem attributed to Vincent Novello, and music for Vespers.[28]

Singing schools were organized in Boston to teach the music in the new volume, and well-attended concerts were given of its contents. In January 1836, a Boston Gregorian Society was formed—centered at the Cathedral of the Holy Cross and consisting of singers from the city's Catholic church choirs—to learn and perform music that they could use back in their own parishes.

Relatively few copies of the 1833 collection were printed, however, before fire destroyed the printing shop and plates. A revised and retitled compilation, *The Morning and Evening Service of the Catholic Church*, was finally issued in 1840, and subsequently reprinted through 1910.[29] Its editor was Richard Garbett (1789–1881), a native of Exeter and an Anglican who had arrived in Boston around 1839 and had been appointed organist of the Cathedral. He revised the material from the 1833 book, placing the chants into regular meter, adding the necessary accidentals to fit the melodies into major or minor, and filling out harmonies in the accompaniments.[30] Some pieces were removed and many more were added, including a number of English-texted pieces from the collections of Aitken and Carr.[31]

Although most Catholic choirs had a limited repertoire and modest libraries, by the 1840s, Catholic choir directors had begun investigating the Viennese mass repertoire, and some groups were attempting to follow the example of metropolitan parish choirs. St.

---

[28] See Grimes, "How Shall We Sing," 152–53, for a table of contents.

[29] Richard Garbett, *The Morning and Evening Service of the Catholic Church* (Boston: Oliver Ditson, 1840).

[30] Grimes, "How Shall We Sing," 220–22 compares Fenwick's 1833 setting of the Gregorian *Veni Creator* with Garbett's 1840 version. See also 216–28 for a further discussion of chant during the period.

[31] Among other things, Allegri's *Miserere* was dropped from the 1840 edition. A critical discussion of the two collections appears in Grimes, "How Shall We Sing," 136–66. The contents of *Morning and Evening Services* are given on 159–61.

Peter's in Lowell, Massachusetts, for instance, performed the "Twelfth Mass" on 15 October 1842. In general, however, the drain on most church budgets for the support of immigrants who were now flooding into the parishes and for the building of parochial schools precluded adequate support for music. Moreover, tastes were changing among many in the congregation.

Beginning in the 1830s, there was a resurgence of interest in the music of "primitive" Christianity. Much more pronounced in America, however, were the effects of the Catholic revival movement that gained momentum during the same years. In many parishes, missions, as they were called, were held regularly, every couple of years. Although Catholic missions did not last as long as the "protracted meetings" of the Protestant revivals, they did go on for a week or so with the visiting missioner, usually an "order" priest such as a Jesuit or Redemptorist, preaching in a direct and emotional manner every night.[32]

Such missions engendered the composition and adaptation of hymns and religious ballads in the style of the secular parlor song. Secular melodies from the Irish and French traditions—Thomas Moore's well-known "Last Rose of Summer," for example—were fitted with sacred texts. Intended like their Protestant counterparts for informal meetings and family devotions, such pieces were widely disseminated in cheap editions and quickly found their way into the regular worship of many parishes.[33]

---

[32] The best known Catholic hymn from that period and one that still holds a well-deserved place in hymnals of many denominations is the Redemptorist import "Holy God, We Praise Thy Name." The text is a paraphrase of the *Te Deum* by the convert priest Clarence Walworth, whom Finney recalled having first met in 1842 at a revival in Rochester, New York. At the time Walworth was a young lawyer and Protestant. Finney was later to encounter Walworth, by then a Redemptorist priest, in England. Walworth was one of the first and foremost missioners in America. Since 1850, the text has been coupled with the eighteenth-century Austrian tune, *Grosser Gott.*

[33] Grimes, "How Shall We Sing," 241–54, cites Edward J. Sourin, *The Sacred Wreath: or A Collection of Hymns and Prayers* (Philadelphia, 1844); and Edward Caswell, *Lyra Catholica* (New York, 1851) reprinted from the London edition. On missions, see Dolan, *Catholic Revivalism.*

At its best then, Catholic church music by "cultivated" European composers appealed far more to cultivated young urban romantics like Strong than the metrical psalmody and occasional hymns that were standard fare in urban Episcopal churches. Special events brought forth special music, of course. The 1820 dedication of St. Paul's Church in Boston, a bastion of Episcopal evangelicalism, had featured a full orchestra and choir of sixty (largely made up of members of the Handel and Haydn Society) under the direction of George K. Jackson, performing music by Jackson himself and Handel, including the opening chorus of the *Dettingen Te Deum*.[34]

In New York, churches hosted concerts, and musical societies were associated with church musicians of Peter Erben's generation. S. P. Taylor, organist of St. Paul's Chapel during Strong's youth, had involved himself from his arrival in 1806 with New York's Handel and Haydn Society, leading concerts of "sacred" music. One such, given 8 March 1814 at the French Huguenot church, St. Espirit, included parts of Handel's *Messiah* and Haydn's *Creation*. The New-York Choral Society and New-York Sacred Music Society were both formed in 1824. The former was under the leadership of James Swindells, music director at St. George's and editor of *The Lyre*. Its first performances in April and May 1824 drew small audiences, and the society (and *The Lyre*) ceased operation a year later. The Sacred Music Society, formed at Zion Church but disassociated from that parish when its vestry denied the group use of the building for a performance, was somewhat more long-lived.[35]

---

[34] Unsigned, "Consecration of St. Paul's Church," *Euterpeiad* 1/14 (1 July 1820): 55.

[35] Lawrence, *Resonances*, xxxiii-xxxviii. It bears repeating that the terms "oratorio" and "sacred music" had different meanings from their modern usage. An oratorio was essentially a concert of "sacred" music that might or might not consist of excerpts from (and seldom if ever a complete performance of) a single work. "Sacred music," in addition to having a text suitable for performing in a church building, also made primary use of amateurs, with only the soloists professional musicians, if indeed even they were. The result was that music making was an activity involving many in the community and therefore eliciting the support of many. By the 1840s, things had begun to change. Touring European soloists and companies, performing in theaters, halls and "gardens," set a professional standard that amateurs

But the music of regular worship remained plain, and even the least attempt at change was generally resisted by the older generation. John Pintard (1759–1844), influential member of St. Thomas, Ascension and St. Espirit in New York (and rapidly losing his hearing at the time) wrote his daughter 3 June 1830, extolling "[the] old solemn tunes of Church psalmody, wh. for devotional excitement far surpass any of the modern more scientific arias. Luther's [*sic*] Old Hundred can never cease to inspire as long as sober chaste tastes shall prevail, and so of many others. Church music to me as cultivated here, is absolutely screeching, but this no doubt is owing to my decayed hearing."[36]

The fifty-one hymn texts and eight pages of tunes that Francis Hopkinson had prevailed upon Bishop White and the General Convention to include as ancillary to the 1786 Prayer Book had been reduced in 1789 to twenty-seven hymns (in addition to the Psalter in metrical setting). In 1808, thirty-one more hymns were added, twenty-six of them written by Baptists and Independents. This evident hesitancy regarding hymns on the part of many Episcopal clergy and bishops was clearly related to their mistrust of religious "enthusiasm," which they saw in the revival fever that was abroad in America and especially among the evangelicals of their own denomination.

Thus, it was only after three years' work that the General Convention accepted an official collection of 212 hymn texts in November 1826 and had it published the next year.[37] No tunes were supplied or authorized; rather, individual parishes were left to select their own, and a number of unofficial collections were compiled in the usual manner of the time. The resulting use of secular "airs" distressed some churchmen who would have preferred to see a similarly "authorized" collection of tunes to go with the texts. In

---

could not meet and fostered a taste for a more European, secular repertoire.

[36] John Pintard, *Letters from John Pintard to his Daughter, Eliza Noel Pintard Davidson, 1816–1833*, 4 vols. (New York: New-York Historical Society, 1940–1941) 3:50.

[37] Notwithstanding, the metrical psalms of Tate and Brady continued in semi-official use right up to 1886.

general, however, congregations made use of a small number of melodies. In the preface to his compilation, *Sacred Harmony, or Elegant Extracts of Sacred Music*, William Nash wrote, "Not one twentieth part of the tunes published in most singing books are ever sung, or worth singing."[38]

The beginnings of a distinctively Episcopal musical practice in America appeared in the early 1840s. The first wave of the Oxford movement reached this country several years before; however, its initial effect on music, if any, was minimal. The reformers had no real interest in ceremony; rather, the Oxford divines and the tracts they produced concentrated on matters of faith and doctrine. Indeed, before his conversion to Roman Catholicism, Newman himself conducted simple services, devoid of extra color or music.

The most controversial, and ultimately the most far-reaching of Oxford reformers' publications, was *Tract 90*, which appeared in 1841. It held that nothing in the history or teaching of Anglicanism, as found in its *Thirty-Nine Articles*, was inconsistent with historic Catholic teaching and practice. In other words, Anglicanism was as much Catholic as it was Protestant. Consequently, Anglicanism was also heir to the historic Catholic ritual. Naturally, the evangelical wing, which sought closer ties with other evangelical Protestant denominations, reacted sharply against the idea of holding anything of substance in common with Roman Catholics. Non-evangelicals, those for whom the authority of Anglicanism lay in its doctrine and its bishops especially, were not inclined see themselves as sharing a religious tradition with the immigrant Germans and especially the Irish they so often despised. Nevertheless, the beginnings of ritualism began to surface among the younger clergy, especially the faculty and students at New York's General Seminary. The result was a controversy within American Episcopalianism that lasted through the first half of the twentieth century.[39]

---

[38] William Nash, *Sacred Harmony, or Elegant Extracts of Sacred Music* (Cincinnati: printed by author, 1836); Rasmussen, *Musical Taste as a Religious Question*, 182. Rasmussen's work is the best available source on the topic. See especially, 129–222.

[39] The issue lies outside the scope of this book. See, however: E. Clowes

Anglicanism in England had long had two distinct church music practices. The cathedrals maintained their established choirs and daily choral services. Even though, by the fourth decade of the nineteenth century, the quality of cathedral choirs was indifferent at best, at least in theory, they served as some sort of musical model for parish churches to emulate. In practice, however, most parish churches made do with metrical psalmody, sometimes led by poorly trained children from the local charity school. Some parish churches had adult choirs who occasionally attempted "cathedral" anthems or services, but such choirs, with few exceptions, were just as poorly trained as the charity school children.

Although America had no cathedrals with endowed musical programs and daily sung services, a number of Episcopal clergy and laymen had visited England and come away awed by cathedral music, mediocre though it might have been by any objective standards. Moreover, the Gothic revival was beginning to take hold in church design. Buildings became larger and more ornate from the 1840s onward. Pulpit and reading desk, which were hitherto combined in a single furnishing—a so-called "three-decker"—with, or at least in close proximity to, the communion table, were now at some distance from each other. The logistics of moving from one place to another during the service, combined with the mystical, neo-Medievalism of the newly fashionable Gothic architecture, probably had as much to do with the growth of an Episcopal musical and ceremonial tradition as did the implications of *Tract 90*.[40]

Chorley, *Men and Movements in the American Episcopal Church* (New York: Charles Scribner's Sons, 1946) and George E. DeMille, *The Catholic Movement in the American Episcopal Church* (Philadelphia: Church Historical Society, 1941, 1950). Both are now out of print but relatively accessible in libraries.

[40] The Cambridge Camden Society was organized in 1836 and formally reorganized in 1839 to foster a revival of Gothic architecture and ritual in the Anglican Church. Its effects were felt almost immediately in America. The bishop of New Jersey, George Washington Doane, had become a patron member by the time the first issue of its periodical, the *Ecclesiologist*, appeared in November 1841. An American counterpart, the New York Ecclesiological Society was formed in 1848; however, by that time, Gothic revival after the English style had become virtually standard for Episcopal churches in the United States. See James F. White, *The*

Three men were especially prominent during this period: two clergymen—Jonathan Mayhew Wainwright and William Augustus Muhlenberg—and a middle-aged expatriate English organist named Edward Hodges. All three were converts, Wainwright from Presbyterianism, Muhlenberg from Lutheranism, and Hodges from British Independent non-conformism. And all three made their mark in New York.

The eldest of the three was Wainwright (1792–1854). His father was a Liverpool merchant, possibly related to a family of church musicians active in that city during the eighteenth century. His mother was descended from a line of Puritan ministers who had been especially active among the Native Americans on Martha's Vineyard during the late seventeenth and eighteenth centuries. Her father was the Reverend Jonathan Mayhew, pastor of Boston's Old West Church and an ardent opponent of Anglican inroads in the old Bay Colony.[41]

Wainwright was born in Liverpool and spent his childhood there. In 1803, the family returned to Boston. In 1808, he entered Harvard, and during his four years as a student there, he served as organist and lay reader at nearby Christ Church in Cambridge. After

---

Cambridge Movement (Cambridge: Cambridge University Press, 1962, 1979); Phoebe Stanton, *The Gothic Revival in American Church Architecture* (Baltimore: Johns Hopkins Press, 1968).

[41] A number of pieces by John Wainwright of Liverpool are to be found in eighteenth and early nineteenth-century collections in England and America. See Allen Perdue Britton, Irving Lowens, and Richard Crawford, *American Sacred Music Imprints 1698– 1810* (Worcester MA: American Antiquarian Society, 1990) (Hereafter cited as *ASMI.*); also see Watkins Shaw, *The Succession of Organists* (New York: Oxford University Press, 1991) 186–88. On Jonathan Mayhew, see Charles W. Akers, *Called unto Liberty: A Life of Jonathan Mayhew, 1720–1766* (Cambridge: Harvard University Press, 1964); and Carl Bridenbaugh, *Mitre and Sceptre* (New York: Oxford University Press, 1962). As of this writing, there is no other biography of Wainwright than John Nicholas Norton's hagiographic *Life of Bishop Wainwright* (New York: General Seminary, 1858) and Bishop G. W. Doane's prefatory "Memoir" in the posthumous book of his sermons edited by his wife: Amelia M. Wainwright, *A Memorial Volume* (New York: n.p., 1857). See also William Rhinelander Stewart, *Grace Church and Old New York* (New York: E. P. Dutton, 1924) 393–95.

his graduation in 1812, Wainwright studied law for a brief time and then turned to theology. He prepared for orders under the guidance of Dr. S. J. Gardiner, Rector of Trinity Church in Boston, at the same time serving as a proctor and instructor in rhetoric at Harvard.

In 1817, he was ordained, and that year, he became rector of Christ Church, Hartford. In 1819, his last year in that post, he published his first collection of church music, titled *A Set of Chants*. His purpose, set forth in the preface, was to furnish choirs with a "comprehensive system of chant" as a better vehicle for preserving the true meaning of the text. "Chanting," wrote Wainwright, "is but another name for reading to a tune," a compromise between the musical and the rhetorical.[42] The music included eleven chants for Morning Prayer, nine for Evening Prayer, and a single set of chants for communion. The texts were underlaid across facing pages, and the music laid out on four staves, the usual alto and tenor above treble (air) and bass. The bass part contained figures (G. K. Jackson is credited with the accompaniments.), with small notes added to the treble and bass staves for organists unable to realize the continuo.

In December 1819, Wainwright became an assistant at Trinity Church in New York, and just over a year later, in January 1821, rector of Grace Church, at that time on the opposite corner of Broadway and Rector Street from Trinity. During the next thirteen years, he gained a reputation as one of New York's leading preachers as well as a patron of the arts and literature, and Grace Church became known for the beauty of its music and worship. One of Wainwright's first acts was to do away with the office of clerk.[43] He

---

[42] Jonathan Mayhew Wainwright, ed., *A Set of Chants Adapted to the Hymns in the (Old English) Morning and Evening Prayer and to the Communion Service of the Protestant Episcopal Church in the United States of America* (Boston: Thomas Badger, Jr., 1819). Wainwright's name does not appear on the title page of the only copy known to the author, in the American Antiquarian Society Collection, Worcester.

[43] This according to J. Newton Perkins, *History of St. Stephen's Parish in the City of New York, 1805–1905* (New York: Gorham, 1906) 37; and judging by Wainwright's subsequent actions, it certainly seems plausible. See also James Elliot Lindsley, *This Planted Vine* (New York: Harper and Row, 1984) 96.

then introduced a small choir to lead in the singing, paying for them out of his own pocket.[44]

His years at Grace saw the publication of his second collection, *Music of the Church*, published in 1828. Unlike his 1819 *A Set of Chants, Music of the Church*,[45] was a compilation of tunes for use with metrical psalms and the hymn texts authorized the previous year. The book was patterned on Gardiner's *Sacred Melodies* (1815), and its contents resembled those of Mason's *Boston Handel and Haydn Society Collection of Church Music* with tunes from some eighty composers and sources, among them Haydn, Beethoven, Paisiello, and Clementi. Each tune was headed with the psalm or text to be sung to it, and none of them was used for more than three texts. As with his earlier publication, Wainwright acknowledged professional assistance, this time from his own organist at Grace Church, James Gear, and from Peter K. Moran of St. Paul's Chapel.

Wainwright had kept touch with his English roots and was certainly a keen observer of the Oxford movement in England during the early 1830s. He may have been among the earliest to foresee its musical and liturgical implications. By 1834, he had apparently begun efforts to recruit the English organist Aaron Upjohn Hayter (1799–1873) for Grace Church. A pupil of A. T. Corfe at Salisbury Cathedral, Hayter must have been a formidable talent in his youth, for he was appointed organist of Hereford Cathedral in 1818, at the age of eighteen. Possibly the prestige was too much for one so young, for he somehow ran afoul of the authorities over a lapse in personal conduct and was dismissed in 1820. His next fifteen years were spent

---

[44]Stewart, *Grace Church and Old New York*, 107. The attraction in the choir was María Málibran, the great operatic soprano, who was at the time financially pressed to pay off the debts of her husband, a failed merchant. She probably sang the psalms alone much of the time; crowds came to Grace to hear her, not to observe her leading congregational singing. Opera was among Wainwright's passions, then and afterward. See Lindsley, *This Planted Vine*, 161–64; and Carl Carmer, *The Years of Grace (1808–1958)* (New York: Grace Church, 1958) 14.

[45] Jonathan M. Wainwright, *Music of the Church. A Collection of Psalm, Hymn, and Chant Tunes, Adapted to the Worship of the Protestant Episcopal Church in the United States* (New York: Samuel Bradford, 1828). The book went through eight editions, the last of which was published in New York by James A. Sparks in 1843.

as organist of the not insignificant collegiate church at Brecon in Wales, and it was thence that he was called to Grace Church.

Hayter accepted the offer and arrived in New York in 1835, but Wainwright had left Grace Church to succeed his old mentor as rector of Trinity Church in Boston. At the same time, Wainwright had begun making overtures to Edward Hodges (1796–1867), holder of a Cambridge music doctorate and modestly renown as an essayist, composer, and organist of St. Nicholas and St. James' Churches in Bristol. The initial approaches were made through a Baptist minister, John Overton Choules, during the latter's 1835 trip to Europe. Some sort of correspondence developed, and Wainwright and Hodges finally met in late autumn 1836, during Wainwright's own trip to England to contract with Gray of London for Trinity's new organ.

Hodges was a Bristol native, son of a paper merchant and religious Independent. Although he himself became an Anglican, the fact that he had not been born one and thus had not gone the normal professional route of chorister and then assistant organist, barred him from succeeding to the post of organist at one of the cathedrals and chapels royal for which he competed. His earning of the Cambridge doctorate, his several articles on church music, his acknowledged expertise in organ design, his published compositions, and his reputation as an erudite musician did not improve his situation. By 1835, Hodges, who was a widower with five children aged from a few months to fifteen years, knew he had no real professional prospects as long as he remained in Britain.

Possibly because he was even then contemplating his move from Boston back to New York, Wainwright suspended negotiations with Hodges. Instead, the nod once more went to Hayter in New York, and he moved to Trinity Church in Boston; yet again, by the time Hayter arrived, Wainwright had moved back to New York and his old post as assistant in Trinity Parish. Hayter remained at Trinity in Boston the rest of his career, serving also from 1839 to 1848 as organist and conductor of the Handel and Haydn Society.

Meanwhile, Hodges had accepted an offer from St. James Cathedral in Toronto. He moved there in fall 1838, but stayed scarcely a month because of the political and economic turmoil in

Canada. By November, he was in New York; and in January 1839, almost certainly through Wainwright's intervention, Hodges was appointed organist of Trinity and assigned to St. John's Chapel, where Wainwright officiated.[46]

Over the six years or so that Hodges and Wainwright worked together at St. John's, their relationship seems to have cooled. Both men were strong-minded, and Wainwright, whose *Music of the Church* was by now in its eighth edition, considered himself as knowledgeable in church music matters as Hodges. With the completion and dedication in 1846 of the new Trinity Church, a Gothic building designed by Richard Upjohn (again, probably chosen as architect by Trinity's vestry on the recommendation of Wainwright, who had known him in Boston), the two were finally freed from working together every week. Hodges took up the duties of organist at Trinity, playing the instrument he had designed and that Henry Erben, son of his predecessor Peter Erben, had built.[47]

By the time he moved to Trinity Church, Hodges had become a fixture in New York church music. In addition to his Sunday morning duties at St. John's, now relinquished, he was teaching at the nearby Trinity School, where in 1843 he had persuaded Trinity's vestry to establish music scholarships for boy choristers.

As a church organist, Hodges was a sharp contrast to most of his colleagues and predecessors. In the first place, church music was one of several activities they combined to eke out a living in music. Hodges's predecessor Peter Erben carried on a music publishing business, imported pianos, probably built organs, organized concerts, and gave lessons. Others spent their weekdays in theater orchestras.

---

[46] On this episode, see Ogasapian, *English Cathedral Music in New York*, 83–100.

[47] For an overview on the Trinity organ and controversies surrounding it, see Ogasapian, *English Cathedral Music in New York*, 143–60. Hodges chronicled the affair in a notebook titled "Memoranda and Copies of Documents connected with the Proposed New Organ for Trinity Church," now in the Library of Congress. For text and commentary, see John Ogasapian, "Toward a Biography of Henry Erben, Part 2," *The Tracker* 22/1 (Fall 1977): 3–13 and "Toward a Biography of Henry Erben, Part 3," *The Tracker* 22/2 (Winter 1978): 10–22.

Hodges, on the other hand, considered himself a full-time member of Trinity's staff, except for some private teaching and accompanying.

Second, other organists, even English immigrants like Hayter, were sensitive to their status as employees of the churches they served. They had always taken things as they found them and sought to please their clergy and congregations. Hodges considered himself an English cathedral organist, temporarily exiled in something akin to a missionary field, but ready to return should the opportunity present itself. Meanwhile, he kept faith with his professional ideal, passed it on to his students, and preached it in numerous speeches and articles aimed at other denominations, as well as his own.

He attended and addressed the American Musical Convention, held at the Broadway Tabernacle during autumn 1845. Among the topics debated were quartet choirs, the use of instruments in church, and the benefit of secular music study on the improvement of sacred music. Hodges urged the group to teach the "science of music" (theory) as well as the art, and he came out strongly for large choirs rather than quartets and for oratorio performances in church. He deplored the number of tunes and indifferent quality growing out of the variety of tune books in circulation, observing how, other than Old Hundredth, few if any tunes were used by all denominations: "Instead of eight or ten tunes adapted to about half as many meters, we have almost innumerable collections, each containing not merely dozens, or scores, but generally hundreds of tunes." Hodges pointed to the twenty-six different meters in the collection used by his own Trinity Church and its chapels as an example of the reason that congregational singing was in "paralyzed and degraded condition."[48]

But most of all, Hodges sought to put his ideal into practice by creating an English cathedral music program in America's largest and wealthiest church.[49] In the end, of course, he could not achieve all his

---

[48] *Proceedings of the American Musical Convention Held in the Broadway Tabernacle on the 8th, 9th and 10th of October, 1845* (New York: Saxton & Miles, 1845) 31–43.

[49] It helped, of course, that he had remarried well. His second wife, Sarah Moore, was of old and prosperous New York stock. Her social connections and money gave him security and shielded him from arbitrary chastisement or dismissal, thus enabling him to effect changes in Trinity Parish's music that were not always to

objectives. An English-style choir of men and boys would always lie beyond his reach. He could not dispense with the adult women, for he did not know how to train boys' head register. For that matter, the new Trinity was not configured like a cathedral with choir stalls in the chancel as the Cambridge Camden and New York ecclesiologists would have preferred; instead, the choir and organ were in a rear gallery. Neither Trinity's congregation nor its clergy, although it was among the more ceremonially progressive Episcopal churches of the time, were ready to allow a choir to be vested or robed and seated in the chancel in the manner of an English cathedral.

By the time such ritualism gained a foothold in America, Hodges and his music were old-fashioned. The collection he compiled for his own use at Trinity contained not only service music and chants but also the usual selection of tunes suitable for the singing of metrical hymn and psalm texts; in short, it consisted of the usual, practical, conservative fare for churches of the era.[50]

Even at his most ideal, Hodges's repertoire and the type of anthems and service music he wrote were that of a Georgian cathedral rather than Victorian; harmonized Anglican chant rather than plainsong; and accompanied multi-movement anthems modeled on Handelian lines rather than motet-style pieces modeled on Tudor polyphony. In short, it was the music of St. Paul's Cathedral, London, under Attwood rather than Goss. Musically, his English colleagues were passing him by. In London, Novello had begun printing individual anthems in octavo in 1844, distributing them with copies of *The Musical Times*. By 1852, the publishing house had established a New York office to open the American market, particularly Episcopal churches.

What Hodges had begun would only be accomplished by his successor Henry Stephen Cutler. Cutler was appointed in 1857; the

the liking of the clergy and congregation.

[50] Edward Hodges, *Trinity Collection of Church Musi:; Containing All the Psalm and Hymn Tunes, Chants, &c. Used in Trinity Church, New York, or in Either of its Three Chapels* (Boston: Oliver Ditson, 1864). The volume was published after his retirement and seen through the press by his young friend, S. Parkman Tuckerman, who edited it and provided "valuable additions."

women in Trinity's choir were gone by 1859, and only boys and men remained. That same year, Cutler was able to institute sung services at Trinity's regular worship. After October 1860, the vested choir of men and boys sang from the chancel of Trinity Church every Sunday.

Still, in the end, Hodges's influence was crucial in professionalizing the practice of church music and as a transition from the indifference of metrical psalmody, occasional Anglican chant, and colorless service music of early-nineteenth-century Episcopalian worship in America to the solemn music and ritual that characterized—or, more accurately, was the ideal of—liturgical worship in the late nineteenth century. Hodges may not have been able to introduce a full-sung service at Trinity, including the intonations of versicles, responses, and psalm, but he did organize the Church Choral Society out of a group of interested clergy, seminarians, and laymen in December 1851 for the express purpose of mounting occasional fully sung services. The society was short-lived; its first rehearsal was held 7 January 1852, and its fourth and final service was sung at Trinity on 17 March 1853. The young clergymen and seminarians who took part imbibed the lesson well; not many years later, they would establish sung services as regular worship in their own parishes after the example Hodges had set.

Hodges was also successful over a longer term in a way that surely would have surprised him. The English cathedral standard, adjusted to the needs of other denominations, become the ideal to which most professional church musicians aspired, and indeed still aspire if truth be told. Much of what he espoused for church music as a profession in the series of articles he wrote for the *New York Musical World* during 1856 and 1857 came to pass in the century after his death. Colleges and seminaries established programs to train and credential musicians for church work; a number of church musicians were able to derive their income mainly or totally from their parish work and to be considered on a level with clergy, even to bearing the title "minister of music."

The remaining member of the three, William Augustus Muhlenberg (1796–1877), may well have been the most distinctive. A little over a century ago, one who remembered him called Muhlenberg "perhaps the most original character in the American church,"[51] and indeed, in retrospect, he presents an extraordinary set of contradictions and combinations.[52]

A theological evangelical, he established a school and then a church, both of which quickly became known for ritual and music. A Lutheran by birth, baptism, family, and tradition, he sponsored the first sisterhood in the American Episcopal Church and then introduced a resolution to permit the bishop of the Episcopal Church to bestow orders on clergymen of any denomination. Far in advance of his time, he made his parish a center of community activity and founded a hospital and a retirement community.

Muhlenberg was born in Philadelphia, the great-grandson of the eminent Lutheran clergyman Henry Melchior Muhlenberg. He was baptized by the hymn writer and pastor of St. Michael's and Zion, J. C. F. Helmuth, but because his family spoke English, the boy and his mother began to attend the Episcopal Church. Muhlenberg graduated from the University of Pennsylvania in 1815. That year, he began the study of music, and like Strong, he took to attending Catholic services for the music. At the same time, he began reading theology under Bishop William White.

In 1815, Muhlenberg was ordained a deacon and took over the music at St. James in Philadelphia at the request of Bishop White. With White's approval, Muhlenberg did away with the position of clerk in 1818, rehearsing the choir of boys and "giving out" the psalms during services himself. In 1820, he was ordained a priest and went to St. James' Church, Lancaster, as rector. Over the next few years, he was tireless in championing the adoption of more hymn texts in place of metrical psalms. In 1821, he published his pamphlet *A Plea for Christian Hymns*, pushing for a hymnal commission. The pamphlet drew attention to the 1817 hymnal of the Lutherans (which

---

[51] Frederic Cook Morehouse, *Some American Churchmen* (Milwaukee: Young Churchmen, 1892) 125.

[52] A considerable amount has been written on Muhlenberg. The definitive biography is Alvin W. Skardon, *Church Leader in the Cities: William Augustus Muhlenberg* (Philadelphia: University of Pennsylvania Press, 1971).

he characterized as a "sister church"), suggesting that "their example may be of weight." The next year, he wrote to a friend and delegate to General Convention, chafing at the limitations of Tate and Brady as "casting a veil over Christianity" and affirming his preference for Watts, Cowper, Newton, and so-called "hymns of human composure."[53]

By 1823, an exasperated Muhlenberg published his *Church Poetry*.[54] The hymns were those used in his church in Lancaster, but the collection was quickly adopted by other parishes in the area. That year, the General Convention set up the committee, including Muhlenberg, that prepared the hymnal that was adopted in 1826 and published in 1827. By then, however, Muhlenberg had turned his energies into another field.

In 1826, he became rector of St. George's Church, Flushing, New York. Two years later, he founded the Flushing Institute, a boy's school that quickly attracted attention and support. John Pintard wrote his daughter on 28 April 1828: "I contemplate placing Marney at an excellent new Institution at Flusing [*sic*] under the sup.intendence of the Rev. Mr Muhlenbergh [*sic*], an Episcopal Clergyman, easy in circumstances, of high classical attainments & devotedly attached to education." Over a year later, Pintard's initial impression of Muhlenberg and his school had been vindicated. In a letter on 14 September 1829, he wrote, "Mrs Brinley, a delicate English lady…has 2 sons for education & enquired my opinion about Mr Muhlenberghs Institute, in praise of wh I told her from my experience as to Marney, I cd not speak too high."[55]

---

[53] William Augustus Muhlenberg, "A Plea for Christian Hymns in a Letter to a Friend," *Evangelical Catholic Papers* (New York: Thomas Whittaker, 1877) 18–19. See also Ann Ayres, *The life and Work of William Augustus Muhlenberg* (New York: Harper & Bros., 1880) 45–47.

[54] William Augustus Muglenberg, *Church Poetry, Being Portions of the Psalms in Verse and Hymns Suited to the Festivals and Fasts and Various Occasions of the Church. Selected and Altered from Various Sources* (Philadelphia: S. Potter & Co., 1823). The collection was admittedly patterned after an English model: Thomas Cotterill, *A Selection of Psalms and Hymns for the Use of St. Paul's and St. James' Churches*, 9th ed. (Sheffield: Montgomery, 1820). See Skardon, *Church Leader*, 35–37.

[55] Pintard, *Letters* 3:30, 97.

Students at the institute were taught sacred music and singing, and the talented ones formed into a choir for the Sunday chapel services. Those services were very advanced for their time, incorporating processional cross, flowers, and candles: normal parts of modern Episcopal worship, but highly controversial in the years after 1828, when Muhlenberg introduced them at the Flushing Institute. Among the boys educated at Flushing and influenced by the ritual was John Ireland Tucker. Years later, as a young priest, he would both take part in Hodges's Church Choral Society and its sung services in New York, and he would establish sung services at the Church of the Holy Cross in Troy, where he was rector.[56]

In 1838, Muhlenberg established a college at Flushing. Jonathan Wainwright was one of its board of visitors and a member of the faculty. He and Muhlenberg apparently met and become friends in the mid-1820s, in all probability drawn together initially by their interest in sacred music and especially their distaste for metrical psalmody. It will be recalled that both men favored suppressing, or at least supplementing, the use of metrical psalmody as the official and authorized music of the Episcopal Church with hymns and chant.

St. Paul's College lasted only a few years. The state legislature hesitated to grant degree authority to an exclusively denominational institution, and Muhlenberg's financial backing faltered in the economic climate that followed the so-called Panic of 1837. But by 1843, he had all but lost interest in the college, and that year departed for Europe, leaving Wainwright in charge of its operations. In Europe, Muhlenberg met the Oxford reformers and briefly came under their sway; however, he turned away from the movement probably because of the defection to Rome of some of its members, particularly John Henry Newman. He returned to New York City with a new vision: to build a "free" church in which the pews were not owned or rented (as was the case in most Protestant churches at the time) but rather were free and open to all.

Underwritten by his sister's fortune, Muhlenberg engaged Upjohn, who was then supervising the construction of Trinity's new

---

[56] Skardon, *A Leader*, 98; Moorehouse, *Some American Churchmen*, 127.

edifice, to prepare a design. He also solicited a scheme for the organ from Edward Hodges, whom he probably met through Wainwright; at the time, Hodges was playing at St. John's Chapel where Wainwright was officiating. In 1844, the cornerstone for the church was laid, and by 1846, the Church of the Holy Communion at Sixth Avenue and Twentieth Street was ready open for worship.[57]

Muhlenberg instituted daily sung services and a weekly celebration of Holy Communion in an era when most Episcopal churches had communion services three times a year or, in the case of more liturgically advanced parishes, once a month. He trained his own vested choir of men and boys, the first such in New York, which sang from the floor and a gallery at the south side of the chancel across from the organ, a position that would certainly have met with approval among the Cambridge Camden and New York ecclesiologists.

The role of the choir at Holy Communion, however, was solely to support congregational singing. Neither then nor later did Muhlenberg care for the sound of boys' voices alone. He prepared his own collections for the use of the congregation.[58] By 1857, the *Church Journal* characterized Holy Communion as "A church whose high standing in congregational music is now known throughout the whole country."[59]

In 1851, Muhlenberg and Wainwright collaborated on a collection titled *The Choir and Family Psalter*. Its purpose was to encourage the use of chant as a vehicle for psalmody, as distinct from hymns or religious poetry, which might appropriately be sung to

---

[57] Ogasapian, *English Cathedral Music in New York*, 163–64; also Stanton, *The Gothic Revival and American Church Architecture*, 68–70.

[58] William Augustus Muhlenberg, *The Psalter; or Psalms of David, together with the Canticles...Figures for Chanting* (New York: D. Appleton, 1849) and *The People's Psalter, Being the Psalms of David, Arranged for Chanting, with an Appendix Containing Hymns from Holy Scripture, and a Selection of Chants* (New York: Stanford & Swords, 1854).

[59] *Church Journal* 27 (May 1857): 141. See also William Augustus Muhlenberg, *A Primer of Church Music* (New York: S. W. Benedict, 1845); Ayres, *William Augustus Muhlenberg*, 222–24.

tunes in meter. Psalms, being scripture, should have their meaning preserved faithfully. As the preface put it, "[Chant] expresses more fully and more accurately the meaning of the inspired original than language transmitted by metre and rhyme can do."[60] The tunes were grouped together; however, blank staves were provided over the psalm texts onto which a preferred tune could be copied. The psalms themselves were arranged on facing pages, odd verses on the left and even on the right.

No composers were given for the seventy-five single and forty-three double chant tunes, but the harmonizations were by George F. Bristow. The chants themselves were arranged in a similar manner to that adopted by Wainwright in his 1819 collection, except that the voices were dispersed over three staves: the middle and lower staves contained the treble and bass parts respectively, with the alto under the treble and the tenor over the bass in small notes. The top staff contained the tenor and alto. Thus, the organist could read all the parts from the lower two staves, and if four voice parts were available, the tenor and alto could read from the top staff.

Although Muhlenberg's religious and social projects continued unabated into his old age,[61] for all practical purposes, his musical activities ended with the 1850s. In the years immediately following his return from a second visit to Europe in 1855, he served on the committee that prepared the first authorized book of hymn tunes. Some years later, he joined in the editing of yet another collection.[62]

---

[60] Rev. Jonathan M. Wainwright and Rev. William A. Muhlenberg, *The Choir and Family Psalter: Being the Psalms of David; Together with the Canticles of the Morning and Evening Prayer and Occasional Offices of the Church, Arranged for Chanting. To Which is Prefixed A Selection of Chants* (Boston: Ditson, [1851]; New York: Stanford & Swords [1851]) 6.

[61] In 1852, Muhlenberg founded the first Episcopal women's order in America, the Sisterhood of Holy Communion. An exponent of ecumenism in a period of denominational rivalry, he gained support for a "memorial" or resolution he introduced in General Convention in 1853, proposing that bishops of the Episcopal Church be authorized to confer orders on ministers of other denominations. He founded St. Luke's Hospital in New York, opened in 1858.

[62] W. A. Muhlenberg, G. T. Bedell, and G. J. Gear, *A Tune Book Proposed for the Use of Congregations of the Protestant Episcopal Church, Compiled by a Committee,*

During the 1850s, both worship ritual and music were undergoing rapid change with attendant conflict in the Episcopal Church and other denominations.[63] A passing remark in *The Message Bird*, dated 15 June 1850, touched off a minor controversy. Characterizing it as "everlasting pruning and cropping going on in church music, just like stripping a stately tree," Miss Augusta Browne described the setting of sacred text to secular music as "an evil more to be deplored than any other...a sacrifice to Cain." She complained of "too many illiterate and utterly incompetent [compilers trying to] level everything to their own less intellectual standard, spoil...the works of the great masters." Wainwright's *Music of the Church*, however, was an exception "occupy[ing] worthily the first place in all regular church libraries." Not all the journal's readers shared her opinion of the volume. Characterizing it as "musical pretentiousness," one respondent declared that although the collection might be a favorite with some, among knowledgeable men the collection was "held in *exceedingly low estimate*."[64]

In a letter to *Dwight's Journal of Music*, a New Englander signing as "X" wrote that while chanting might be a "devotional and impressive" alternative to metrical psalmody, choirs erred in making use of anthems set to music from the Italian operatic repertoire. "All this shows, I think, among other things, the want of a proper school of Church Music." But the answer was not the old English repertoire because "Purcell, Gibbons, Boyce, &c. require for their proper effect means which we have not at command.... I cannot help thinking that if our choirs would take the old [Lowell Mason] 'Handel and Haydn

---

Appointed for the Purpose by the House of Bishops (New York: The Committee, 1859); George Burgess [compiled by Members of the Protestant Episcopal Church as a contribution to any addition that may be made to the hymns now attached to the Prayer Book] (Philadelphia, J. B. Lippincott & Co., 1861).

[63] As if to complicate the situation, a new wave of revivals appeared among the evangelical groups late in the decade.

[64] Miss Augusta Browne, "Musical Reminiscences," *The Message Bird* 1/24 (15 July 1850): 390–91; A constant reader, "To the Musical Editor of the *Message Bird*" [Disagreement concerning the popularity of church music repertoire], *The Message Bird* 2/25 (1 August 1850) 410.

Collection,' published many years ago, and discard all the rest, they would find there all that is really needed for this part of the musical service."[65] As the presiding bishop, the cultivated and educated John Henry Hopkins summed it up in endorsing the publication, at long last, of the authorized tune book: "The 'Lyres,' 'Harps,' and 'Zion Song Books' of the nineteenth century school of Church music have flooded the land and corrupted the tastes of our choristers."[66]

That Wainwright's two New York parishes evolved musically in opposite directions serves to illustrate Episcopal church music at mid-century. As Edward Hodges put it in 1850, "[Trinity's music is] modelled strictly for what may be termed the English Cathedral School...pure, simple devout and grand; and the movements usually in the simple modes of equal time.... [The music at Grace Church] partakes of the Oratorial and serious Opera case."[67] And indeed, *The Grace Church Collection of Sacred Music,*[68] compiled by the church's organist, William A. King for his quartet choir, did indeed contain a large amount of music from the Italian, German, and Austrian repertoire, necessarily adapted for use at Grace Church.[69] But King denied the operatic cast of Grace's music in his preface.

The comparison of music at Grace and Trinity was again the subject of an often venomous exchange of letters in *The Churchman,* reprinted in the *Brooklyn Daily Eagle* between 10 and 19 December 1856. The two opposing views are clearly enough articulated in the first letter and response. "A Daughter of the Church," as she signed herself, termed Grace's "theatrical" music a "mockery of public worship.... Grace is not the only church from which light and fashionable music drives out all devotional feeling."[70] Defender

---

[65] X [pseudo.], "Church Music," *Dwight's Journal of Music* 1/24 (18 September 1852): 186–87.

[66] N.a., "The Music of the Church," *Church Journal* (21 October 1857): 308.

[67] *New York Musical Review* 1/18 (15 March 1850): 297–98.

[68] William A. King, *The Grace Church Collection of Sacred Music* (Boston: Oliver Ditson, 1852).

[69] King, *The Grace Church Collection.*

[70] A Daughter of the Church [pseudo.], "The Churchman," *Brooklyn Eagle* (10 December 1856): 2.

"Goethe" responded, "Whatever tends to make religion more general and less austere and bitter, adds to its influence."[71]

By 1860, Jonathan Wainwright and Edward Hodges were gone from the American church music scene. Wainwright had been elected provisional bishop of New York in 1852 and died in 1854, largely of exhaustion from two strenuous but critical years of holding a contentious diocese together. As for Hodges, a series of strokes forced him to take leave of Trinity in fall 1857. He was never able to return and finally retired formally in 1861. A year later, widowed yet again, he returned to England, where he died 1 September 1867.

Muhlenberg lasted a bit longer. By 1870, his interests lay in the establishment of a Christian community on Long Island with schools and even a home for the elderly, to be called St. Johnland. In 1872, he traveled to Europe for the last time. Two years later, he contracted malaria, from which he never recovered. In real sense, Muhlenberg had outlived his era. By the time of his death, musical tastes had bypassed him. Episcopal congregations in cities like New York and Philadelphia were listening silently either to highly paid professional quartets or highly trained choirs of men and boys.

---

[71] Goethe [pseudo.], "The Churchmen," *Brooklyn Eagle* (15 December 1856): 2.

7.

Black Spirituals and White Gospel Hymns

African-American Church Music

Through most of the eighteenth century, blacks attended the same churches as whites, sitting in segregated sections and learning and singing the psalm texts of Tate and Brady, Watts, Wesley, and other hymnodists to the same tunes as whites. After 1800, most slaves in the South continued to attend church where their owners had decided; however, in the North, groups of urban blacks, most of them free, began to form separate congregations during the 1780s and 1790s. In Philadelphia, they withdrew from St. George's Methodist Episcopal Church and from John Street Methodist Episcopal Church in New York, and they founded the first African Methodist and African Methodist Episcopal Zion churches, respectively. By the end of the first quarter of the nineteenth century, African Americans in the two cities and elsewhere had their own Baptist, Episcopal, and Presbyterian congregations as well.[1]

---

[1] See Daniel Alexander Payne, *Recollections of Seventy Years* (Nashville: Publishing House of the African Methodist Episcopal Sunday School Union, 1888); C. S. Smith, ed., *History of the African Methodist Episcopal Church* (Nashville: Publishing House of the African Methodist Episcopal Sunday School Union, 1891). On Philadelphia's African-American community, see Gary B. Nash, *Forging Freedom:*

Most whites considered African Americans to have a natural affinity for music. As Thomas Jefferson wrote, "[Blacks] are more generally gifted than the whites with accurate ears for tune and time."[2] A number of black singing masters taught schools for whites in the eighteenth century, among them a former student of tunesmith Andrew Law, who seems to have been especially successful. As Law wrote: "This evening I opened to see if I could get a school, but very few attended. Frank, the Negro who lived with me, has about 40 scholars which he engaged to give up when I came, but he does not incline to now…. Everyone to whom I bestow favors takes the bread out of my mouth."[3]

In early summer 1819, John Pintard, the prominent New York Episcopal layman, attended the consecration of St. Philip's, a black parish, and was especially taken with the singing. On 13 July, he wrote his daughter in New Orleans, "The Africans sung the concluding hymn themselves with great effect, for they have fine voices." On Sunday afternoon, 7 May 1826, he was again part of an overflowing congregation at St. Philip's that saw Bishop Hobart confirm a class of 120, and the next day wrote his daughter again of the impressive singing he had heard: "As to chanting, singing & responding, they beat us out of sight. A delightful organ well performed [on] by a brother African, conducts the choir. Indeed, the latter is composed of the whole congregn."[4] Years later, a visiting Scottish Presbyterian clergyman recorded a similar impression of the music in a black Methodist church he attended in Savannah, in 1848.

the Formation of Philadelphia's Black Community, 1720–1840 (Cambridge: Harvard University Press, 1988). On the music in general, including sections on religious and church music, see Eileen Southern, The Music of Black Americans (New York: W. W. Norton, 1971).

[2] Robert Stevenson, Protestant Church Music in America (New York: W. W. Norton, 1966) 93; Lawrence W. Levine, Black Culture and Black Consciousness (New York: Oxford University Press, 1977) 5.

[3] Richard Crawford, Andrew Law, American Psalmodist (Evanston: Northwestern University Press, 1968) 53.

[4] John Pintard, Letters from John Pintard to his Daughter, Eliza Noel Pintard Davidson, 1816–1833, 4 vols. (New York: New-York Historical Society, 1940–1941) 1:203–204; 2:262.

He wrote, "The deacons in the African Church act as our Scotch elders, not only waiting on the members at communion, but holding prayer meetings. They are all practised singers."[5]

Most black congregations formed out of white churches adopted the hymnody of their parent churches and denominations, at least initially. Episcopal parishes especially maintained a traditional decorum in their music.[6] As the century progressed, however, African-American congregations added new hymns.

Richard Allen (1760–1831), founding pastor of the first African Methodist Episcopal church, Mother Bethel in Philadelphia, compiled and published the first African-American hymnal in 1801. His *Collection of Spiritual Songs and Hymns* did not depart from typical fare to be found in any Methodist hymnal of the time; it contained fifty-four texts by such writers as Watts and Wesley. In a second edition, published later the same year, Allen modified some of the existing texts for relevance to his black congregation. He also added to a total of sixty-four texts, some of them possibly his own work.[7]

---

[5] George Lewis of Ormiston, *Impressions of America and the American Churches* (Edinburgh: W. P. Kennedy, 1845; repr., New York: Negro Universities Press, 1968) 170.

[6] With possible exceptions: for example, Robert A. Bennett, "Black Episcopalians: A History from the Colonial Period to the Present Day," *Historical Magazine of the Protestant Episcopal Church* 43/3 (September 1974): 239, suggests that the spiritual "Let Us Break Bread Together on Our Knees" might have grown out of and been used in the context of Episcopal practice in receiving Communion; on the other hand, it may as well reflect Methodist practice. In either case, its content is distinctive in that it bespeaks a particular liturgical practice. On the other hand, Miles Mark Fisher, *Negro Slave Songs in the United States* (Ithaca: Cornell University Press for the American Historical Association, 1953) maintained that the communion stanzas were added later and that the piece was actually a signal to gather. See Marilyn Kay Stulken, *Hymnal Companion to the Lutheran Book of Worship* (Philadelphia: Fortress, 1981) 293.

[7] Richard Allen, *Collection of Spiritual Songs and Hymns Selected from Various Authors by Richard Allen, African Minister* (Philadelphia: John Ormrod, 1801); Richard Allen, *A Collection of Hymns and Spiritual Songs from Various Authors, by Richard Allen, Minister of the African Methodist Episcopal Church* (Philadelphia: T. L. Plowman, 1801). For the contents and sample texts, see Eileen Southern, ed., *Readings in Black American Music* (New York: W. W. Norton, 1971) 53–61. See also: Southern, *The Music of Black Americans*, 85–89, and her "Musical Practices in Black Churches of

In the South, conversion to Christianity among African Americans had increased noticeably by 1760, probably as a function of the Great Awakening. Black preachers worked effectively and with little opposition at first. By the end of the century, however, their independence had been curbed by increased opposition from slave owners, who saw Christianity rather as a means of more effective control over their slaves' behavior.[8]

The camp meetings of the early nineteenth century involved both races, although slaves attended at the sufferance of their owners and all blacks were housed in their own section of the campground. Owners who were converted in the course of the Second Great Awakening often took upon themselves the responsibility of providing places for worship—"praise houses"—and religious instruction for their slaves; however, the slaves also took to holding their own semi-secret "bush meetings."

Given the choice (and they often were), most blacks were drawn to the Methodists and especially the Baptists. There was something resonant for slave congregations in the belief of most Baptists that any man, black or white, could be "called" to preach and ordained. Indeed, a number of blacks were thus called; such slave preachers were allowed a measure of liberty, and some even gained a following among whites. Moreover, Baptist worship itself was uncomplicated,

---

Philadelphia and New York, *ca.* 1800–1844," *Journal of the American Musicological Society* 30/2 (Summer 1977): 297–310; Jon Michael Spencer, "Black Denominational Hymnody and Growth toward Religious and Racial Maturity," *The Hymn* 41/4 (October 1990): 41–45, and his "The Hymnody of the African Methodist Episcopal Church," *American Music* 8/3 (Fall 1990): 274–93. The major study is Spencer, *Black Hymnody: A Hymnological History of the African-American Church* (Knoxville: University of Tennessee Press, 1992).

[8] Eugene D. Genovese, *Roll Jordan Roll: The World the Slaves Made* (New York: Random House, 1974) 185; James Hammond, for example, made especial note of how he had curbed his slaves' "night meetings" when he took possession of his Silver Bluff, South Carolina, plantation in 1831. See Drew Gilpin Faust, *James Henry Hammond and the Old South: A Design for Mastery* (Baton Rouge: Lousiana State University Press, 1982) 73–74.

the preaching easy to understand, and salvation was experiential and emotional.[9]

Black congregations developed a distinctive singing style, often accompanied by movement. White writers recorded their impressions, and often their disapproval, of that style. As early as 1817, John Fanning Watson of Philadelphia observed at a camp meeting, "In the *blacks'* quarter, the coloured people get together, and sing...short scraps...lengthened out with...choruses...in the merry chorus manner of the southern harvest field." He described the alternating call-and-response style of the slave song, and indeed, of African music.[10] Henry Russell, famed in his time as a singer and composer of parlor songs, recorded his impressions of the singing in a black church in Vicksburg, Mississippi, during the 1850s: "When the minister gave out his own version of the Psalm, the choir commenced singing so rapidly...[that] the fine old psalm tune became thoroughly transformed. For a moment I fancied that not only the choir, but the little congregation intended to get up a dance as part of the service."[11]

---

[9] Nathan O. Hatch, *The Democratization of American Christianity* (New Haven: Yale University Press, 1989) 102–104; Cushing Strout, *The New Heavens and New Earth: Political Religion in America* (New York: Harper & Row, 1974) 110–11; Genovese, *Roll Jordan Roll*, 186–89, 232; Peter Kolchin, *American Slavery, 1619–1877* (New York: Hill & Wang, 1993) 143–45. In the early stages, a number of preachers in those denominations welcomed blacks with a measure of equality, and some even preached openly against slavery, at least prior to the 1820s. Part of the reason for "bush meetings" was that black-led slave gatherings at "worship houses" were often required by law to have one or more whites present—Alabama required five slaveholders to be in attendance when a black preached—to prevent any talk of flight, or worse, of insurrection. Still, whites usually respected black slave preachers to the extent that they were allowed to dress relatively well and spared from hard labor in the fields. See Levine, *Black Culture and Black Consciousness*, 44–47.

[10] John Fanning Watson, *Methodist Error, or, Friendly Christian Advice to Those Methodists Who Indulge in Extravagant Emotions and Bodily Exercises* (Trenton: D. & E. Felton, 1819) 30. The complete passage is most readily accessible in Southern, *Readings in Black American Music*, 62–64.

[11] Henry Russell, *Cheer! Boys, Cheer!: Memories of Men and Music* (London: J. Macqueen, 1895) 84–85, quoted in Irene V. Jackson, "Music among Blacks in the Episcopal Church: Some Preliminary Considerations," *Historical Magazine of the*

Shouting

White clergy were especially put off by the blacks' most distinctive African-rooted worship practice, the so-called ring shout. Watson described the ring shout he witnessed at a camp meeting in 1817: "With every word so sung, they have a sinking of one or [the] other leg alternately, producing an audible sound of the feet at every step.... If some, in the meantime, sit, they strike the sounds alternately on each thigh."[12] A half-century later during the Civil War, Unitarian minister Henry George Spaulding described a similar ritual, which he characterized as a "religious dance of the negroes," in Port Royal, South Carolina: "Three or four, standing still, clapping their hands and beating time with their feet, commence singing in unison one of the peculiar shout melodies, while the others walk around in a ring, in single file.... They will often dance to the same song for twenty or thirty minutes."[13]

Thomas Wentworth Higginson, white Colonel of the black South Carolina Volunteers during the Civil War, later recalled evocatively: "Often in the starlit evening I have returned from some lonely ride by the swift river, or on the plover-haunted barrens, and, entering the camp, have silently approached some glimmering fire, round which the dusky figures moved in the rhythmical barbaric dance the negroes call a 'shout,' chanting, often harshly, but always in the most perfect time, some monotonous refrain." Higginson had noted some of the texts sung during ring shouts and that they singled out members of the circle by name, in turn:

"Hold your light, Brudder Robert, Hold your light..." would be sung for half hour at a time, perhaps each person being named in turn. It seemed the simplest primitive type of "spiritual." The next in popularity was almost as elementary, and, like this, named successively each one of the circle...:

Protestant Episcopal Church, 49/1 (March 1980): 21–22. See also Albert J. Raboteau, *Slave Religion* (New York: Oxford University Press, 1978) 243–46.

[12] Watson, *Methodist Error*, 30–31.

[13] Genovese, *Roll Jordan Roll*, 233.

"Jordan River, I'm bound to go...
My Brudder Robert, I'm bound to go...
My sister Lucy, I'm bound to go..."[14]

Black urban clergy, many of them as well trained as their white colleagues and sensitive to public image, took a dim view of the shout. Daniel Alexander Payne—free-born, well educated, and a bishop in the African Methodist Episcopal Church—attempted to suppress the practice among congregations in his charge. Describing a bush meeting around 1842, Payne wrote:

After the sermon they formed a ring, and with coats off sung, clapped their hands and stamped their feet in a most ridiculous and heathenish way. I requested the pastor to go and stop their dancing. At his request they stopped their dancing and clapping of hands but remained singing and rocking their bodies too and fro.... In that instance, they broke up their ring, but would not sit down, and walked sullenly away.... These "Bands" I have had to encounter in many places, and...I have been strongly censured because of my efforts to change the mode of worship or modify the extravagances by the people.... By the ignorant masses, as in the case mentioned, it [the ring-shout] was regarded as the essence of religion.... Some one has even called it the "Voodoo Dance." I have remonstrated with a number of pastors for permitting these practices, which vary somewhat in different localities, but have been invariably met with the response that he could not succeed in restraining them, and an attempt to compel them to cease would simply drive them away from our Church.[15]

---

[14] Thomas Wentworth Higginson, *Army Life in a Black Regiment* (Boston: Fields, Osgood & Company, 1870) passages reprinted in Southern, *Readings in Black American Music*, 164–92. The quoted material appears on 173–74.

[15] Payne, *Recollections*, 254–55; here again, the most accessible source is Southern, *Readings in Black American Music*, 65–70.

The Spiritual

The main music of the slaves' own worship was the spiritual, most often in the call-and-response form. Such pieces bore a similarity to lined-out psalmody, which persisted in Southern churches long after it had died out in the north, but were more closely allied to the responsorial work songs that drivers and the slave gangs themselves used to coordinate the effort and exertion required for a particular jobs and to the African tradition of antiphonal and responsorial singing.[16]

Over the past few years the debate over the precise relationship between white and black spirituals has given way to an emerging consensus that the two influenced each other in both form and style.[17] And in fact, there is significant evidence that the independent chorus, usable as a refrain with any number of hymns and a significant trait of early nineteenth-century camp-meeting hymnody, originated in the black quarters of the camp grounds.[18]

Black spirituals were open-ended, continuous, and often quasi-improvisatory, especially on the part of the leader to whose call the group responded with a set phrase. But even in the group singing improvised ornamentation abounded, such as melodic turns, held

---

[16] For contemporary descriptions, see Southern, *Music of Black Americans*, 91–96; Stephen A. Marini, *Sacred Song in America: Religion, Music and Public Culture* (Urbana: University of Illinois Press, 2003) 108, astutely observes that "the story of black church song is a compelling journey from West African roots through Evangelical Protestant hymns and slave spirituals to the gospel songs of the twentieth century."

[17] George Pullen Jackson's assertion that the black spiritual was a copy of the white is in no way credible. See Dena J. Epstein, *Sinful Tunes and Spirituals: Black Folk Music to the Civil War* (Urbana: University of Illinois, 1977) and "A White Origin for the Black Spiritual? An Invalid Theory and How It Grew," *American Music* 1/2 (Summer 1983): 53–59; William H. Tallmadge, "The Black in Jackson's White Spirituals," *The Black Perspective in Music* 9/2 (1981): 139–60; John F. Gast, "Mutual Reinforcement and the Origins of Spirituals," *American Music* 4/4 (Winter 1986): 390–406.

[18] Hatch, *The Democratization of American Christianity*, 157.

notes, and quarter-tones. Sections of different hymns and spirituals, black or white, might be interpolated, and choruses borrowed from other pieces. The effect could be chant-like and hypnotic. The texts of black spirituals reflected very real, day-to-day, earthly trials. Blacks identified with Old Testament figures Jonah, David, and the Israelites enslaved in Egypt; their deliverance was seen as prefiguring their own; accordingly, the spirituals' subject matter more often derived from the Old Testament—as in the following verses from two popular spirituals—than the New, except for the Book of Revelation, describing the Day of Judgment on which they would be freed:

> Go down, Moses; Way down in Egypt-land
> Tell Old Pharaoh, "Let my people go."

> Didn't my Lord deliver Daniel,
> And why not every man.[19]

Such spirituals yield an insight into the religious discourse of the slaves and also freedmen subjected daily to indignities from whites. Deliverance signified freedom, not from the undefined evil of earthly sin, but from a physical, spiritual, and psychological state of bondage. Hell was not a future to be dreaded, but a present to be endured. Heaven was a place, not so much of transcendent joy, but of respite from their condition and from subservience to whites. Death meant passage home.

Thus, Old Testament places and terms took on special meaning—more palpable, physical, and even real. To the slaves, Canaan—the "promised land"—signified flight to free soil. Indeed, many texts encoded signals for forbidden activity. "Steal away home"

---

[19] Given the improvisatory nature of spirituals, recorded texts vary; for instance, the variant "O my Lord delivered Daniel/ O why not deliver me too." Unless otherwise indicated, the texts here are as printed some years later in Hampton Institute, *Jubilee and Plantation Songs...As sung by the Hampton Students, Jubilee Singers, Fisk University Students, and Other Concert Companies* (Boston: Oliver Ditson, 1887) 4, 24.

and "Crossing Jordan," for instance, suggested escape or at least the summons to a surreptitious meeting. "Deep river, my home's across the Jordan./ Deep river, I want to cross over into campground."[20]

The sense of individual sin and repentance that characterized white evangelical hymnody and doctrine figured far less in the black spiritual; black texts did not reflect the Calvinist sense of personal unworthiness and judgment dread. Salvation came at death, not after; the day of jubilee brought rest from the white man's lash or oppression; Jesus, often merged with Moses as a single symbol of deliverance, is victorious not through suffering on the cross but at the head of an army: "Ride on, King Jesus! Ride on Moses, Ride on King Emanuel/ No man can hinder me. Want to go home in the morning."[21] Black spiritual texts, as Thomas Wentworth Higginson put it, spoke of "nothing but patience for this life,—nothing but triumph in the next."[22]

White Audiences and the Black Spiritual

Several factors contributed to an increased interest in the black spiritual among whites during the 1860s and 1870s. The first printed collection appeared in 1867.[23] In 1871, nine students from Fisk University formed the Jubilee Singers under the direction of a white faculty member and toured the northern states giving concerts of

---

[20] Levine, *Black Culture and Black Consciousness*, 52. Paul Oliver, "Spiritual," in *New Grove Gospel, Blues and Jazz* (New York: Norton, 1986) 11–13. On spirituals as a surreptitious means of signaling, see M. M. Fisher, *Negro Slave Songs in the United States* (New York: Russell & Russell, 1968). In 1892, Frederick Douglass, *The Life and Times of Frederick Douglass* (London: Collier-Macmillan, 1962) 159–60, recalled that "Canaan" was a code word for Northern freedom for him and other slaves planning escape; see Raboteau, *Slave Religion*, 247. On the general issue of signifiers in music, see Roger D. Abrahams, *Singing the Master: The Emergence of African Culture in the Plantation South* (New York: Pantheon, 1992).

[21] Southern, *Readings in Black American Music*, 176; Hampton Institute, *Jubilee and Plantation Songs*, 79.

[22] See also Levine, *Black Culture and Black Consciousness*, 22, 39–44; the quoted passage appears on 43.

[23] William Francis Allen, Charles Pickard Ware, and Lucy McKim Garrison, *Slave Songs of the United States* (New York: A. Simpson & Co., 1867).

spirituals to raise money for the institution. Hampton Institute formed a similar ensemble two years later, and in the years that followed, the two groups developed a following for spirituals among Americans and then Europeans.

White audiences, however, were neither accustomed to nor willing to embrace the improvisatory character and rhythmic freedom of the original folk spirituals. Rather, the pieces sung on tour by both groups were recast into concert versions whose formal European harmonies and organized rhythms were more in keeping with the cultivated tastes of the era. It is in these arrangements, adopted for concert by white and black college choirs, that many black spirituals have come down to the present.[24]

Ironically, even as they gained a following among whites in the years after the Civil War, the use of spirituals in black churches declined. Newly emancipated blacks, anxious to leave behind them the cultural artifacts of their bondage, moved more toward the adoption and adaptation of white gospel songs that had gained currency late in the century.[25]

Revivals and Evangelical Music: The Gospel Hymn

Although one must be careful of making facile comparisons between the Civil War and the crusading spirit of the revival, for those who looked on and many who took part, there was about it something of the aura of a great camp meeting in the struggle. In an era in which Americans were far more overtly and self-consciously religious than they had been since the age of the Puritans in the seventeenth century, many a foot soldier went into battle, and to his death, fresh from one of the frequent revival meetings held in the camps of both

---

[24] Levine, *Black Culture and Black Consciousness*, 166. There is, of course, no denying that the choral arrangements and solo versions of spirituals by a genius of the level of Henry T. Burleigh or William Dawson were and are unsurpassingly beautiful; but they are nevertheless far from the original worship music of nineteenth-century African Americans.

[25] Oliver, "Gospel," *New Grove Gospel, Blues and Jazz*, 190.

armies, with a Bible or a hymnal (that is, a collection of religious poetry) in his pocket.[26]

The Southerners, whose heritage was generally and distinctively that of the camp-meeting, were led by such generals as the dourly pious Thomas "Stonewall" Jackson and Episcopal bishop Leonidas Polk of Louisiana, who had himself been converted in a revival held at West Point during his student years there. At the same time, many Northerners saw the war as a sign of both of God's judgment and of his intent to "purify" the land, ideas whose roots went back even further than the urban revivals and rural camp meetings to the philosophy of the Puritans.[27]

A Civil War song like "We are coming, Father Abraham" was clearly and intentionally a religious metaphor. "Tenting Tonight on the Old Camp Ground" evoked sentimental memories of other camps and camp meetings. Marches like "Battle Cry of Freedom" and especially the tune "Glory, Glory Hallelujah," sung by the North variously to "John Brown's Body" and after 1861 to Julia Ward Howe's "Battle Hymn of the Republic," resonated with the spirit of camp meeting torch-light marches.[28]

At the same time, a more sentimental type of song, expressing an uncomplicated experiential faith in simple, direct words and set to an engaging and singable melody with simple harmonies and catchy rhythm, had become popular. Patterned on popular parlor songs, marches, and quicksteps, the genre had appeared in the 1840s as part of the Sunday School movement, which had been founded in 1817, among other things to provide Christian education for poor children. During the 1850s, collections of Sunday school hymns were published quarterly and sold by subscription in series.[29] Although his

---

[26] See Steven E. Woodworth, *While God Is Marching On: The Religious World of Civil War Soldiers* (Lawrence: University Press of Kansas, 2001).

[27] Cushing Strout, *The New Heavens, and New Earth; Political Religion in America* (New York: Harper & Row, 1974) 198.

[28] "Battle Cry of Freedom," composed by George F. Root, appeared in 1862. On the other hand, "Glory Hallelujah" probably originated as a camp-meeting chorus.

[29] See Paul Gaarder Kaatrud, "Revivalism and the Popular Spiritual Song in

teacher disapproved of the form, one of the most active composers was Lowell Mason's pupil, William Batchelder Bradbury (1816–1868).[30] Bradbury, a native of Maine, was by no means a naïve successor to the tunesmiths. He had studied composition with Moscheles in Germany, and teamed up with Mason and Hastings to promote music education in New York.[31]

In the post-war decades, such pieces would be christened "gospel songs" after the title of a popular collection published by Philip Paul Bliss (1838–1876) in 1874.[32] Such hymns readily found a place in the revivals that began in 1857 among adults, many of whom had fond memories of the genre from their childhood in Sunday schools. The revivals continued beyond the war years. In other words, the revivals grew out of the Sunday School movement and simply took over the songs of that movement. Post-war America was becoming an urban culture, and the focus of these new revivals was the city.[33]

Unlike the earlier urban revivals of Finney and his generation of evangelists, religion was now the means of developing both a

---

Mid-Nineteenth Century America: 1830–1870" (Ph.D diss., University of Minnesota, 1977).

[30] Kaatrud, "Revivalism and Popular Spiritual Song," 224–28, 265–83. Mason and Thomas Hastings objected particularly to the adaptation of secular melodies, even though Mason himself set Sarah Adams, "Nearer my God to Thee" to the tune of Thomas Moore's "Oft in the stilly night," renaming the tune *Bethany*. Hastings, *The New York Musical Review and Choral Advocate* 4/5 (May 1853): 74, called such pieces "the lowest dregs of music...poisonous trash." Bradbury's *Oriola* (New York: Ivison & Phinney, 1859) contained both Sunday school and usual-style hymns. His rival in the Sunday school song publication was Horace Waters. Waters's extremely successful two-volume set *The Sabbath School Bell* (Chicago: Biglow & Main, 1859, 1860) made heavy use both of secular melodies and of refrains. Bradbury followed suit with *The Golden Chain* in 1861, *The Golden Shower* (1862), and *The Golden Censor* (1864), publishing the three volumes in 1867 as *The Golden Trio*. Waters kept pace with *The Golden Harp* and *The Athenæm* of 1863, containing music by Stephen Foster, and *The Diadem* (1865).

[31] See Alan B. Wingard, "The Life and Works of William Batchelder Bradbury" (DMA diss., Southern Baptist Theological Seminar, 1973).

[32] Philip P. Bliss, *Gospel Songs* (Cincinnati: J. Church & Co., 1874). Bliss was supposedly inspired to write his still popular "Hold the Fort," by a Civil War event.

[33] Donald P. Hustad, *Jubilate II: Church Music in Worship and Renewal* (Carol Stream IL: Hope Publishing Co., 1993) 231–35.

personal religious commitment and social virtues—temperance, domesticity, and social responsibility—among young workers and a bulwark against the temptations of the city. The vehicle for the movement was the newly established Young Men's Christian Association, and its services took the form of prayer meetings, often held several times a week and even during midday lunch hours. Such meetings placed less emphasis on preaching and no emphasis on exhortation. Instead, they aimed at inspiring personal moral and religious sentiment with their format of song, prayer, and individual testimony.[34]

The hymnody and its worship context also reflected an urban, middle-class focus, combined with the rural flavor of the camp-meetings, which continued being held through the century. Whereas the texts of white spirituals focused on grace and salvation, gospel hymns and songs were intimate testaments of faith with texts that were personal, submissive, and often sentimental. For instance, compare the allegorical text from *The Sacred Harp*:

> The Lord into his garden come,
> The spices yield a rich perfume,
> The lilies grow and thrive.
> Refreshing showers of grace divine
> From Jesus flow to every vine,
> And make the dead revive.

with the intensely personal text from *Gospel Hymns*:

> O I love to talk with Jesus,
> for it smooths the rugged road;
> And it seems to help me onward,
> when I faint beneath my load;

---

[34] On the social aspects, see Sandra Sizer, *Gospel Hymns and Social Religion* (Philadelphia: Temple University Press, 1978); David Stowe, *How Sweet the Sound: Music in the Spiritual Lives of Americans* (Cambridge: Harvard University Press, 2004) 116.

When my heart is crushed with sorrow,
and my eyes with tears are dim,
There's nought can yield me comfort
like a little talk with him.[35]

Gospel hymns had melodies that were easy to sing and immediately attractive. They had simple harmony and the regular, infectious rhythm of a march or waltz. Their overall form was strophic, usually with a refrain. In other words, the gospel hymn was similar in form and style to the parlor songs that were widely popular with the urban middle class. Indeed, the solo gospel song—in effect, a parlor song with sacred words—became a distinctive device of the new movement. Camp meetings had used solo songs for entertainment and as part of altar calls; however, Philip P. Bliss and Ira Sankey, following the example of the first solo evangelist Peter Phillips (1834–1895), made dramatized songs and "singing sermons" an extremely popular institution after the Civil War, one that took its place in the worship of evangelical Protestantism, especially in the South and West.[36]

Stephen Foster published solo religious songs with his own texts and also settings of texts by other composers. His pieces appeared in Horace Waters's two 1863 collections, *The Golden Harp* and *The Athenæum*, and his pieces served as models for others. Lowell Mason's assistant, George Frederick Root (1820–1895) wrote a large number, many to texts by the blind poet Fanny Crosby (1820–1915).[37] Crosby also collaborated with Bradbury from 1864 on, and their *Fresh Laurels for the Sabbath School* sold over a half-

---

[35] B. F. White and E. J. King, *The Sacred Harp*, 3rd ed. (Philadelphia: S. C. Collins, 1860) 64. Ira D. Sankey, James McGranahan, and George C. Stebbins, *Gospel Hymns, Nos. 1 to 6 Complete* (New York: Biglow & Main and Cincinnati: John Church, 1894) 511.

[36] Kaatrud, "Revivalism and Popular Spiritual Song," 48.

[37] On Foster's sacred songs, see William W. Austin, *"Susanna," "Jeannie" and the "Old Folks at Home": the Songs of Stephen C. Foster from His Time to Ours* (New York: Macmillan, 1975) 185–93, 261–63.

million copies.[38] Bradbury's collections contained hymns specifically intended for use at adult prayer meetings.[39]

It bears repeating that composers of gospel hymns were by no means unskilled musicians. To be sure, William H. Doane (1832–1915) was a successful industrialist and inventor, but he was also a well-trained amateur. Bradbury and Root had studied in Europe. All three were capable composers in their chosen style and idiom, and they wrote for a specific purpose. Bradbury's setting of the text "He leadeth me," for instance, has found its way over the years into virtually every denominational hymnal.

Philip Paul Bliss (1838–1876) was a fellow Pennsylvanian and Sankey's only rival during the early years of the latter's career as a gospel singer. Bliss was a trained singer, singing school teacher, and student of Bradbury. He took up composition in the mid-1860s. In 1874, he gave up his professional activities for revival music and entered into a partnership with the revival preacher D. W. Whittle. Such Bliss hymns as "Hold the fort," "Let the lower lights be burning," and "Wonderful words of life" still hold a firm place in modern evangelical hymnody. Bliss's career was cut short by his death in a train wreck at Ashtabula, Ohio, on 29 December 1876. His successors as Whittle's musical partners were George C. Stebbins (1846–1945) and James McGranahan (1840–1907). Among other composers and compilers of gospel songs were Robert Lowry (1840–1907), William Howard Doane (1832–1915), and Charles H. Gabriel (1851–1921).[40]

---

[38] William Batchelder Bradbury and Fanny Crosby, *Fresh Laurels for the Sabbath School* (New York: Biglow & Main, 1867).

[39] For instance, William B. Bradbury, *Pilgrim Songs* (New York: Iverson & Phinney, 1863). See Bernard Ruffin, *Fanny Crosby* (Westwood NJ: Barbour, 1976).

[40] Austin, "*Susanna*," 272–77. On Bliss, see Bobby Joe Neil, "Philip P. Bliss (1838–1876) Gospel Hymn Composer and Compiler" (DMA diss., New Orleans Baptist Theological Seminary, 1977); and D. J. Smucker, "Philip Paul Bliss and the Musical, Cultural and Religious Sources of the Gospel Music Tradition in the United States, 1850–1876" (Ph.D. diss., Boston University, 1981).

Dwight L. Moody and Ira D. Sankey

The major figure in these revivals was Dwight L. Moody, a Boston shoe salesman who, having become involved in the YMCA movement, moved to Chicago and established both a thriving church and the pattern of carefully planned and executed traveling "crusades" emulated by later evangelists such as Billy Sunday and Billy Graham. Moody's musical partner was Ira D. Sankey (1840–1908), son of a Pennsylvania state legislator.[41]

An active Methodist layman, Sankey was blessed with a fine singing voice. As a young man, he attended a musical convention taught by Bradbury in 1860. Shortly thereafter, he entered the Union Army and rose to the rank of sergeant. After the Civil War, he took a job with the federal government and married the daughter of a United States senator. In 1867, he became secretary of the YMCA in New Castle, Pennsylvania, and in that capacity attended the 1870 convention in Indianapolis where he met Moody.[42]

Moody himself was neither especially musical nor especially well-educated. He had no particular interest in music for its own sake, but he recognized the drawing power of a talent like Sankey's and recruited him. Their 1873 and 1875 campaigns in England were resounding successes. Sankey warmed up audiences, singing his own gospel songs and those of Bradbury and Bliss. His appeal was directed at his listeners' emotions. He used semi-spoken *parlando*, dramatic pauses, abrupt tempo changes, and other effects, accompanying himself on a small reed organ. He also directed the singing of such hymns by the assembly.[43]

So popular was Sankey's music that a twenty-four page pamphlet of his songs was combined with a collection published by Bliss and issued as the first of six books of gospel songs that appeared from

---

[41]Sankey chronicled his own life and work in *My Life and the Story of the Gospel Hymns and of Sacred Songs and Solos* (New York: Harper and Brothers, 1907; repr., New York: AMS, 1974).

[42] Sankey, *My Life and the Story of the Gospel Hymns*, 15–19.

[43] Sankey's use of a small reed instrument can probably be credited with breaking down the last remnants of resistance in denominations that still held out against the use of organs in worship.

1875 to 1891 and then combined into a single collection.[44] Among his numerous gospel hymns, still sung are "Softly and tenderly Jesus is calling" and "Faith is the victory." In his last decades, Sankey enjoyed immense popularity; indeed, he probably sang before the largest audiences assembled at any one time during the era. His *Gospel Hymns and Sacred Songs* sold over 50 million copies by 1900. From 1895 until his death in 1908, Sankey was president of Biglow & Main, his publisher for several years.[45]

Gospel Hymns and Evangelical Worship

Gospel hymns served a direct purpose in giving a musical voice to the emotion and personal testimony of evangelical worship, conveying that emotion clearly and simply. As such, issues of musical quality and even substantive theological discourse are simply irrelevant. Sankey never thought of himself as performing music for his crowds, but rather of singing them the Gospel, as he himself put it. Such music accorded well with the spirit of the late-nineteenth-century revivals. As Homer Rodeheaver, musical partner of the early-twentieth-century evangelist Billy Sunday would later explain it, the gospel hymn was intended "to give men a simple, easy, lilting melody which they could learn the first time they hear it and which they could whistle and sing wherever they might be."[46]

---

[44] Ira D. Sankey, *Sacred Songs and Solos* (London: Morgan and Scott, 1873) and P. P. Bliss, *Gospel Songs* Cincinnati: John Church, 1874) combined into *Gospel Hymns and Sacred Songs* (Cincinnati: John Church, 1875) It and the five subsequent volumes were republished as a single volume, Ira D. Sankey, James McGranahan, and Geo. C. Stebbins, *Gospel Hymns, 1 to 6 Complete* (Chicago: Biglow & Main, 1894; Philadelphia: Theodore Presser, 1894).

[45] In addition to Sankey, *My Life and the Story of the Gospel Hymn*, see Robert Stevenson, "Ira D. Sankey and the Growth of Gospel Hymnody," *Patterns of Protestant Church Music* (Durham: Duke University Press, 1953); and Mel R. Wilhoit, "A Guide to the Principal Authors and Composers of Gospel Song in the Nineteenth Century" (DMA diss., Southern Baptist Theological Seminary, 1982), which also contains material on other figures.

[46] Quoted in Charles Hamm, *Music in the New World* (New York: Norton, 1983) 277–78.

Rodeheaver's is as good a description as any of gospel hymns and solo gospel songs: emotional texts—personal testimonies on one hand, martial statements on the other—set to singable melodies, stirring or sentimental depending on the type of text, with driving or lilting rhythms and simple harmonies. Most, like popular parlor songs of the time, had stanzas that could be sung as solos with a refrain for the group (the "chorus"). Gospel hymns met, and still meet, the need for a simple type of heartfelt music that could be learned quickly and sung by a large number of people with a variety of talents in an evangelical worship context.

Moreover, it is simply inaccurate to dismiss composers of such music as ignorant or inartistic, as did many later church musicians in academic settings. On the contrary, few were amateurs, and most were educated and cultivated, both in music and in other areas. W. H. Doane, for instance, was an art collector. Fanny Crosby, who supplied texts for Doane as well as Root and Bradbury, was a talented pianist and soprano. They shared a primary commitment to religious revival, and they gave voice to that commitment in a vernacular style of hymnody without lofty artistic pretense: a style that still holds a significant place in the evangelical worship tradition, both in America and abroad.

8.

The Solo Quartet and Its Music

By the time of the Civil War, the solo quartet—or "quartette," as it was usually spelled—either alone or with a chorus of volunteers, reigned pre-eminent in churches of all denominations (and synagogues), especially in cities. Such groups of professionals had appeared early in the nineteenth century to lead congregational psalmody where there was no choir. As rector of Grace Church in New York during the 1820s, Jonathan Mayhew Wainwright paid out of his own pocket for a handful of soloists to lead congregational psalmody. The group included the eminent operatic soprano María Málibran and the locally celebrated Emma Gillingham (later Bostwick).[1]

In some cases, soloists were engaged in the hopes of bringing order and discipline in both the music and deportment of singing school adolescents for whom choirs were more often social outlets than spiritual ones or of improving on the singing of children. As it turned out, the soloists, usually a quartet, frequently displaced the chorus. Around 1840, for instance, just as the movement to establish boys' choirs in Episcopal churches was about to pick up momentum, St. Michael's in Charleston disbanded its boys' choir, by then in

---

[1] William Rhinelander Stewart, *Grace Church and Old New York* (New York: E. P. Dutton, 1924) 107; see also Carl Carmer, *The Years of Grace, 1808–1958* (New York: Grace Church, 1958) 14.

existence for decades, and replaced it with a solo quartet. The arrangement continued at St. Michael's until 1926.[2]

In many churches, especially from the 1840s on, the installation of a newer and larger organ behind the pulpit, where it could be seen and admired by the congregation, occasioned the relocation of the choir from its usual position in the rear gallery where the old organ had been situated to a much smaller choir loft in the front of the church near the new organ. In view of the reduced space, the volunteer choir (if one existed) was often simply disbanded, leaving only the quartet and organist. Where the volunteer chorus choir had sung from the gallery *with* the congregation; quartets—or "quartet choirs," as they were often termed—now sang from the front *for*, and eventually *to*, the congregation. Even where they were engaged as section leaders in a volunteer or "chorus choir," the four soloists almost always regarded themselves as a group within a group.[3]

Before the Civil War, most quartets sang only hymns and service music. By the 1860s, there was a growing repertoire of church music especially for soloists and quartets. In general, this music was in the fashionable, quasi-operatic style that signified culture and taste on the part of singer and listener alike, much to the delight (although not always for the religious edification) of the Sunday congregation. From time to time, ministers complained in their sermons about the prominence of music and its entertaining distractions. The hard-headed church authorities, in whose eyes the "finer music" to be had from professionals constituted an added attraction for new members and a consequent rise in pew rents, generally turned a deaf ear to such protestations.

Words of caution about the replacement of choirs with quartets were also voiced by prominent church musicians, although here too there was often a tinge of self-serving concern that the demand for their services to form and teach singing schools for churches was being reduced by the quartet vogue. As early as 1845, the American

---

[2] Leonard Ellinwood, *The History of American Church Music* (New York: Morehouse-Gorham, 1953; repr., New York: Da Capo, 1970) 73.

[3] Ellinwood, *History of American Church Music*, 73–74.

Musical Convention, meeting in Broadway Tabernacle in New York, resolved that any and all advantages of a quartet could be had with a chorus choir.[4]

Still, the quartet reigned supreme in most city parishes by 1861. A survey of over 130 New York churches, for instance, showed seventy-two of them with solo quartets or double quartets. Of seventeen Roman Catholic churches, fourteen used quartets, as did twenty-four of the thirty-one Episcopal parishes. Grace Church was especially famed for the "attractive quality of its music" as sung by a quartet under the direction of its English organist George Washburne Morgan. *Dwight's Journal of Music* reported that "the style of music [of Grace Church] is less ecclesiastical, and more ornate...and consists mainly of selections from the works of Beethoven, Mozart, *et al*, interspersed with the compositions of Mosenthal [organist of Calvary Church in New York, the former organist of Grace Church, William A.] King, and Mr. Morgan."[5]

Among non-liturgical Protestant churches surveyed, there was some denominational difference in the presence of quartets as opposed to volunteer choirs. Only seven of twenty-four Presbyterian churches employed quartets, compared to twelve with chorus choirs (the rest had only congregational singing); on the other hand, eight of eleven Dutch Reformed congregations employed quartets. Only among Baptists and Methodist churches, with their tradition of lusty congregational hymnody, was the balance tilted heavily in favor of volunteer chorus choirs; the former showed four churches with quartets and nine with choruses, and the latter four quartets as opposed to sixteen churches with large volunteer groups.[6]

---

[4] *Proceedings of the American Musical Convention: Held in the Broadway Tabernacle, on the 8th, 9th and 10th of October 1845* (New York: Saxton & Miles, 1845) 7. Clearly, a larger chorus provided better leadership for congregational singing, one of the convention's main concerns. The root of the problem was probably an increasing sentiment among the early Victorians that singing in public was an improper activity for girls and women.

[5] N.a., "Church Music in New York," *Dwight's Journal* 18/23 (9 March 1861): 396.

[6] N.a., *The American Musical Directory* (New York: Thomas Hutchinson, 1861)

Many churches were without quartets only until they could afford them. In 1861, Fourth Universalist Church in New York had to make do with congregational singing only. By 1864, however, it was able to announce that "the old system of congregational singing...will be abandoned, the [double] quartet and organist previously officiating at St. Ann's in Eighteenth street having been engaged."[7]

As professionals, the singers often viewed their church work as nothing more special than any other engagement. Young singers sought church positions for the experience as well as the remuneration. The steady work and amount of music to be learned in a comparatively brief rehearsal time helped them to sharpen their musical and sight-reading skills. The pay averaged about $250 a year, not an insignificant sum in the 1860s and 1870s considering the few hours required. Moreover, a top singer in Boston might make $750—a generous amount during the 1870s—and at least one New York church made the amazing offer of $3,000 and more to lure an especially outstanding singer. By the 1870s, it was possible for a singer with no operatic aspirations to live quite well (if nowhere near as opulently as an opera star) on earnings from a church solo position, supplemented by some teaching and concert work. It was not unusual for all four singers in a quartet to move as a unit at the end of a season, often along with the organist, if another church in the same city had made a higher bid for their services.[8]

On the other hand, church music committees contracted with quartets and organists for a year at a time, often through agents, and had no hesitation about making a change to gain more public notice for their music or to save money. New York was a buyers' market for music committees. Aspiring vocal students, who were in the city to

---

215–33.

[7] This quote and those that follow are from n.a., "Organists and Singers in New York," *Dwight's Journal* 24/15 (14 May 1864): 236. St Ann's had switched to a choir of boys and congregational singing.

[8] Stanley Robert McDaniel, "Church Song and the Cultivated Tradition in New England and New York" (DMA diss., University of Southern California, 1983) 343–46, 70.

study with well-known operatic and concert singers, eagerly auditioned for church jobs to support themselves. In 1876, there were some 200 applicants for a tenor post at Plymouth Church in Brooklyn; a similar opening at St. Bartholomew's in Manhattan in 1910 drew 200 candidates. Auditions were often open to the public or at least to such members of the congregation who might wish to attend and voice their preferences. In short, the arrangement was often purely mercenary on both sides.[9]

During the 1860s and 1870s, *Dwight's Journal of Music* regularly reported such activities, comings and goings in its "Church Music" column:

> At Christ Church, the entire choir, including the *prima donna* Isadora Clark has left, Miss Scondra taking the place of the leading soprano…. At St. Marks…the system of a single quartet, so generally popular, will be maintained, and the music will continue, as hitherto, to elicit the admiration of strangers and others visiting the church….
>
> In the meantime…the late organist of St. Stephen's [Roman Catholic Church] has gone to Zion Church…with Centemeri as basso, or rather, baritone. This importation of an Italian Roman Catholic element into a Protestant Episcopal Church, as well as the very large salaries to be paid is exciting considerable comment in choir circles; and it is expected that Zion Church will have about as "stylish" music as any in the city.[10]

---

[9] McDaniel, "Church Song and the Cultivated Tradition," 346, 357–58.

[10] Zion's rector, Bishop Horatio Southwick, had come from Boston's Church of the Advent, a seedbed parish of Oxford ceremonial whose choir of men and boys had been directed by Henry Stephen Cutler before he moved to Trinity a few years earlier. One may wonder what both Cutler and Southwick thought of this "importation of an Italian and Roman Catholic element." On the other hand, as will be seen, several of the most ritualistic Episcopal parishes aped the music of contemporary Roman Catholic churches, abuses and all. Ellinwood, *History of American Church Music*, 95, observes that the heavily operatic bent of many Roman Catholic churches was probably due to the availability of opera singers who were Catholic and could be called on to serve their parishes at no cost, or at least less cost

As the century went on, a large amount of music was produced with professional quartets in mind. The repertoire included service music, solo songs with refrains for chorus or quartet, and anthems for the full quartet. Some of it was adapted from operas by such composers as Rossini and Gounod; other pieces were written in pallid imitation of the fashionable European operatic style or in the style of the popular, sentimental parlor songs with which middle class families of the era entertained themselves and each other. The composers were for the most part Americans, several of them with European training.

The quality of the music varied. A fairly low, but not atypical, level is represented in the works of George William Warren (1828–1902). Warren was a native of Albany, New York, and self-taught in music. Although he dropped out of Racine College after only a short time, the school later conferred an honorary doctor of music degree on him. He served churches in Albany and then Holy Trinity Church in Brooklyn. In 1870, he began a thirty-year tenure as organist and music director of St. Thomas Church in New York. For a period, he was also professor of music at Columbia University.

Warren is remembered nowadays only for his hymn, "God of Our Fathers"; however, in his day he was highly regarded for such works as his *First Easter Cantata* (1875) for solo quartet.[11] The piece is a sort of verse anthem in a lilting compound meter. Each stanza of the text, a piece of devotional doggerel by Bishop Arthur Cleveland Coxe, closes with the refrain: "The singing of birds, a warbling band/ and the Spirit's voice./ The voice of the truth is heard in our land," garnished with appropriately pictorial trills and bird call effects. Warren's *Second Easter Cantata* (1878) was a setting of the text "Fill

---

than they might otherwise command.

   [11] The William Pond publication bears a copyright date of 1876; however, the piece was first sung at St. Thomas on Easter of 1875 (cf. the order of service for that day). Although it has a marked—if shoddy—resemblance to their style, it actually antedates the popularity of Gilbert and Sullivan in America by a several years.

the font with roses" by the popular sentimental poet Mrs. Lydia Sigourney.[12]

The music of Dudley Buck (1839–1909)[13] represents the best work in the genre. Buck was born in Hartford and entered Trinity College in 1855, at age sixteen; at the same time, he began the serious study of music. Buck dropped out of college only two years later and went to Leipzig, where he studied with organ first with Moritz Hauptmann and then Johann Michael Schneider; he also studied piano with Ignaz Moscheles.[14] When Schneider moved to Dresden, Buck followed him and continued as his pupil for a year. After two additional years of study in Paris, Buck returned to Hartford in 1862 to become organist of the North Congregational Church.

Buck quickly acquired a reputation as a concert organist, composer, and conductor. He removed to Chicago as organist of St. James' Church in 1869 and set up a studio there; however, church, home, and studio were lost in the great fire of 1871. Buck moved to Boston, where he joined the faculty of New England Conservatory and became organist of the Music Hall. Four years later, he was in New York as assistant conductor of the renowned Theodore Thomas Orchestra, at the time the best in America. By 1877, he had decided to devote himself to church music. He moved to Brooklyn and

---

[12] Warren's son, Richard Henry Warren, served St. Bartholomew's Church at the same time his father was at St. Thomas.

[13] William K. Gallo, "The Life and Church Music of Dudley Buck (1839–1909)" (Ph.D. diss., Catholic University of America, 1968) remains the only book-length study as of this writing. More recent research may be found in N. Lee Orr's lengthy article, "Dudley Buck: Leader of a Forgotten Tradition," *The Tracker* 38/3 (Fall 1994): 10–21.

[14] On Schneider, see Henry C. Lahee, *The Organ and Its Masters* (Boston: L. C. Page, 1903) 139–45. Schneider (1789–1864) was organist of the University Church in Leipzig at age twenty-two and was much in demand as a recitalist. He was highly esteemed both for his improvisations and his readings of Johann Sebastian Bach's organ music. Buck was among his last pupils, but one of the first American natives to study music in Germany. The group later included the future founder of Harvard's music department, John Knowles Paine, who was exactly Buck's age. Paine (and later his student, Whitney Eugene Thayer) studied with Schneider's pupil in Berlin, Karl August Haupt (1810–1891).

became organist and director of music at Holy Trinity Church, a position held by Warren a few years earlier. At the same time, he published a small practical book for the organist.[15]

Buck's own view of the quartet as a musical medium was unenthusiastic but pragmatic. As early as 1877, he wrote: "Quartet singing *alone* [that is, apart from a chorus] narrows down the scope of much good music composed for the church service.... We do not propose, however, to argue the much-discussed topic of Quartet *versus* Chorus Choirs. We have simply to deal with the fact the former exist, and whatever the signs of the future may be, they unfortunately form at present the majority."[16] Nevertheless, over the next decades, he wrote a large amount of service music and numerous anthems for quartet, many published as part of Gustav Schirmer's series *Episcopal Church Music, Designed for Either Quartette or Chorus Choir.*

Buck's music enjoyed immense popularity and a secure place in the repertoire of American church choirs. At its height, his work was exceeded in frequency of performance only by Mendelssohn's music and that of the English composer Joseph Barnby. Although he had declined the offer of a professorship there shortly before, Yale conferred an honorary doctorate on him in 1884. The *New York Herald* for 5 July 1890 said, "Few would deny Dudley Buck's claim as foremost writer of Protestant Church Music." From 1896 to 1899, Buck held the honorary title of president of the newly formed American Guild of Organists.[17]

Buck's pieces make generous use of solo sections; nevertheless, they are usually structured so as to be usable by choir if such were available along with, or instead of, the quartet. His style is melodic with light touches of chromaticism in the harmony. Although the pieces are definitely examples of their period and genre, they are seldom trite and never cheaply sentimental. Buck had the skill to

---

[15] Dudley Buck, *Illustrations in Choir Accompaniment, with Hints in Registration* (New York: G. Schirmer, 1877).

[16] Buck, *Illustrations in Choir Accompaniment*, 1877, 19. See Elwyn A. Weinandt and Robert H. Young, *The Anthem in England and America* (New York: Free Press, 1970) 330.

[17] Orr, "Dudley Buck," 18–19.

handle his materials with an effortless competence and occasionally, even inspiration. His melodies are graceful and immediately attractive; his harmonies and counterpoint are sure-footed, and his structures well put together.

Buck remained at Holy Trinity until 1902, and then he took a similar position at Plymouth Church, from which he retired in 1903. He lived his last years in Orange, New Jersey. Buck's pupils—including R. Huntington Woodman (1860–1943), William H. Neidlinger (1863–1924), and Harry Rowe Shelley (1858–1947)—carried on in his favored style and genre, but without his inspiration (if not genius). Woodman and Shelley lived to see their music and Buck's fall out of favor as larger churches replaced their quartets with volunteer and professional chorus choirs and as more church musicians sought out—and publishers began issuing—European choral music from as far back as the sixteenth century. With his talent, Buck might have been able to respond to the challenge of writing in a new, more historically informed style; his students, less gifted, could not.

Probably the most talented, and certainly the most popular, of the three was Shelley. He served in turn the Fifth Avenue Baptist Church in New York and from 1877 to 1881 at the Church of the Pilgrims in Brooklyn. He moved to Plymouth Church in Brooklyn for six years, and then he returned to Church of the Pilgrims where he served from 1887–1899. Shelley was one of the founders of the American Guild of Organists and held in high regard by his professional colleagues.

Among choirs and quartets, as well as the church-going public at large, Shelley's music enjoyed a measure of popularity comparable to that of his teacher's. Nevertheless, his was a more modest talent than Buck's, and his work relied more on facility and cliché than on inspiration. His melodies are especially attractive—indeed, in some cases more immediately appealing than Buck's—but his harmonies tend more to the saccharine, with passages in thirds and sixths, chromatically altered dominant and secondary seventh chords and passing tones, and fulsomely dramatic use of diminished seventh chords on one hand and unison passages on the other.

Like Buck, Shelley crafted his anthems for use by quartet or chorus. Sections for one or another solo voice abound; and like Buck, Shelley took special care to see that the vocal part with the solo played an all-but-dispensable role in the ensemble accompaniment and would not be missed in a quartet performance, as for instance in his still popular setting of Frederick William Faber's 1854 text, "Hark, hark, my soul."[18]

Many voices were raised in criticism against the quartet. As is clear from the entries in the *American Musical Directory* of 1861, noted above, Methodist churches were among the few in New York that held out against the quartet and maintained their volunteer chorus choirs. Yet that same year, Henry Ward Beecher was on vacation in Matteawan, New Jersey, and was discouraged by the singing in a Methodist church he attended:

> Imagine my chagrin when, after reading the hymn, up rose a choir from the shelf at the other end of the church, and began to sing a monotonous tune of the modern music book style. The patient congregation stood up meekly to be sung to.... Scarcely a lip moved. No one seemed to hear the hymn or care for the music. How I longed for the good old Methodist thunder! One good burst of old fashioned music would have blown this modern singing out of the window like wadding from a gun! Men may call this an improvement, and genteel. Gentility has nearly killed our churches.[19]

It should be observed that Beecher's own Plymouth Church in Brooklyn had a superb organ and organist, a highly acclaimed and highly paid solo quartet, and a chorus of seventy volunteers and was without a doubt one of the city's premiere bastions of musical gentility. At the same time, however, Beecher insisted on

---

[18] Harry Rowe Shelly, *Hark! Hark, My Soul!* (New York: G. Schirmer, 1887).

[19] Rev. H. W. Beecher, "Church Music," *Dwight's Journal* 19/15 (13 July 1861): 116.

congregational singing, and the primary obligation of the choir at Plymouth Church was to support and lead congregational hymns.[20]

A decade later, an English visitor, Howard Glover, faulted the secular character of music in New York City, in the London *Musical Standard*, singling out Christ Church as a place where "various airs from Italian operas are sung to words selected by the organist from the Holy Scriptures." Glover observed tartly, "Verdi is evidently the favorite church writer of America." He blamed the situation on a lack of authority—the absence of cathedral establishments able to exert pressure on parish churches—and the need to meet expenses by attracting people, selling pews, and collecting rents. "They are compelled to pander to the tastes of the congregations, lest the main source of their income should fail.... I don't think it possible to find one [city in the world] in which [church] music is so thoroughly debased."[21]

An unsigned letter in an 1875 Methodist periodical complained that the purpose of music had become more "to show off some prima donna or fine basso than to worship God in Spirit and in Truth." Christian writers were not the only ones concerned. The same periodical quoted an item in the *Jewish Messenger*: "Some of our congregations compete like rival tradesmen, each to outdo the other in...the splendor of its choir, the resonance of its organ."[22]

The next year an unfavorable economy had forced reductions of a third to a half in the music budgets of many New York churches, and a lengthy list of them—mainly Presbyterian, Methodist, and Baptist—were dismissing their paid quartets and seeking either less expensive singers, volunteers, or going to chorus choirs or even all-

---

[20] McDaniel, "Church Song and the Cultivated Tradition," 495.

[21] Reprinted in Howard Glover, "Church Music in New York," *Dwight's Journal* 33/13 (4 October 1873): 99–100. The writer goes out of his way to exempt Trinity Church—which he characterizes as similar in its music to an English cathedral—from his general disapproval.

[22] Unsigned letter, *New York Christian Advocate* 50 (11 February 1875): 42; *New York Christian Advocate* 48 (4 December 1873): 338, both quoted in Paul A. Carter, *The Spiritual Crisis of the Gilded Age* (DeKalb: Northern Illinois University Press, 1971) 11–12.

congregational singing.[23]

But the ebbing of the quartet was only temporary. As soon as the economy rebounded, the churches reestablished their quartet programs. In an 1880 address to the Music Teachers' National Association meeting in Buffalo, W. Eugene Thayer—highly regarded organist, church musician, composer, and music journalist—suggested that a "true choir" consisted of more than a quartet or double quartet.[24]

Thayer was not alone in his view; nevertheless, the solo quartet did have positive aspects. It provided professional singers with performing experience and exposure and gave the congregation a taste of—and for—professional quality musicianship. Soloists within a volunteer chorus choir set a musical standard for the volunteer singers around them and enabled the choirs in which they sang to attempt more difficult music. Few singers made more than a token amount; however, some, like Emma Thursby in New York, were by talent or—as in Thursby's case, inclination—not engaged in opera work and were still able to live comfortably, if less than opulently, on a relatively generous church stipend along with private teaching and recitals.[25]

---

[23] Eugene Thayer, "Church Music in New York," *Dwight's Journal* 36/3 (13 May 1876): 228–29.

[24] Reported in n.a., "Reform in Church Music," *Dwight's Journal* 40/1025 (31 July 1880): 126–28; and Eugene Thayer, "Reform of Church Music," *Dwight's Journal* 40/1026 (14 August 1880): 132–33. Interestingly, Thayer recommended the double quartet configure itself so that one male and one female voice sang each part; i.e. that all the parts be doubled at the octave. Thayer's most pungent comments were directed toward hymns. The Sunday school variety he dismissed as "twaddle" and "driveling nonsense." He had, he said "seen and played from a Sunday-school book which had the words of 'Jesus is my Savior' set to that drunken melody 'We won't go home till morning,' with three or four notes changed, but the rest note for note." Thayer, who had been trained in Germany, declared a pronounced preference for a smaller number of hymns, 25–50, most of them German chorales rather than English psalm tunes and American adaptations. And Dwight himself, in a comment on Thayer's speech, agreed with the "infinite superiority of the chorale to the humdrum modern psalm-tune with its would-be melody and its helpless monotony of harmony."

[25] Richard McCandless Gipson, *The Life of Emma Thursby, 1845–1931* (New

In any case, the effect of Thayer's words was negligible. With some marked exceptions among Episcopal and Roman Catholic parishes—the latter mostly of German tradition—who established boys' choirs between the Civil War and the turn of the century, solo quartets continued strong in both Protestant and Catholic churches well into the 1920s.

Music in Smaller Churches

Professional quartets were, for the most part, to be found in city churches that could afford them. In smaller churches from city to village, where the gospel hymn tradition had taken hold, amateur choirs and untrained directors clamored for appealing music in a similar style that could be easily learned. From mid-century on, their demand was met by a regular flow of pieces with simple texts set syllabically to repetitive melodies with engaging rhythms, uncomplicated harmony, and a generally sentimental style harking back to that of such composers as the extremely popular Isaac Woodbury (1819–1858).

Individual octavo size copies of anthems had appeared in the 1840s in England. In 1844, J. Alfred Novello bought a three-year-old magazine that was published each month with an anthem bound in it. Novello had renamed it *The Musical Times and Singing Class Circular* and made multiple copies of the pieces available for churches as an alternative to the costly hardbound collections used by cathedral choirs. In 1852, Oliver Ditson (1811–1888), a Boston organist, became Novello's American representative as well as a leading publisher in his own right. With the establishment of White, Smith & Co. and B. F. Wood over the next decades, Boston became a center for choir music publishing.[26]

In America, in the larger city churches as well as smaller ones, separate volumes of hymns and choir music were replacing the earlier oblong collections with their mix of congregational hymns and choir

York: The New York Historical Society, 1940) 68, 83, 114.
[26] Weinandt and Young, *The Anthem in England and America*, 244–50; McDaniel, "Church Song and the Cultivated Tradition," 643–44.

anthems.[27] Lowell Mason's *The Sabbath Hymn and Tune Book* appeared in 1855; that same year, John Zundel of Brooklyn's Plymouth Church issued *The Plymouth Collection*.[28] The most significant innovation for smaller churches was the serial publication of choir music, a counterpart to the gospel song collections being issued periodically in series.

The first such periodical appeared in 1874 and was titled *The Parish Choir*. In 1892, John P. Vance (1867–1897) of Chicago offered by subscription his *Choir Herald*, each issue of which contained anthems, most by Vance himself. Edmund S. Lorenz (1854–1942) founded what has become the largest supplier of church music by subscription in 1894, when he issued the first number of *The Choir Leader*. The periodical was aimed at volunteer choirs and contained a column of advice and "music of a simple or only moderately difficult character." Vance died in 1897, and Lorenz bought the *Choir Herald* and began publishing it with music a grade easier than *The Choir Leader*. In 1913, Lorenz added a periodical with still easier music, *The Volunteer Choir*.

Lorenz's music was specifically targeted at small churches with unsophisticated congregations, untrained and unbalanced choirs, and volunteer directors with minimal background and neither the time nor the knowledge to select individual pieces of music for their choirs from the usual catalogues. Lorenz's periodicals offered such churches music for every Sunday of the year with a consistent level of difficulty and a consistent style of composition. Most of the pieces were written by in-house composers to fairly transparent formulas or adapted from

---

[27] Among the most popular were George F. Root's *The Diapason: A Collection of Church Music* (New York: Mason Brothers, 1860); Luther O. Emerson's *The Jubilate: A Collection of Sacred Music for Choirs, Singing Schools, Musical Conventions, etc.* (Boston: Ditson, 1886) the latter containing some European pieces. On these collections, see Weinandt and Young, *The Anthem in England and America*, 308–309. The same book contains a full discussion of the anthem periodicals (310–26), and the paragraphs that follow rely heavily on that discussion.

[28] Henry Ward Beecher and John Zundel, *Plymouth Collection of Hymns and Tunes* (New York: Barnes & Co., 1855). For a contemporary commentary on the *Plymouth Collection*, see n.a., "Congregational Music," *Dwight's Journal New York Musical World* 16/290 (18 October 1856): 507.

the classical repertoire, instrumental and vocal. In some cases, popular anthems—from the "Hallelujah Chorus" from Handel's *Messiah* to Shelley's "Hark, hark my soul" and "The King of Love my shepherd is," for instance—were simplified and shortened for use by more modest groups.

Lorenz neither apologized nor made excuses for his techniques. He considered himself to be the sole steady source of usable music for small rural churches, far from music stores and professional assistance. In a very real sense, he was right. A large number of such churches and their choirs formed a fierce loyalty to Lorenz over years, decades, and generations, relying on the company's periodicals for all their music and building their libraries from accumulated issues.

9.

Male Choirs, Historical Tradition, and Liturgical Revival

If the mid-nineteenth century saw the rise of professional quartets in most churches, in many Episcopal churches, a historicist movement was rallying sentiment for the displacement of women's voices with boys' voices. Richard Storrs Willis, editor of the *New York Musical World*, endorsed children's choirs over quartets in churches of all denominations as a means of improving the worship atmosphere. He especially recommended that singing be taught at least a half-hour a day as a part of a parish school curriculum.[1] A letter in *The Churchman* for 9 April 1857 asked if, instead of paying a quartet, "would not an appropriation of some money expended on Sunday services be better employed in providing, by means of a boys' school, a suitable choir?" And in the 18 June 1857 issue, yet another correspondent assailed the "unwarrantable and often mischievous practice of having women in choirs."[2]

---

[1] Richard Storrs Willis, *Our Church Music* (New York: Dana & Co., 1856) 34–35.

[2] Jane E. Rasmussen, *Musical Taste as a Religious Question in Nineteenth Century America* (Lewiston NY: Mellen, 1986) 335–38. The writer of the first letter signed it "Helmore," adopting as a pseudonym the name of a well-known British choir reformer, church music compiler, and composer of the period Thomas Helmore (1811–1890).

Art, Architecture, and Ritual

In a real sense, the American boy-choir movement (like the generally increased attention to ceremony and beauty in worship)[3] may be seen as a function of the mid- and late-nineteenth-century American neo-medievalism, itself a far different affair from the medievalism of the English romantic period fifty years earlier. During the Civil War and in the years after, immense fortunes were being made, and many successful capitalists and their wives began to see themselves as latter day barons; indeed, that was the term applied to them. They began to collect art in the manner of a European aristocrat. Manuscripts, tapestries, reliquaries, sculpture, and paintings crossed the Atlantic in an unprecedented volume. As might be expected, the tastes of such men and women were to be seen in the churches they built, supported, and attended.

Like their predecessors of six centuries earlier, they underwrote the construction of large churches, and not surprisingly, they favored neo-medieval gothic and Romanesque edifices[4] with striking stained glass, elegant decoration, and luxurious furnishings. Such neo-medievalism affected urban and suburban churches of virtually all denominations. More neo-gothic Presbyterian, Methodist, and even Unitarian churches were built from the 1870s on. But many, if not most, of the latter day barons favored the Episcopal Church because it represented an aesthetic as close to the medieval baronial (and Catholic) spirit as their Protestant sensibilities and social peers would tolerate.

These larger churches housed larger organs. During the decades after the Civil War, American organ builders were heavily influenced by the instrument installed in 1863 in the Boston Music Hall. The so-called "Boston organ," the work of E. F. Walcker of Ludwigsburg,

---

[3] The Oxford movement of thirty years earlier had essentially been concerned with the recovery of doctrine and tradition, not of ceremonial; however, out of the Oxford reforms emerged the Cambridge ritualist movement, the Camden Society, whose publication, *The Ecclesiologist*, inspired a similar movement and periodical in the United States.

[4] Henry Hobson Richardson, neo-Romanesque architect, whose work included Trinity Church in Boston, was fond of relaxing his immense bulk in a monk's habit.

Germany, had a reedy sound and a variety of novel solo colors and quasi-orchestral effects.[5] Up to that time, the largest organs in America were three-manual instruments of thirty to thirty-five stops, such as the one in Trinity Church, New York, built by Henry Erben in 1846, to a design of Edward Hodges.[6]

Erben (1800–1884) had been the most prominent and arguably the finest builder in America prior to the Civil War, approached only by the brothers Elias and George Hook of Boston. By the mid-1860s, Erben's firm was in decline largely because he alone among the major American builders resisted the influence of the Boston Music Hall organ and the changes in public taste that it brought about. Hook (and its successor, Hook & Hastings) and Hall & Labagh and George Jardine, Erben's closest competitors in New York, quickly outstripped him. In 1868, for instance, Temple Emanu-El in New York turned to Hall & Labagh for its four-manual instrument of sixty-six stops. A year later, Jardine installed a four-manual of fifty-two stops, its uncased pipes brightly decorated in painted stripes and stenciling, in the rear gallery of St. George's Church in New York.

Erben stayed in business until his death in 1884; however, his mantle of preeminence had by then fallen to another New Yorker. The heir to Erben's prominence in the last years of the nineteenth century was Hilborne Roosevelt (1850–1886), a first cousin of Theodore Roosevelt. Roosevelt's family fortune enabled him to study European organ-building firsthand, and his name certainly provided him an advantage in gaining local commissions in the New York area. But it was the superb quality of Roosevelt's instruments, large and small, that earned his reputation and clientele. At its height, the Roosevelt Organ Works had plants in New York, Baltimore, and Philadelphia and instruments in churches as far away as San Francisco and Rome, Italy.[7]

---

[5] The instrument exists, heavily rebuilt and altered, most recently during the 1940s by the Boston firm Æolian-Skinner.

[6] On the Trinity Church organ, see John Ogasapian, *Organ Building in New York City, 1700–1900* (Braintree MA: Organ Literature Foundation, 1977) 77–96.

[7] After Hilborne's death, the firm continued to operate until 1893 under the ownership of his youngest brother, Frank Roosevelt (1862–1894) building another

Roosevelt was a skilled engineer, and his instruments incorporated an electrical key-and-stop action he had perfected before 1870.[8] The use of electricity enabled even larger organs to be built and their separate divisions of pipes to be dispersed at some distance from one another and from the organist. Roosevelt's largest was a huge four-manual instrument, which was built between 1879 and 1895 for the exquisitely proportioned Episcopal Cathedral of the Incarnation in Garden City, Long Island. Its 114 stops were separated into twelve divisions, dispersed among the chancel, tower, and adjoining chapel.[9]

Larger churches and their antiquarian furnishings also brought about increased ceremonial. The separate lectern, altar, and pulpit required that the clergy move a number of times during worship; music and ritual clothed these movements in formality and decorum. As might be expected, the trend was most pronounced in Episcopal churches. The Oxford movement, which had appeared in England in the 1830s and crossed the Atlantic almost immediately, had drawn in its wake a so-called Ecclesiology movement now impelling Anglicans and Episcopalians to seek their historical traditions, not only in theology, but also in worship ritual.

---

178 organs in that time.

[8] Roosevelt was not the inventor of electric organ action. The first patent was issued in England to Alexander Bain, as early as 1847. A Britisher, Charles Barker, had been issued another patent early in 1868, and that same year a Philadelphia builder, J. C. B. Standbridge, incorporated electricity into one division of an organ he was rebuilding for St. Augustine's Church in that city. Roosevelt was one of the earliest to develop and apply a practical system, however. See Ogasapian, *Organ Building in New York City*, 160–62.

[9] The cathedral is 188 feet long with a 109-foot transept span at the crossing—by no means small, but certainly not of European cathedral proportions. The instrument's effectiveness was hampered because it was simply too large for the space it occupied. In 1925, it was finally rebuilt and drastically reduced in size to suit better the building and space. See Ogasapian, *Organ Building in New York City*, 172–74, 237–39.

Male Choirs

Although the *American Musical Directory* showed quartets in all but a handful of New York's thirty-two Episcopal churches in 1861, choirs of boys and men were, in fact, gaining a foothold in what was considered the proper Anglican tradition.[10] Of course, many such male choirs did little more than sing the same type of music their congregations had been used to hearing from the solo quartets or mixed choirs that had heretofore held sway; however, a number of churches established men-and-boys' choirs specifically to chant the psalms and canticles after the model of an English cathedral or collegiate church.[11]

The choir at Holy Innocents was described as consisting of "several boys,"[12] and the music at Church of the Transfiguration—better known even then as the Little Church around the Corner—was "congregational singing led by eight boys and two men." It is highly unlikely that the boys in either choir were trained after the English model. Rather their tone was almost certainly that of the old-fashioned charity school children, attempting to lead congregational psalmody by singing with their harsh juvenile voices at the top of their lungs. Nor is it likely that even William Augustus Muhlenberg

---

[10] *American Musical Directory* (New York: Thomas Hutchinson, 1861) 216–19, 220–24,

[11] Of course, the choral services, even on Sundays, were Morning and Evening Prayer (or "Evensong"). Rarely, if ever, did such choirs venture onto the far more hazardous, Romanizing ground of singing the Communion service, beyond the basic parts of the Ordinary—the Kyrie, Gloria, Sanctus, and Agnus Dei, all in English—and the term Mass was used only toward the end of the century and only in the most ritualistic churches.

[12] Although the *Directory* makes no mention of men with the boys, Rasmussen (*Musical Taste*, 375) supplies evidence that some use was made of men. Moreover, the choir at Holy Innocents was vested, or robed, at least three years before Trinity Church in New York vested its men and boys. In a letter dated 31 October 1857, J. H. Perrine, lately appointed lay reader under John J. Elmendorf, rector of Holy Innocents, writes Bishop William Whittingham of Maryland: "He [Elmendorf] may also ask me to take part in his choir. I will take this occasion to ask if there is any objection to the practice of having the men and boys of his choir dressed in the surplice."

cultivated an English-style head tone in the choir of boys he trained to lead his congregation's singing at the Church of the Holy Communion.

Some churches who could afford it retained their quartet in the gallery and instituted a choir of men and boys in the chancel. Still others introduced a choir of men and boys but continued to use women who were hidden behind a curtain. St. Michael's in New York had a choir of girls and women hidden behind a screen to support the boys who were in view of the congregation.[13]

Under the direction of Henry Stephen Cutler, Trinity Church in New York instituted a choir of men and boys, functioning on the English cathedral model and supplanting Hodges's group of men, women, and boys.[14] Indeed, even as S. P. Tuckerman was publishing *The Trinity Collection of Church Music*,[15] the repertoire in that book—Edward Hodges's repertoire—had been discarded by Cutler and out of use in Trinity for over five years. So distinctive was Trinity's choir and music that the *American Musical Directory* felt called upon to comment further on them, making an especially careful point that the boys were not the charity school inmates of earlier times. The *Directory* records:

> The service here is what is termed the "Cathedral" or "Choral Service," that is, the clergy *intone* the prayers, and the *Amens* and all other responses are by the choir and people in full harmony. This is the only church in this country, where the English cathedral service is presented in its integrity [*sic*], although an approximation to it is attempted at

---

[13] Stanley McDaniel, "Church Song and the Cultivated Tradition in New England and New York" (DMA diss., University of Southern California, 1983) 558–61.

[14] It was probably Edward Hodges's main failing in his efforts to develop an English cathedral-style program at Trinity Church that, never having been a choirboy himself, he did not know how to develop the English chorister's characteristic head register.

[15] S. Parkman Tuckerman, *The Trinity Collection of Church Music* (Boston: Ditson, 1864).

the Church of the Holy Communion...and at the Church of the Advent, Boston.

The choir is composed of male voices exclusively. The parts usually sung by females are here sustained by boys. These boys are most carefully selected, with reference to musical aptitude and refinement of character, and belong to the higher walks of life. Their musical training is of the most thorough description. Daily they are practiced at the choristers music room in the most intricate vocal exercises, as well as the classical works of Handel and the cathedral composers; anything, however, which resembles in style the modern Italian is carefully avoided. These boys are trained to read the most difficult music at sight, even before they attain the age of thirteen. Their voices are, with the exception of the altos, purely soprano, reaching to C *in altissimo* without difficulty.[16]

Henry Stephen Cutler (1824–1902),[17] a native of Boston, had studied there with George F. Root and Aaron Upjohn Hayter, organist of Trinity Church. Hayter may have had a significant part in the development of Cutler's interest in English cathedral music, although Hayter himself had neither a boys' choir nor such program at Trinity in Boston. In 1844, Cutler went to Germany, where for the next two years he studied piano and violin. He also spent time studying English boys' choirs, an institution then in early stages of a revival after a lengthy period of institutional indifference and incompetent leadership.[18] Cutler was back in Boston by 1847, and

---

[16] *American Musical Directory*, 247–48. John Ireland Tucker's Holy Cross Church in Troy, New York, was by this time singing daily services; in fact, as will be noted presently, both Trinity and Advent had used Holy Cross as their model.

[17] On Cutler, see W. S. B. Mathews and Glanville Howe, *A Hundred Years of Music in America* (Chicago: G. L. Howe, 1889) 270–72; Leonard Ellinwood, *The History of American Church Music* (New York: Morehouse-Gorham, 1953; repr., New York: Da Capo, 1970) 206–207.

[18] Although noted above, it bears repeating here that the classic study on the English choir movement at mid century is Bernarr Rainbow, *The Choral Revival in the*

shortly thereafter he became organist of Grace Church in that city. In July 1852, he was appointed organist and choirmaster of the Church of the Advent, one of the earliest parishes of the so-called ritualist movement.

The Reverend William Croswell, rector of Church of the Advent, had tried to replace the church's volunteer adult quartet with boys as early as 1849; however, it was not until Cutler was hired that the boys' choir was established.[19] Two years later, the *New York Musical World* reported that Cutler had both the regular choir and a group of probationers and had rehearsals and services daily except for three weeks of vacation in August. The group's repertoire included at least five English anthems and five services, among them one each by Tallis and Byrd.[20]

In 1858, Cutler was called to Trinity, New York, to take over the duties of the incapacitated Edward Hodges. A year later, he had weeded out the women left over from the regime of his predecessor, and shortly thereafter, he moved the choir out of the west gallery. Instead, the sixteen boys and six men were divided on either side of the chancel, in spite of the difficulties of coordinating and supporting the group with the gallery organ, which was some 150 feet away.[21]

Anglican Church (New York: Oxford University Press, 1970). See also Nicholas Temperley, *The Music of the English Parish Church* (New York: Cambridge University Press, 1979); William Gatens, *Victorian Cathedral Music in Theory and Practice* (New York: Cambridge University Press, 1986); and John Ogasapian, *English Cathedral Music in New York: Edward Hodges of Trinity Church* (Richmond: Organ Historical Society, 1994).

[19] Church of the Advent, Boston MA, *The Parish of the Advent in the City of Boston: A History of One Hundred Years, 1844–1944* (Boston: Parish of the Advent, 1944) 42–43, 124–26. A similar effort under S. P. Tuckerman at nearby evangelical St. Paul's failed, allegedly because of "Puritan prejudice."

[20] Edward Hodges, "Choristers," *New York Musical World* 16/294 (22 November 1856): 627.

[21] See Arthur H. Messiter, *A History of the Choir and Music of Trinity Church, New York* (New York: Edwin S. Gorham, 1906) 72–112. Not until 1865, the year Cutler was dismissed by Trinity's vestry, was an organ ordered for the chancel. Awarded an honorary doctorate by Columbia in 1864, Cutler went from Trinity to Christ Church in New York, where he maintained a vested male choir in the chancel and a mixed choir in the gallery.

Although the boys were visible to the congregation, they sang in street clothes. Vestments, long white surplices, had been donated in 1859, but not until the visit of the Prince of Wales in October 1860 was the choir allowed to wear them for the first time.[22]

By the late 1860s, Trinity's choir had become a tourist attraction in New York. One 1868 tourists' guide, *Sunshine and Shadow in New York*, not altogether approvingly, records:

> The choral service is one of the specialties of Old Trinity. It was introduced, in its present order, by Dr. Cutler, who succeeded Dr. Hodge [*sic*] as organist. A choir of boys was introduced in connection with the voices of men. The whole, dressed in white surplices, make quite a show in the chancel.... Everything is sung in the service that can be sung—the Psalter, the Creed, as well as other parts of the service. The people are mere spectators. The ministers and choir within the chancel rail have it all to themselves. The music is very difficult and it is sung at such a rapid time that an untrained voice cannot keep up. The service opens on Sunday with a thronged house—aisles and vestibules full. The crowd remains till the singing is over and the sermon begins. Then it disappears as if the performance was complete.

---

[22] Messiter, *A History*, 84. The prince worshiped at Trinity on 14 October; however, the choir wore vestments for the first time the previous Sunday, in order to accustom the boys to the surplices and prevent any awkwardnesses in the presence of the distinguished visitor. Ellinwood, *History of American Church Music*, 82, reports that the choir of another church was so affected the first Sunday its members wore vestments that they were unable to sing as they marched in procession. Cutler's choir at Church of the Advent may have been vested as early as 1856; however, such is not documented for certain until 1859, after he had left. St. James the Less in Philadelphia had vested its choir in 1857. By the 1860s, a number of Episcopal choirs were vested; however the movement engendered much controversy; as late as 1868, a resolution was introduced into the General Convention of the Episcopal Church, against ritualistic ornaments in general, and specifically directing in part that "no Ecclesiastical vestments shall be worn...by Choirs..." See Rasmussen *Musical Taste*, 371–78.

The piece goes on to describe the processional, as led by the "leader of the music," and how the "priest intones the service after the manner of the Catholic Church."[23]

Four years later, yet another guide, *Lights and Shadows of New York Life*, observed less testily: "Trinity has long been famous for its excellent music. The choir consists of men and boys, who are trained with great care by the musical director. The service is very beautiful and impressive, and is thoroughly in keeping with the grand and cathedral-like edifice in which it is conducted."[24]

Outside New York, in addition to Church of the Advent in Boston and Tucker's Holy Communion in Troy, male choirs had been organized in the late 1850s at both St. Mark's and St. James the Less in Philadelphia, at St. John's in Detroit, Church of the Advent in Boston, at parishes in western New York, and elsewhere. By the 1860s, the movement had spread to Chicago, where Church of the Atonement, St. James, and several other churches dispensed with their quartets in favor of boys and men.[25] In 1873, the Reverend John Sebastian Bach Hodges (1830–1913), son of Edward Hodges, established a vested choir of men and boys at St. Paul's Church Baltimore in 1873, backing it with a day school for the first time in America.[26]

That same year, J. Kendrick Pyne (1852–1938), organist and choirmaster of Chichester Cathedral, moved to St. Mark's in Philadelphia. In a very real sense, he was the first musician with significant and authentic cathedral boy-choir experience to work in an American church. Pyne was a student of Samuel Sebastian Wesley at Winchester and followed him to Gloucester as his assistant. Pyne was appointed to the Chichester post in May 1873; he had thus been

---

[23] Matthew Hale Smith, *Sunshine and Shadow in New York* (Hartford: J. Burr, 1868) 281–82.

[24] Michael McCabe, *Lights and Shadows of New York Life* (Philadelphia: National Publishing Co., 1872) 566.

[25] Rasmussen, *Musical Taste*, 356–62, 549. Ellinwood, *History of American Church Music*, 77–78.

[26] Francis F. Beirne, *St. Paul's Parish, Baltimore: A Chronicle of the Mother Church* (Baltimore: Horn & Shafer, 1967) 126–32.

there only a few months when he accepted the offer from St. Mark's. And indeed, he remained in Philadelphia scarcely two years, and then he returned to England in 1875 as organist and choirmaster of Manchester Cathedral. He spent the rest of his career as cathedral, city, and university organist in Manchester. Like Cutler, Pyne knew how to train the head register, and his methods were closely copied by such men as George LeJeune of St. John's Chapel, in New York.[27]

Liturgical Music

Although the male choir movement in the Episcopal Church coincided both with an increased use of early church music and with the ritualism movement, the three phenomena were not necessarily a function of one another. While choirs of boys and men sang the canticles, psalms, and even responses of the Morning and Evening Prayer to such settings as that of Thomas Tallis in an increasing number of Episcopal churches as the century wound down, so did some mixed choirs and even quartets. Some churches, for example Holy Trinity Church in Brooklyn under Dudley Buck, maintained a double quartet, seated liturgically on opposite sides of the chancel, *decani* and *cantoris*; some such antiphonal quartets sang psalms, canticles, and responses in the cathedral style.

Ironically, unlike Church of the Advent in Boston and St. Mark's in Philadelphia, the most advanced ritualistic Episcopal parishes in New York—St. Mary the Virgin and Church of the Resurrection—had patterned their music after stylish urban Roman Catholic churches. Their mixed quartets sang Italian masses in the inappropriately operatic style and tradition.

Conversely, some churches instituted boys' choirs without changing either ritual or music. Instead, the boys sang the same sort of music as the quartets they replaced. Even the best choirs in Episcopal churches, mixed or male, rarely sang anthems drawn from

---

[27] Watkins Shaw, *The Succession of Organists* (New York: Oxford University Press, 1991) 189. Pyne's brother, Minton, also emigrated and became organist and choirmaster of St. Mark's in 1881. He remained in that city until his death in 1905, establishing the cathedral choir and service tradition at St. Mark's.

the motets of Tallis and his contemporaries. Rather, if their anthem repertoire did not coincide with, or at least overlap, that of the quartets in other fashionable urban churches, they drew on eighteenth- and nineteenth-century oratorios and masses (the latter in suitably appropriate English texts or translations), middle and late English Victorians such as Goss and Stainer, and a very few American composers best exemplified by George Whitefield Chadwick (1854–1913) and his student Horatio Parker (1863–1919).

Parker's early training was with his mother and under Chadwick's tutelage. In 1881, he went to Munich to study with Josef Rheinberger for three years. Upon his return, he taught at two private Episcopal schools on Long Island and at the National Conservatory in New York. In 1893, he returned to Boston as organist and choirmaster of Trinity Church, and that year produced his oratorio *Hora Novissima*. In 1894, he was appointed Battell Professor of Theory at Yale, and from then until his retirement, he commuted between Boston and New York, teaching, conducting, and composing. In 1902, Cambridge awarded him the Mus.D. degree.

Parker was a major figure in American concert music at the turn of the century; however, throughout his life, he continued to write church music. Parker's work was consistently at the level of the best English cathedral musicians and composers of his time: Charles Villiers Stanford and C. Hubert H. Parry. His anthem style, like theirs, is characterized by strong diatonic melodies and harmonies, excellent counterpoint often contrasted with unison passages for all voices, and independent organ accompaniments. In fact, his music was popular enough in New England to be carried in Novello's catalogue alongside the works of Stanford and Parry.[28]

As late as the 1890s, the music in New York's churches was still worthy of mention as a tourist attraction, and especial distinctions

---

[28] As of this writing, the best study of Parker is William K. Kearns, *Horatio Parker (1863–1919): His Life, Music, and Ideas* (Metuchen NJ: Scarecrow, 1990). On Parker's anthems, see Elwyn A. Weinandt and Robert H. Young, *The Anthem in England and America* (New York: Free Press, 1970) 342–45.

were drawn relative to Trinity and its chapels. The *Sun's Guide* records:

> The most complete illustration of the choral, or Cathedral, school known outside of St. Paul's in London or Westminster Abbey, is found at the mother church of Trinity Parish—"Old Trinity".... Here too, the introduction of "surpliced" choirs, composed exclusively of boys and men, was successfully accomplished...with the result that hardly more than a quarter of a century [later] more than one half of the [Episcopal] churches...or forty out of seventy-five have followed....
>
> A full Cathedral morning and Communion service is sung at Trinity every Sunday in the year, and a Complete choral service in the afternoon.[29]

The organist and choirmaster of Trinity was now Arthur Messiter (1834–1916). Messiter was born in Somersetshire, England, and studied in Austria. He came to New York in 1863 and sang in Trinity's choir under Cutler before taking over the music at St. Mark's in Philadelphia, later that year. In 1866, he was called back to Trinity, succeeding Cutler after a one-year hiatus.[30]

Meanwhile, at St. John's Chapel, the choir music was "of a somewhat lighter character," and Trinity Chapel's music was "a happy medium between the Cathedral and modern school." Both chapels had choirs of men and boys. St. John's music was under the direction of George LeJeune (1841–1904). LeJeune was a native of London and student of Joseph Barnby and George MacFarren. He had studied the boy-choir techniques of J. Kendrick Pyne during the

---

[29] Colin H. Livingstone, *The Sun's Guide to New York* (New York: R.Wayne Wilson & Co., 1892) 263. By this time, the choir had gone from floor length surplices to the current style of vestment, a short white cotta over a dark colored cassock. Trinity may be seen to have progressed by 1892 to sung Communion services in addition to Morning and Evening Prayer.

[30] Messiter completed his *History of the Choir and Music of Trinity Church* in 1906, a decade after his retirement.

latter's year in Philadelphia. In 1876, he took over the music at St. John's and built an excellent choir of men and boys; however, his repertoire consisted largely of fashionable pieces from Mozart and Haydn, as well as some American anthems, rather than the liturgically more appropriate music from the Anglican tradition. Although somewhat less "light" than that of the St. John's choir, the choir at Trinity Chapel, which also sang a less formal repertoire than the mother church's, was under the direction of Walter B. Gilbert (1829–1910). Gilbert was born in Exeter and studied with S. S. Wesley. He served Trinity Chapel from 1870 to 1897, when he returned to England.[31]

Roman Catholic Music

In the second half of the nineteenth century, Roman Catholic churches in urban areas held for the most part to what had come to be their customary music: operatic-style masses sung by solo quartets, with or without volunteers. In 1861, according to the *American Musical Directory* survey, almost all the Catholic churches in New York, including St. Patrick's Cathedral, had a small solo group: a quartet, quintet, or double quartet. The few who had chorus choirs recruited from the congregation were ethnic German parishes, whose members cultivated singing as a part of their culture: Most Holy Redeemer, St. Vincent de Paul, and St. Nicholas. A fourth German parish, St. Francis Xavier, maintained a double quartet and a volunteer chorus.

The few exceptions elsewhere in America were also primarily German churches. In the Midwest, St. John's Abbey was established in the 1850s in Collegeville, Minnesota, as a monastery and seminary. By the 1870s, the community was using Gregorian chant and polyphony under the influence of a movement that had begun in Europe a decade earlier. Founded in Germany, the Caecilian movement sought to recapture the historical spirit of Catholic

---

[31] Ellinwood, *History of American Church Music*, 222–23, 214–15; Livingstone, *Sun's Guide*, 261. Only at St. Paul's Chapel was there still a quartet and mixed choir, under one Leo Kofler.

liturgical music. Its view of church music was probably best summed up nearly a century later by an American scholar Archibald T. Davison: "The ideal which persisted throughout the best years of Roman Catholic composition was that the music should never be an end in itself; that it should exist to heighten the significance of the great liturgical texts to which it was set, that it should be an ally, selfless, inconspicuous of the attitudes of worship."[32]

Under the influence of Karl Proske (1794–1867) and his pupil Franz Xavier Witt (1834–1888) in Regensburg, German Catholic scholars had been recovering masses, motets, and other settings of liturgical Latin texts by such composers as Palestrina, Victoria, Lassus, and others of their generation. They published them from 1853 in a subscription series titled *Musica Divina*.[33] At the same time, the Benedictine monks of Solesmes in France were engaged in the recovery and editing of the Gregorian repertoire.

In 1868, Witt and others founded the Caecilia Society; its aims were to revive the use of Gregorian chant and such liturgical polyphony as the masses of Palestrina and to promote the composition of new mass settings in the style of Palestrina. The society also sought to foster vernacular congregational singing. Witt's student, the Swiss-born John Baptist Singenberger (1848–1924), brought the Society to America when he became professor at the Catholic Normal School in St. Francis, Wisconsin, in 1873. Singenberger himself wrote masses, vespers, motets, and instruction books, including one on the singing of chant. The American Caecilian Society held its first annual convention in Milwaukee on 17 June 1874; earlier the same year, it had begun the publication of its journal, *Caecilia*. By 1878, it had some 3,000 members.[34]

---

[32] Archibald T. Davison, *Church Music, Illusion and Reality* (Cambridge: Harvard University Press, 1966) 26.

[33] On the subject, see John Ogasapian, "The Restoration of Sacred Music in Romantic Germany," *Journal of Church Music* 30/3 (March 1988): 9–12, 30.

[34] See Ellinwood, *History of American Church Music*, 99–107; Mathews and Howe, *A Hundred Years of Music in America*, 280–82.

The first issue of *Caecilia* set forth the Society's aims: "Banishing from our churches, all music of a profane and worldly character, and to substitute the sublime compositions of such authors as Palestrina." Among the styles to be thus banished were, not only "soft, sentimental duets, solos and opera melodies," but also sacred masterworks by such composers as Haydn, Mozart, and Beethoven, which made "scarcely any difference between the church and the concert-hall." Women were not to be allowed as singers or organists, except in convents.[35]

The reaction from American Catholics was mixed. A small number of churches embraced Caecilian tenets; a far larger number either ignored or rejected them. Chicago's Cathedral of the Holy Name adopted a number of reforms, much to the irritation of some in its congregation. A letter in the *Chicago Tribune* dated 17 November 1878, signed "A Parishioner," declared: "Caecilian, Gregorian, anti-Catholic stuff...is simply no music, and is a disgrace to the name, and certainly a disgrace to the Cathedral of the Holy Name,...this unholy, unheavenly substitute for the grand old Catholic music."[36]

For the most part, the hierarchy ignored the movement and its aims, and the society had no power itself to enforce them, even though the principles it espoused had been specifically mandated by Rome. By the 1890s, New York's Catholic churches still had quartets or double quartets, in many cases backed by mixed choirs, some of which were as large as eighty voices. The major exception was St. Francis Xavier, whose "admirable male-voice choir" featured "unique church music," mainly Gregorian chant.[37]

On 22 November 1903, the feast day of St. Caecilia, Pope Pius X issued his *Motu Proprio* on church music, affirming the principles of the society (including the controversial ban on women in the organ- and choirloft). Although the encyclical was no more successful in

---

[35] Ronald Damian, "A Historical Study of the Cæcilian Movement in the United States" (DMA diss., Catholic University, 1984) 19–23.

[36] Damian, "Cæcilian Movement," 38.

[37] Livingstone, *Sun's Guide*, 265–66.

gaining conformity to its directives than the Caecilians had been, Singenberger determined that the society had accomplished its purpose. Accordingly, no more conventions were held.[38]

Lutheran and Reformed Musical Renewal

At the same time, the Lutherans in America were undergoing a recovery of their historic doctrine and practice, similar to that of the Episcopalians. A number had been reminded of their traditions by the influx of traditionalist European immigrants into New York, Pennsylvania, and the Midwest. These immigrants had no experience with, and little sympathy for, the shifting winds of American Protestantism that had characterized most of the century. Under their influence, Lutheranism turned away from the revivalism that had threatened to submerge its distinctiveness and returned to its historical roots. After 1850, stained glass, altar crosses, and paintings increasingly appeared in Lutheran church design, even as kneeling and chanting reappeared in worship.[39]

Similarly, the German Reformed Church was moving away from the emotional and experiential ethos that characterized general Protestant worship in the wake of the early nineteenth-century revivals and attempting to move toward a more formal liturgical tradition based on history. The movement began in the 1840s, spearheaded by two professors at the denomination's seminary at Mercersburg, Pennsylvania: American-born theologian John Williamson Nevin (1803–1886) and Swiss-born historian Philip Schaff (1819–1893). The pair shared in common with their Oxford-movement contemporaries a respect for historically and theologically informed worship and a certain empathy with Roman Catholicism.[40]

---

[38] Damian, "Cæcilian Movement," 84–86.

[39] On the Lutheran controversy of the period, see E. Clifford Nelson, *The Lutherans in North America* (Philadelphia: Fortress Press, 1980) 210–51. The best comprehensive study of the phenomenon as a whole is Ralph Gerald Gay, "A Study of the American Liturgical Revival, 1825–1860" (Ph.D. diss., Emory University, 1977) 98–99.

[40] Gay, "A Study of the American Liturgical Revival," 116–39. For a general overview of the Mercersburg movement and theology, see Paul K. Conkin, *The*

The renewed interest in tradition and ceremony fueled changes in congregational hymnody as Protestant denominations sought to recover their own artistic and historical heritage and to borrow, sometimes eclectically, from others' traditions. Several denominations issued new hymnals with a breadth of material absent from earlier collections.[41] Chorales appeared in more American collections along with their tunes. Musical figures like John Sullivan Dwight and W. Eugene Thayer came out squarely for their adoption as superior to metrical psalmody and its tunes, especially those adapted from secular music. Thayer, who had received a goodly amount of his training in Berlin, was especially vocal.[42]

In 1860, the Pennsylvania Ministerium had issued an English version of the 1748 Muhlenberg liturgy, and in 1862, it set about the preparation of an English language hymnal to go with it. A year later, several confessional synods, including the Pennsylvania Ministerium, broke away to form the General Council, and in November 1867, the council met in Fort Wayne to prepare a liturgy and worship book. The result was the *Church Book*.[43] The collection contained no music; however, its texts included, in addition to the usual Watts and Wesley texts, a selection of German texts and nearly 200 Latin and Greek texts in translation. A German collection appeared just over a decade later. John Endlich's *Choralbuch mit Liturgie und Chorgesänge*

Uneasy Center: Reformed Christianity in Antebellum America (Chapel Hill: University of North Carolina Press, 1995) 169–76; see also Sidney E. Ahlstrom, *A Religious History of the American People* (New Haven: Yale University Press, 1972) 615–21.

[41] Perhaps the best resource on the subject is the set of essays collectively titled "A Historical Survey of Christian Hymnody in the United States and Britain," in *The Hymnal 1982 Companion*, ed. Raymond F. Glover (New York: Church Hymnal Corporation, 1990).

[42] See, for instance, Eugene Thayer, "Reform in Church Music," *Dwight's Journal* 40/1025 (31 July 1880): 126–28 and Eugene Thayer, "Reform of Church Music," *Dwight's Journal* 40/1026 (14 August 1880): 132–33.

[43] General Council of the Evangelical Lutheran Church in North America, *Church Book for the Use of Evangelical Lutheran Congregations by Authority of the General Council of the Evangelical Lutheran Church in America* (Philadelphia: Lutheran Book Store, 1868).

zum Kirchenbuch der Allgemeinen Kirchenversammlung contained music as well as text.[44]

From 1855 to 1857, Schaff compiled a new hymnal for the German Reformed churches. The *Deutsches Gesangbuch* contained a fine selection of German hymns and metrical psalmody.[45] It remained in use among German-speaking congregations even after Schaff joined the Presbyterian church in 1862 and left for the faculty of Union Seminary in New York. Sixteen years later, an equally fine English-language Reformed hymnal appeared. *Hymns for the Reformed Church* was edited for the Eastern Synod by Elisha Higbee (1839–1899).[46] It contained the usual texts by Watts and Wesley, but it added to them translations of medieval Latin texts by John Mason Neale (1818–1866) and German chorales translated by Catherine Winkworth (1827–1878). The English-speaking Reformed were less conscious of, or interested in, historical tradition; accordingly, *Hymns for the Reformed Church*, excellent though the collection was, did not gain a significant level of acceptance.

Hymnody

Although metrical psalms remained the officially sanctioned ideal virtually up to the Civil War, in practice, Episcopal hymnody was similar to that which was found in such non-Episcopal collections as Beecher's *Plymouth Collection*, which was compiled for the congregation of Plymouth Church in Brooklyn, and Lowell Mason's *Sabbath Hymn and Tune Book*, which was prepared for the Fifth Avenue Presbyterian Church in New York.[47] These contained mostly

---

[44] Marilyn Kay Stulken, ed., *Hymnal Companion to the Lutheran Book of Worship* (Philadelphia: Fortress, 1981) 95–96; John Endlich, *Choralbuch mit Liturgie und Chorgesänge zum Kirchenbuch der Allgemeinen Kirchenversammlung* (Philadelphia: United Lutheran Publication House, 1879).

[45] Philip Schaff, *Deutsches Gesangbuch* (Philadelphia: Lindsay und Klakiston, 1859).

[46] Elisha Higbee, ed., *Hymns for the Reformed Church in the United States* (Philadelphia: Reformed Church Publication Board, 1874).

[47] Henry Ward Beecher, *Plymouth Collection of Hymns and Tunes* (New York: Barnes, 1855); Lowell Mason, *Sabbath Hymn and Tune Book* (New York: Mason Bros., 1859). For a contemporary view of the *Plymouth Collection*, see n.a., "Congregational

texts by Watts, Wesley, and similar authors, which were set to tunes from the common repertory or well-known adaptations by such composers as Mason and Hastings. In the 1840s and 1850s, Lutheran choral tunes and texts in translation had also come into use, although not necessarily together. Some collections set choral texts to English tunes, rather then their usual ones, and conversely, they used choral tunes for other than their customary texts.[48]

An unofficial Episcopal collection, *Hymns for Church and Home*, appeared in 1860. Prepared by a committee of clergy and laymen, it contained 417 hymns and was intended as a supplement and model for a new official collection.[49] That same year saw perhaps the signal event in Anglican and Episcopal hymnology. In London, the Church of England published *Hymns Ancient and Modern* in 1861, with tunes edited by William H. Monk (1823–1899). Its reception was immediate; in fact, so good was the collection that the compilers of the Lutheran *Church Book* of 1868 drew on it, as did the editors of *The Presbyterian Hymnal.*[50]

Music," *New York Musical World* 16/290 (18 October 1856): 507.

[48] For instance, the text "O Sacred Head," translated by the pastor of Fifth Avenue Presbyterian Church, James Waddell Alexander, appears as 356 of that church's hymnal, Mason's *Sabbath Hymn and Tune Book*, not to its traditional tune, but rather to a metric tune of uncertain pedigree, titled *Canonbury*. The six choral tunes in S. P. Tuckerman's *Trinity Collection*, 273–77, include those that traditionally go with such well-known texts-in-translation as "O Sacred Head" and "A Mighty Fortress"; however, in each case a new text has been fitted: "Send out thy light and truth, O God," to *Ein Feste Burg*; and "From ev'ry earthly pleasure, From ev'ry transient joy," to *O Haupt voll Blut. Jesu Meine Freude* is used twice; one of the texts (273) approaches here and there a very loose transliteration of the German: "Jesu, king of glory,/ Thou whose brow was gory,/ Jesu, look on me./ Ah, my heart desiring,/ Humble yet aspiring,/ Fain would soar to Thee," etc.

[49] George Burgess, ed., *Hymns for Church and Home, Compiled by Members of the Protestant Episcopal Church, as a Contribution to Any Addition that May be Made to the Hymns Now Attached to the Prayer-Book* (Philadelphia: J. B. Lippincott, 1860). See Mason Martens, "Four Centuries of Anglican Hymnody in America," in *Hymnal Studies One: Perspectives on the New Edition* (New York: Church Hymnal Corporation, 1981) 19.

[50] Josepth Tuthill Duryea, The Presbyterian Hymnal (Philadelphia: Presbyterian Board of Publication, 1874).

In 1868, the Episcopal Church's General Convention formed a commission to prepare an official American hymnal. In the meantime, *Hymns Ancient and Modern* was reprinted in this country, and Episcopal bishops were authorized by General Convention to license its use in their parishes pending its completion of the American collection. In 1871, it was determined that the new hymnal, unlike previous collections, would not be bound as a supplement with the *Book of Common Prayer*. A year later, the *Hymnal according to the Use of the Protestant Episcopal Church in the United States* appeared.[51] It contained 520 hymns, which were organized in accordance with the seasons of the church year. Changes and additions in 1874 brought the total to 532.

Unlike *Hymns Ancient and Modern*, no tunes were officially authorized for the American collection; however, publishers were licensed to issue music editions, paying a 10 percent royalty to the church's pension fund. At least five musical editions were published, of which the most widely used was that prepared by the rector and organist of Holy Cross Church in Troy, New York. John Ireland Tucker and William Rousseau's *The Hymnal with Tunes Old and New* went through four subsequent editions, one a year to 1875.[52] "Musical supervision" was credited to William H. Walter (rather than Rousseau himself), and there seems no question that he was the actual editor of the tunes compiled by Tucker and Rousseau.

The 1892 revision raised the number of hymns to 692, once again without official tunes, but with provision for independent musical editions.[53] Some six such were published, including collections by Tucker, Arthur Messiter, and Horatio Parker. Parker's choice of music was severe and his compilation met with little success. Far more eclectic and popular was a collection prepared by Charles L. Hutchins, rector of Grace Church, Medford,

---

[51] Charles H. Hall and S. B. Whitsley, *Hymnal according to the Use of the Protestant Episcopal Church in the United States* (New York: A. S. Barnes, 1872).

[52] John Ireland Tucker and William Rousseau, *The Hymnal with Tunes Old and New* (New York: F. J. Huntington, 1871).

[53] Episcopal Church, *The Church Hymnal Revised and Enlarged* (New York: T. Nelson, 1892).

Massachusetts. Hutchins's volume was highly popular and went through a number of editions even after the Episcopal *Hymnal* of 1916 was supposed to have superseded the 1892 publication.[54]

---

[54] John Ireland Tucker and William W. Rousseau, *The Hymnal Revised and Enlarged as Adopted by the General Convention of the Protestant Episcopal Church in the United States of America in the Year of Our Lord 1892...Modified with Tunes Old and New Including the Morning and Evening Canticles* (New York: various, 1894–1904); A. H. Messiter, *The Hymnal Revised and Enlarged as Adopted by the General Convention of the Protestant Episcopal Church in the United States of America in the Year of Our Lord 1892...Modified with Music as Used in Trinity Church New York* (New York: E. & J. B. Young, 1893); Horatio Parker, *The Hymnal, Revised and Enlarged as Adopted by the Protestant Episcopal Church in the United States of America in the Year of Oour Lord 1892 Including the Morning and Evening Canticles* (New York: Novello, Ewer, & Co., 1903); Charles L. Hutchins, *The Church Hymnal Revised and Enlarged in Accordance with the Action of the General Convention of the Protestant Episcopal Church in the United States of America in the Year of Our Lord 1892 Together with the Morning and Evening Canticles (with Authorized Pointing) with Music.* (Boston: The Parish Choir, 1894–1923). For a full listing, see Raymond F. Glover, *The Hymnal 1982 Companion* (New York: Church Hymnal Corporation, 1990) 670–71.

10.

New Currents in the New Century

Professionalization

Although professional musicians had engaged in church music since Colonial times, church music in America was not a profession in the sense it had been in Europe. There were exceptions, like Edward Hodges at New York's Trinity Church during the mid-nineteenth century, who identified themselves exclusively as church musicians. But even Hodges, whose parish was the wealthiest in America and the *de facto* cathedral of the American Episcopal Church, was forced to depend on private teaching to make ends meet.

But most urban music "professors," as they were often called, counted their stipends for Sunday morning duties at the organ as a steady, if modest, part of their income, and they eked out a living by such additional activities as teaching, performing, and music merchandising. In many cases, they had no particular loyalty to the church they served and moved frequently and at short notice. Consequently, the churches felt no reciprocal loyalty and had no hesitation in making a change if a better prospect or lower honorarium was possible. Ironically, mid-nineteenth-century American culture was self-consciously religious, and church music interested a sufficient number of readers that newspapers and periodicals often commented on Sunday morning music, especially at prominent city churches.

By the late nineteenth century, church music was no longer the primary interest for the musical public or a central activity for many American musicians, performers, and composers. In the years after the Civil War, Americans traveled to Europe, especially Germany, for advanced musical study and returned with the musical tastes of European romanticism. Newly established conservatories and full-time symphony orchestras offered them steady and remunerative employment, enabling them to turn from what had become the backwater of church music. At the same time, the symphonic music those orchestras programmed quickly displaced church music as the focus of public and composer interest in America, much as it had decades earlier in Europe. Concert halls like Carnegie Hall in New York and Symphony Hall in Boston displaced churches that had been the venue for public concerts during much of the nineteenth century. In other words, the musical focus for both audiences and musicians shifted decisively from the church to the concert hall.

In Boston, John Knowles Paine left West Church for Harvard in 1864, after only two years as organist there. In the next generation, Edward MacDowell and Amy Beach had no interest in doing church music as a professional activity, though Beach wrote a good bit of choral music for her own parish, St. Bartholomew's in New York. To be sure, not all of America's leading composers abandoned church work entirely. Chadwick, Foote, and Parker served churches; in fact, Parker wrote some of his best music for the church, but in this he was the exception. Foote's anthems and Chadwick's are of indifferent quality relative to their concert and chamber works.

The greatest American composer of the era, Charles Ives (who was a pupil of Parker's), played the organ in various churches from 1889, when he was fourteen, until 1902, when business success enabled him to give up his Sunday morning obligations at Central Presbyterian Church in New York. By his own admission, Ives the church musician was torn between his inclinations to explore new sounds and his obligation not to upset his congregation's sensibilities. In the end, he opted for the latter course and looked to his teachers—Buck, Shelley, and later Parker—as models for his church music. It may well be an index of his attitude that he left behind numerous manuscripts of choral and organ music he had composed, which were discarded and lost when the church moved to its new edifice on Park Avenue, in 1915. In the final analysis, though, Ives had lost interest in writing church music long before he entered his prime as a composer from 1908 to 1918.[1]

The American Guild of Organists

Meanwhile, church musicians had begun banding together to shore up the prestige of their calling as a profession. The first steps were taken in 1896 with the founding of a society that would certify the proficiency of its members by examination. Gerrit Smith (1885–1912), organist of the South Dutch Reformed Church in New York, had come into contact with the Royal College of Organists while in England during summer 1894 and its system of examinations and certificates.

On his return, he and nineteen other New York City organists met in winter and spring 1896, and on 13 April of that year, they formed the American Guild of Organists: "To advance the cause of worthy church music; to elevate the status of church organists; to increase their appreciation of their responsibilities, duties and opportunities as conductors of worship and to obtain acknowledgement of their positions from the authorities of the Church."[2]

During the remainder of the year, "founders" from several cities were added by vote of the original membership, based on their reputation and accomplishment as perceived by their colleagues. In December, the Guild was chartered by the state of New York to administer examinations and grant certificates; thereafter for some years, membership was by examination to the certificate levels of Associate (AAGO) and Fellowship (FAGO). A Pennsylvania Chapter,

---

[1] Henry and Sidney Cowell, *Charles Ives and His Music* (New York: Oxford University Press, 1969) 43; J. Peter Burkholder, "Ives and the Four Musical Traditions," in *Charles Ives and His World*, ed. J. Peter Burkholder (Princeton: Princeton University Press, 1996) 8–11.

[2] See n.a., "The A.G.O. Chronicles, Part III," *The American Organist* 29/3 (March 1995): 84–88.

centered in Philadelphia, was added in 1902; and a New England Chapter in Boston, in 1905.[3]

Eventually, a non-examination membership category would be added, and certification by examination would no longer be a requirement for guild membership. But in its time the restriction fulfilled an important function. American colleges and universities offered few degree-granting programs in music, let alone church music, and only a small number of organists were able to finish their training with study in Germany or France, or in England if their interest was in church music or boys' choirs. Guild membership by examination certified a level of proficiency in theory as well as organ playing and allowed members to signify that proficiency by adding degree-like letters, English style, after their names. This professional certification by their peers would secure them a measure of recognition and status, like the clergy, in the churches that employed them. As the number of degree-granting academic programs increased over the years, the necessity for guild certification would diminish and a minority of members would take the examinations, but those who took them successfully would continue to be accorded an added measure of prestige and respect by their colleagues in the profession.

An alternative group, the National Association of Organists, was founded in 1908, in Ocean Grove, New Jersey. The association had no examination requirement and thus was able to draw its membership from a far broader base than did the guild. Annual conventions were held at Ocean Grove up to 1915, and thereafter in various cities, as membership increased over a larger geographical area. In 1919, the association adopted as its official journal *The Diapason*, a monthly tabloid founded ten years earlier in Chicago as a periodical aimed primarily at organ builders. In 1935, the association

---

[3] Founders were encouraged to take the examinations, but under no compulsion to because of "the public esteem already enjoyed by those who have a record of years of successful work." Only a handful of founders ever risked that "public esteem" by hazarding the exams, even though there was some pressure to do so as the number of members who were non-founders grew. See Samuel Atkinson Baldwin, *The Story of the American Guild of Organists* (New York: H. W. Gray, 1946).

merged into the American Guild of Organists, and the combined group again adopted *The Diapason* as its official publication.

Choirs and Choral Music

Although church musicians took dynamic strides toward securing professional recognition for their field during the first decade of the twentieth-century, church music itself essentially remained static, maintaining and consolidating both repertoire and trends from the late 1800s. On one hand, quartets and quartet-led choirs remained the musical norm in most urban Protestant and Roman Catholic churches. For most Catholic congregations, the publication of Pope Pius X's *Motu Proprio* had little practical effect. Here and there, a choir of men and boys was formed to supplant the quartet choir, or a handful of urban parishes experimented with chant masses. With few exceptions, however, the American hierarchy opposed, or at best ignored, the encyclical's stringent provisions, and apart from some college chapels and a few progressive parish churches and cathedrals (for the most part in the Midwest, and in areas where ethnic groups with strong musical traditions—Germans, for instance—had settled) who engaged enlightened and educated musicians, there was no discernable change in Catholic church music at the parish level.

Many more Episcopal churches, urban and suburban, had instituted vested choirs of men and boys, although the quality of such groups varied widely. The best of them were to be found in cities, in churches that had established choir schools, or drew their boys from the parish day school. The prejudice against garbing such male choirs in quasi-clerical cottas and cassocks—short white garments over close-fitting black robes—had died out. Vesting mixed choirs, let alone quartets, was somewhat more problematic, however. There was a good bit of resistance from many quarters to "seeing girls and women dressed up in the ecclesiastical attire of men and boys."[4]

---

[4] George Mead, "The More It Changes," *The Diapason* 51/1 (1 December 1959): 6. At the time of the article, Mead was organist and choirmaster of Trinity Church. During the period 1909–1912, he had been a chorister at one of Trinity's smaller chapels, St. Cornelius on Governor's Island. In 1909, Trinity Parish, the wealthiest in the nation, had a total operating budget of about $341,000, of which

The number of such choir schools would decline after mid-century to less than a handful in all the United States, but during the first decades, it was on the rise. In Baltimore, St. Paul's had established its choir and school in the decades after the Civil War under the leadership of its rector, Edward Hodges's son, Dr. J. Sebastian B. Hodges, a composer and musician in his own right. Trinity in New York drew on its school for its choirboys, and Grace Church, New York, exchanged its quartet-led choir for men and boys among much controversy in 1894, at the same time establishing a school for the boys. The newly begun Cathedral of St. John the Divine in New York established its choir of men and boys and English-style choir school as soon as the chancel area of the building was completed in 1901. Eight years later, it moved to put the school on a firm footing by hiring Miles Farrow (1871–1953) away from St. Paul's Church and School in Baltimore. Washington Cathedral started a similar school in 1909. T. Tertius Noble (1867–1953) was recruited from York Minster in 1913 to establish a men-and-boys' choir at St. Thomas in New York, and the school there was opened in 1919. In 1929, the St. Dunstan's School was established in Providence, Rhode Island, to train boys for three of the city's Episcopal churches.[5]

---

music was allotted $63,000, according to Ray Stannard Baker, *The Spiritual Unrest* (New York: Stokes, 1910) excerpted in Robert Cross, ed., *The Church and the City 1865–1910* (New York: Bobbs Merrill, 1967) 79. As late as the turn of the century, Ralph Adams Cram was taking pains in his designs for small Episcopal churches to hide the usual unvested choir from the congregation's view, even when it sang from the chancel rather than a rear gallery. See his *Church Building: A Study of the Principles of Architecture in Their Relation to the Church* (Boston: Small Maynard & Co., 1901) 20.

[5] On American choir schools, see Paul Douglas Criswell, "The Episcopal Choir School and Choir of Men and Boys in the United States: Its Anglican Tradition, Its American Past and Present" (Ph.D. diss., University of Maryland, 1987) 64–80 See also, Leonard Ellinwood, *The History of American Church Music* (New York: Morehouse-Gorham, 1953; repr., New York: Da Capo, 1970) 80. Grace Church, St. Thomas and Washington Cathedral schools are still in operation, though St. Thomas is the only remaining boarding school. St. John-the-Divine did away with its choir of men and boys and turned its choir school into a parish school in 1965. St. Dunstan's school closed after World War II.

Of the group, Noble was by far the most influential. His anthems—with their conservative but strong harmonies; elegant melodies; solid, if typically English, choral unison passages; and effective accompaniments—appealed to competent choirs. His services, broadcast from St. Thomas, soon became the model emulated by many large Episcopal churches and the ideal aspired to by most smaller ones well past mid-century.

Noble was born in 1867, in Bath, and at the age of fourteen, he became organist at All Saints, Colchester. In 1886, he entered the Royal College of Music, where he studied with Charles Villiers Stanford. From 1890 to 1892, he was Stanford's assistant at Trinity College, Cambridge. From 1892 to 1898, he served as organist and choirmaster of Ely Cathedral, and from 1898 to 1912, he served at York Minster, where he revived and conducted the York Music Festival. In 1913, he emigrated to take over the music at St. Thomas and remained there until his retirement in 1943, at age 75 to Rockport, Massachusetts, where he spent the last ten years of his life. During his years in New York, Noble was honored by Columbia University with both the MA (1918) and D.Mus. (1926) degrees. His native England honored him with the Lambeth D.Mus. in 1932. He served on the commissions that prepared both the 1916 and 1940 Episcopal hymnals, and the year of his retirement, he published a book on boy choir training. Although most of his anthems went out of style as years passed, a few—"Grieve not the Holy Spirit," for instance—have held their place in the repertoire.

Noble's influence was limited outside his immediate circle of large parishes, primarily Episcopal. For most Protestant (and Catholic) churches, choir and quartet repertoire remained as they had been in the preceding decades; indeed, for the average choir, there was little change in the music sung from 1900 to the 1930s. Most pieces ranged from simple vernacular style, not far removed from gospel hymns, through orchestral melodies with texts fitted to them, to pieces adapted from or patterned after operatic excerpts by such composers as Gounod. Professionally led choirs in larger and more urbane churches, both mixed and men and boys, sang choruses from oratorios by Mendelssohn and Handel. They also sang pieces by such English musicians as Joseph Barnby, Caleb Simper, J. Varley Roberts, John Henry Maunder, Berthold Tours, and—at a slightly higher level—John Stainer and his predecessor at St. Paul's, John Goss. They sang pieces by their American counterparts: Harry Rowe Shelley, F. Flaxington Harker, and—again, at a somewhat higher level—Dudley Buck.

The best choirs, those with more discerning congregations, turned to such English musicians as Stanford and Charles Wood and to Americans of the level of George Whitefield Chadwick and Horatio Parker. These composers' anthems would hold their place in the repertoire well into the second half of this century, although they would increasingly be supplemented and, in some cases, displaced by the work of younger composers, such as Noble, William C. Macfarlane (1870–1945), Clarence Dickinson (1873–1969), Everett Titcomb (1884–1969), David McK. Williams (1887–1978), and Leo Sowerby (1895–1968).

The only new genre added to the American church choir repertoire during the first third of the century was selected Russian choral literature, adapted for use as anthems in Protestant worship by such musicians as N. Lindsay Norden (1887–1956). A few pieces by Dmitri Bortniansky (1751–1825), music director of the Imperial Chapel, had appeared in nineteenth-century collections.[6] Individual octavos were published after the turn of the century of similar works by Alexei Lvov (1798–1870), Alexander Archangelsky (1846–1924), Alexander Gretchaninoff (1864–1946), and others.

The Russian repertoire was popularized by the concert programs of such touring groups as the Don Cossack Chorus. The style of these pieces especially suited American choirs and congregations. They were chordal rather than contrapuntal, as well as melodic and sectional. The tempi were generally slow, and harmonies were diatonic with octave doublings between men's and women's parts.

---

[6] An arrangement of Bortnianski's "Cherubic Hymn, No. 7" had appeared in Luther O. Emerson's *The Jubilate* (Boston: Oliver Ditson, 1866) 310–11. Actually, it was not until 1880, under Archangelski, that women's voices were used in Russia. See Elwyn A. Weinandt and Robert H. Young, *The Anthem in England and America* (New York: Free Press, 1970) 411–13.

Not only were the pieces themselves generally excellent, but they served to wean choirs and congregations away from the steady diet of vernacular-style sentimental English and American anthems to which they had become accustomed during the last quarter of the century. They aroused at least a measure of interest in unaccompanied music from other periods and places among the more artistically adventuresome groups, especially after touring college choirs made such pieces better known.

The adaptation of secular and concert music to use for choir anthems had its parallel phenomenon in organ repertoire and tonal design. Between 1890 and 1930, transcriptions from the concert and operatic literature were the unvarying staples of organists' repertoire for church and concert, and organs were increasingly designed and built to accommodate the trend. Traditional organ ensemble was attenuated in favor of a collection of varied orchestral voices, distinctive colors in and of themselves but lacking the ability to blend with one another. The trend reached its height in the 1920s, when silent movies were at their height and theater organs became the public's standard for proper organ tone.

Organ repertoire was of far less concern to a number of trained church musicians than the anthems and hymns used even in some of the largest churches. Clearly, professional prestige was at some level connected with the quality of the music being performed. Church musicians could not expect to receive the respect accorded to their colleagues on the concert stage unless they worked with a correspondingly good repertoire. Educated church musicians, particularly those who had studied in Europe, had become familiar with the sacred literature from various periods in Western music history, and many (although by no means all) were inclined to look to that literature as the core repertoire for American choirs and the proper model for American church music composers.

Hymnody and Hymnal Revision

The strongest trend in mainstream Protestant hymnody during the early decades of the twentieth century was consolidation. The phenomenon is clearly to be seen in the several denominational hymnals that were published during that time. On the one hand, each collection reflected the musical tradition of its denomination; on the other, the hymnals borrowed from one another's tradition to a greater or lesser degree.[7] In general, all drew in differing proportions on a collective repertoire consisting of metrical psalmody tunes and texts, eighteenth- and nineteenth-century English hymnody including chant tunes and translations of early Greek and Latin hymns, German chorales in translation, and a handful of favorite gospel hymns, which were so well loved that even in relatively formal and urbane denominations, not even the most ardent disciples of Davison's principles could suppress them.[8]

The earliest major revision was that of the Episcopal *Hymnal*. Having decided to go forward with the revision in 1910, the General Convention established a joint commission in 1913 to undertake the work. A collection of 561 texts appeared in 1916; and in 1918, *The New Hymnal* was issued, the first of the denomination to contain tunes along with the texts. Overall, *The New Hymnal* made no effort to hide its distinctly English roots or its editors' preference for the ideal of Victorian cathedral-style choir hymns, tunes with a range and of a difficulty such that most congregations would be discouraged from attempting to sing them. But it also contained a number of German chorales as harmonized by Johann Sebastian Bach and with texts in the excellent Catherine Winkworth translations.

The editorial committee included T. Tertius Noble and Horatio Parker, who also wrote several of the tunes. Yet another contributor

---

[7] The Hymn Society was founded in 1922 with the purpose of fostering the study, writing, and singing of hymns. Its quarterly journal has become a prime resource for students of hymnody.

[8] Among the most resistant and durable, "What a Friend We Have in Jesus," and "He Leadeth Me." For an excellent, brief study of American hymnody, in the early twentieth century, see David Farr, "Protestant Hymn Singing in the United States, 1916–1943: Affirming an Ecumenical Heritage," in *The Hymnal 1982 Companion*, ed. Raymond F. Glover (New York: Church Hymnal Corporation, 1990) 505–24. A less substantial but nevertheless helpful survey of hymnals during the first half of the twentieth century may be found in Talmadge W. Dean, *A Survey of Twentieth Century Protestant Church Music in America* (Nashville: Broadman, 1988) 88–138.

and member of the committee was a priest, musician, and author, whose influence would be felt on Episcopal church music for well over a generation. Winfred Douglas (1867–1944) was born in Oswego, New York, and graduated from Syracuse University in 1891. After a year as organist and choirmaster at Zion and St. Timothy's in New York, however, he was forced to move to Colorado for his health. He was ordained a priest in the Episcopal Church in 1899, and between 1903 and 1906, he studied church music in Europe, especially chant. In 1907, he became a canon at St. Paul's Cathedral, Fon du Lac, Wisconsin, where he remained until 1934, when he took a similar post at St. John's Cathedral, Denver. Douglas was a major figure, not only in church music, but also in liturgics and education. A fellow of the American Ecclesiological Society, Douglas represented the high church, ritualist wing of Episcopalianism. He lectured widely, and his book *Church Music in History and Practice* became a standard resource in the field.[9]

The General Convention of 1937 resolved to revise the hymnal yet again. A larger commission including Douglas, David McK. Williams, and Leo Sowerby was instituted to prepare the edition, and their work produced what is probably the best-known collection of the century, known as *The Hymnal 1940*.[10] For over forty years, the book was a standard against which new editions of other major denominational hymnals measured themselves. Though more eclectic than its 1916 predecessor, its 600 hymns and service music were also drawn heavily from the English repertoire; however, there were fewer Victorian cathedral hymns, and many of the bellicose texts in vogue during the World War I years, when the earlier hymnal was compiled, were dropped.

Louis Benson's 1911 edition of *The Hymnal* for the Presbyterian Church was superseded by Clarence Dickinson's edition of 1933. The book contained chants, traditional English hymns, metrical

---

[9] Winfred Douglas, *Church Music in History and Practice* (New York: Scribner, 1937); Episcopal Church, *The Hymnal 1940 Companion* (New York: Church Pension Fund, 1949) was dedicated to Douglas's memory.

[10] The book actually appeared in 1943.

psalmody, and German chorales, again in Winkworth translations. Unlike the Episcopal hymnal, there were no "cathedral" hymns. The book went through nineteen printings in the next ten years and remained in use until 1955, when it was superseded with a hymn collection prepared jointly under the sponsorship of several Presbyterian and Reformed groups.

During the early years of the century, American Lutherans were divided into a number of synods along ethnic lines and had several service books and hymnals. Not until 1945 did work begin on a collection, and by 1958, the year the *Service Book and Hymnal* was published, eight of the synods had merged into two. The new volume, about 1,000 pages, contained 602 hymns and chants of the liturgy. It drew tunes from ethnic folk songs, plainsong, and English tunes and included a heavy concentration of traditionally Lutheran chorale melodies and texts.

Evangelical Hymnody

Among independent Protestant congregations—especially numerous in the South, Midwest, and West—hymnal repertoire assumed a far different cast. Gospel hymns, for the most part excluded from mainstream denominational hymnals, constituted the largest proportion of their contents. Hymns from the late-nineteenth-century revivals were augmented with new favorites from later revivals by evangelists following in the steps of Dwight L. Moody. Of this group, the most important was William A. (Billy) Sunday (1862–1935), a player for the Chicago White Sox who had been converted in 1886 and gave up baseball for the sawdust trail five years later. Sunday was a keen student of Moody's techniques and combined the latter's evocation of sentiment with the physical exhortations of a Charles Finney. With his 1917 campaign in New York City, Sunday became famous.

Early in his career, he had teamed up with Charles Alexander (1867–1920), a veteran of evangelistic campaigns who had a special talent for training quickly and conducting large choirs that were formed locally and for the particular set of meetings. But Sunday's most important musical partner was Homer Rodeheaver (1880–1955), who joined his team in 1909.

Rodeheaver was a native of Ohio whose family had moved to Tennessee shortly after his birth. He worked in area coal mines and attended the camp meetings that had never died out in the area. He played the trombone in a local band. He had a special talent for galvanizing a crowd; in fact, his one year at Ohio Wesleyan University, 1902, was distinguished chiefly by his activity as a cheerleader. From 1903 to 1909, he worked with the evangelist William E. Biederwolf, leading the music before and during meetings.

Sunday sought him out in 1909 to replace Alexander as his music director. Over the years, Rodeheaver sang, played his trombone, and led Sunday's crowds in singing. He popularized such hymns as "The Old Rugged Cross" (for many years before the relatively recent rediscovery of "Amazing Grace" by mainstream churchgoers and hymnal editors, voted the favorite American hymn), "In the Garden," "Brighten the Corner," and "Since Jesus Came into my Heart." In 1910, Rodeheaver Ackley Co. began publishing collections of such hymns. By 1945, it had issued nearly 150 collections and books. The firm was the largest publisher of gospel music until it was bought by Word, Inc. of Waco, Texas.[11]

African-American Hymnody

Through most of the nineteenth century, African-American churches made heavy use of white metrical psalmody and hymnody after the model of Richard Allen's *A Collection of Hymns* 1801. Indeed, the archaic practice of lining out "Dr. Watts Hymns," as such music was called, persisted in some African-American churches into the 1920s. Less use was made of spirituals after the Civil War probably because they were a too poignant reminder of the days before emancipation.[12]

By the end of the century, the preferred hymnal among African-American Baptist congregations was W. H. Sherwood's 1893

---

[11] See Dean, *Survey*, 66–77.

[12] Stephen A. Marini, *Sacred Song in America: Religion, Music and Public Culture* (Urbana: University of Illinois Press, 2003) 109.

collection, *The National Harp of Zion*. At the same time, a distinctively
black gospel stream was emerging with such figures as Charles Albert
Tindley (1859–1933), a Methodist preacher in Maryland and
Pennsylvania. His *New Songs of Paradise* (1916), issued at the dawn of
the jazz age, offered an energetic, exciting alternative both to
sentimental white gospel and the careful concert arrangements of
spirituals of such groups as the Fisk Jubilee Singers and Tuskegee
College Choir.

Meanwhile, the Holiness movement was providing yet another
stream of gospel hymnody. Holiness had its origins in the writings of
John Wesley, though the formal movement dates to the years
immediately after the Civil War. During the 1890s, it split over the
charismatic issues of "speaking in tongues" and "spirit-filled
songs"—essentially, singing in tongues. Over the next twenty years,
more than twenty denominations resulted. Whites separated into
Nazarenes and Assemblies of God. Black charismatics established the
Church of God in Christ; conservatives formed the Church of Christ.
Published in 1899, the first edition of their *Jesus Only* song book
included a large number of gospel songs by the evangelist Charles
Price Jones (1865–1949). Supplements to the collection culminated
in the *Jesus Only Songs and Hymns Standard Hymnal* of 1940.[13]

The charismatic Holiness wing became the beginnings of the
Pentecostal movement, particularly during a three-year interracial
revival meeting held in a former Methodist church on Azusa Street in
Los Angeles, beginning in April 1906. The rhythmic movement of
gospel—its sheer physicality—suited the physical dimension of
charismatic worship, both black and white. The Church of God in
Christ embraced the spontaneity of praise and "spirit" songs. It did
not publish an official hymnal until *Yes Lord!* in 1982.[14]

---

[13] Jon Michael Spencer, *Black Hymnody: A Hymnological History of the African-American Church* (Knoxville: University of Tennessee, 1992) 101–104.

[14] Virginia Lieson Brereton, "White Folks 'Get Happy': Mainstream America Discovers the Black Gospel Tradition," in *Wonderful Words of Life*, ed. Richard J. Mouw and Mark A. Noll (Grand Rapids: Eerdmans, 2004) 171; Spencer, *Black Hymnody*, 140–43, 158.

Black gospel reached its height with the work of Thomas A. Dorsey (1899–1993), leader of the Chicago Gospel Choral Union. Dorsey's hymns employed blues and jazz devices and traditional black call-and-response, sung by choir and congregation to free accompaniments on the piano and Hammond organ. The resulting effect has the highly emotional tenor of both blues and its offshoot: early rock 'n' roll. Dorsey, who founded his own publishing house, wrote about 1,000 gospel pieces. "Precious Lord, take my hand" and "Peace in the Valley" quickly crossed the color line during the 1930s, thanks to recordings. Dorsey's later hymns incorporated traits of jazz, swing, and blues, as well as the music of holiness groups, whose worship involved physical activity, cries, and dancing to popular-style music played on such instruments as piano and percussion.[15]

Professional Church Music Training

Even though the repertoire in mainstream Protestant churches was by no means as dynamic as in independent churches during the early decades of the twentieth century, changes were occurring that would begin to be felt especially in the 1930s. Probably the most important of these changes was a concerted move toward the establishment of collegiate-level training programs in church music, out of which would come the full-time Minister of Music on the staff of many large Protestant churches.

By the mid-1930s, New York had become the center of American church music. Not only was it the site of guild headquarters, but as the largest and wealthiest city in the United States, it also had the largest number of wealthy churches, outstanding choirs, and top-flight professionals to lead and accompany them. Perhaps most important of all, New York was the home of Union Theological Seminary with its School of Sacred

---

[15] The definitive study of Gospel is Horace Clarence Boyer, *How Sweet the Sound: The Golden Age of Gospel* (Washington DC: Elliott and Clark, 1995). The best brief source, on which (as can clearly be seen) I have relied heavily, is Paul Oliver, "Gospel," in *The New Grove Gospel, Blues and Jazz* (New York: Macmillan, 1986) 190–215.

Music, at which a large number of organists and choirmasters from the city's most prominent churches taught.

The school had been founded by Clarence Dickinson (1873–1969) and his wife, Helen Adell (Snyder) Dickinson (1875–1957). A native of Lafayette, Indiana, Dickinson had earned master's and doctoral degrees in church music from the School of Music at Northwestern University.[16] After two years of study in France and Germany and nine years at St. James Cathedral in Chicago, he came to New York to take over the music at the Brick Presbyterian Church and at Temple Emanu-El in 1909. On Gerrit Smith's death in 1912, Dickinson succeeded to the instructorship in sacred music at Union Seminary, where his duties involved teaching a course or two, conducting the choir of seminarians, and playing the chapel services. Dickinson steadily enlarged the scope of musical activities at the seminary, and in 1928, he began the School of Sacred Music, which had forty students. The curriculum—leading to masters' and doctoral degrees in sacred music (MSM and DSM)—involved organ and vocal performance, conducting, choral literature and training, theology, and liturgy. The school drew on the regular seminary faculty and church musicians in New York. Dickinson headed the school until his retirement in 1945.[17]

David McK. Williams (1887–1978) was among the prominent church musicians who taught at Union Seminary. Williams was born in Wales, but his family immigrated to Denver when he was an infant. At thirteen, he became organist and choirmaster of St. Paul's in Denver. In 1908, he moved to New York, where he became organist of Grace Church's free chapel. Three years later, he went to Paris, where he studied at the Schola Cantorum under Vincent d'Indy, Louis Vierne, and Charles Marie Widor. In 1914, he was back in New York at the Church of the Holy Communion. In 1920,

---

[16] Northwestern's School of Music, founded by Peter Christian Lutkin in 1896, was one of the earliest in a major university.

[17] On Dickinson and the School of Sacred Music, see David A. Weadon, "Clarence Dickinson (1873–1969) and the School of Sacred Music at Union Theology Seminary in the City of New York (1928–1973)" (Ph.D. diss., Drew University, 1994).

he was appointed organist and choirmaster of St. Bartholomew's Church, where his Sunday morning service music and afternoon oratorio performances with a professional adult choir attracted a good deal of attention. In addition to his work at the seminary, Williams also headed the organ department at Juilliard.

During the next four decades, until it closed its doors in 1973,[18] a casualty of economics—but also the Viet Nam War era's upheavals in religion, society, and culture—the School of Sacred Music conferred a large percentage of the graduate degrees in church music, and its alumni oversaw a disproportionate number of the most active and successful music programs in large, urban, and suburban Protestant churches nationwide.

Union drew its students from the steadily increasing number of undergraduate majors in organ and church music instituted by colleges and conservatories in the years after World War I. Special undergraduate programs were established and were aimed at providing church musicians for particular denominations. St. Olaf College in Northfield, Minnesota, established a curriculum dedicated to the training of Lutheran church musicians, and in 1918, the Pius X School of Liturgical Music was founded for Catholic musicians at Manhattanville College of the Sacred Heart.

Mid-Twentieth-Century Composers

Although the concentration of churches in New York, as well as Union Seminary, made it the center of church music activity during the period, a considerable amount of activity was occurring in other metropolitan areas; indeed, some of the leading composers of church music in the first half of the twentieth century worked outside America's largest city. Leo Sowerby (1895–1968) was a native of Grand Rapids, Michigan, who spent most of his life in Chicago. He graduated from the American Conservatory, where he studied piano with Percy Grainger; he was self-taught in organ. After a term as an army bandmaster during World War I, he was awarded the *Prix de*

---

[18] For all practical purposes, the school and its faculty removed to New Haven as the Yale Institute of Sacred Music.

Rome and studied composition in Europe. He returned to Chicago and the faculty of the American Conservatory in 1925, and a year later became organist and choirmaster of St. James Cathedral. Like Horatio Parker, Sowerby composed a good deal of concert music, especially during his younger years. His *Canticle of the Sun*, on the St. Francis of Assisi text, won the Pulitzer Prize in 1946.

Sowerby is best known for his church music, much of which remains in the active repertoire of capable choirs. His style was distinctive and sharply advanced compared to that of Noble or Williams. He placed elegant melodies over modal and chromatic harmonies, sometimes approaching the popular idioms of the time, even jazz and blues. In Sowerby's hands, such materials were always subtle, finely crafted, and sensitively handled. In retrospect, Sowerby's is best seen as a distinctively American idiom in the manner of a Copland, Ives, or even Gershwin. His materials were traditionally European, but their use was not. In his later years, Sowerby's interests turned more toward church music and away from the concert hall. In 1962, he retired from St. James and removed to Washington, DC, where he founded and directed the College of Church Musicians at the National Cathedral for the rest of his life.[19]

Everett Titcomb (1884–1969) spent his whole career in the greater Boston area. He was born in Amesbury, Massachusetts, and studied with Samuel Brenton Whitney, organist and choirmaster of the Church of the Advent in Boston. His first position was in his home church, St. James in Amesbury; however, in 1903, he moved to Boston and became organist and choirmaster of the Church of the Messiah in Auburndale, and then for a year in 1909, left Boston to serve at Christ Church, Andover. Titcomb's inclinations were strongly toward the music of high-church ritualism, and from 1910, he was able to give full vent to them. That year he was appointed

---

[19] On Sowerby, see Francis J. Crociata, "Leo Sowerby," *American Organist* 29/5 (May 1995): 50–53; and Lester H. Groom, "Leo Sowerby Remembered," *The American Organist* 29/5 (May 1995): 54–55; B. Wayne Hinds, "Leo Sowerby: A Biography and Descriptive Listing of Anthems" (EdD diss., Geo. Peabody [Vanderbilt], 1972); Raymond Durwald Jones, "Leo Sowerby: His Life and his Choral Music" (Ph.D. diss., University of Iowa, 1973).

organist and choirmaster of Boston's Church of St. John the
Evangelist, the church of the Cowley Fathers' order. He remained at
St. John's for the rest of his career, composing, teaching, and writing
on church music. He served on the church music faculties at Boston
University and at New England Conservatory.

Titcomb's music, like his training, was far less sophisticated than
Sowerby's; as a result, it has not held as prominent a place in the
repertoire, with such notable exceptions as his transcendently lovely
short motet "I will not leave you comfortless," his anthems "Jesus,
Name of Wondrous Love" and "Behold Now, Praise the Lord," and
his organ paraphrase on the Gregorian *Regina Coli*. Titcomb's style is
sectional, with abrupt changes and frequent cadences. Within
sections, melodies are simply structured and harmonized. The result
is naïve and scarcely arresting; yet the music lies well for the voice
and is extremely effective, even when done by a choir of limited
capability.[20]

Multiple Choir Systems

Williams, Sowerby, and Titcomb were atypical not only in their
talents but in the kinds of music programs over which they presided
in their own churches. For most large Protestant churches, the major
trend was toward the development of a graded multiple choir system.
Indeed, the Union Seminary School of Sacred Music's closest
undergraduate counterpart was Westminster Choir College, founded
in Dayton, Ohio, in 1926, by John Finlay Williamson (1887–1964).
Williamson was director of music at Westminster Presbyterian
Church in Dayton, where he had established such a graded choir
system with separate choirs for younger and older children, youth,
and adults. Westminster Choir School was established as part of
Williamson's program at Westminster, hence its name. The school
offered a three-year program in choir training techniques at all levels
and granted a diploma.

---

[20] On Titcomb, see Susan Ouellette Armstrong, "The Choral and Organ Music
of Everett Titcomb," *The American Organist* 23/4 (April 1989): 64–69.

In 1929, Williamson moved the school to Ithaca, New York, where it became a full-fledged college, chartered to grant the Bachelor of Music degree; in 1932, Westminster Choir College moved again, this time to its present campus in Princeton, New Jersey. Graduate programs and curricula in other areas such as music education were added; however, Westminster's strength and fame has always rested on its programs in church music, especially its training in the development of multiple choir systems.[21]

Although graded multiple choir programs have held their place in many large churches, the movement probably reached its peak during the 1950s, when church membership and attendance were at their highest. The Chorister's Guild was founded in 1949 to support such children's choirs, and a number of books on multiple choir training and administration appeared around the same time. The most successful of these was certainly Donald D. Kettring's *Steps toward a Singing Church*, describing the manner by which the author built and administered such programs at a number of churches he served.[22]

Children's choirs in such graded systems should not be confused either with boys' choirs or with the charity school-based children's choirs of the eighteenth and early nineteenth centuries. Children's choirs in multiple graded systems provided a musical outlet and musical training for children and youth from the congregation, often aimed at preparing future members of the "flagship" adult choir. At least as important, such youth and younger children's groups (all the way down to "cherub choirs" for pre-schoolers) provided a church-centered social outlet for their members.

Early children's and boys' choirs had no such purposes. Rather, they were ends in and of themselves; that is, they existed to lead the

---

[21] See Charles Harvey Schisler, "A History of Westminster Choir College, 1926–1973" (Ph.D. diss., Indiana University, 1976). Westminster is now the school of music of Rider University. On Williamson, see David A. Wehr, "John Finley Williamson (1887–1964): His Life and Contribution to Choral Music" (Ph.D. diss., University of Miami, 1971).

[22] Donald D. Kettring, *Steps toward a Singing Church* (Philadelphia: Westminster Press, 1948).

congregational psalmody or to sing the service music after the European or English cathedral model. As such, they fulfilled their full purpose in the Sunday morning service. Occasional contrary rhetoric and incidental practical outcomes notwithstanding, such choirs did and do not exist explicitly to provide musical education for the children who sang in them, and they were not an outlet for recreation under church auspices.

Equally significant, early children's choirs and boys' choirs in the late nineteenth and twentieth centuries sang the same repertoire that contemporary adult choirs did: canticles, chants, hymns, and anthems. Other than the gospel hymns of the Sunday school movement, no special pieces were composed or adapted for children's groups. Graded children's choirs, by contrast, were a ready and well-funded market for a special repertoire, and publishers moved to supply that repertoire as the movement grew. Pieces for treble voices in one to four parts, in varying degrees of difficulty and often of indifferent quality or worse, were and are composed, adapted, and arranged specifically with various ages and competence levels of children's choirs in mind.

Critiquing Church Music

Perhaps the most articulate, acerbic, and influential critic of American church music during the first half of the century was Archibald T. Davison (1883–1961). Davison had studied at Harvard with John Knowles Paine and gone on to earn the first Ph.D. in musicology conferred by an American university (Harvard) with a dissertation on the music of Claude Debussy. As a professor at Harvard, he continued his original research in music history,[23] but he also had charge of the Harvard-Radcliffe choir and took an active interest in the problem of American church music and how to

---

[23] One major effort was the two-volume anthology of pieces from classical Greek music through the mid-eighteenth century that Davison prepared in collaboration with Willi Apel, *Historical Anthology of Music* (Cambridge: Harvard University Press, 1949–1950) better known to a generation of undergraduate music history students and their teachers as *HAM*.

improve it, and in 1933, he set forth his views in a widely read and influential book *Protestant Church Music in America*.[24]

For Davison, proper worship, regardless of denomination, was mystical and unworldly; as such, he allowed no room for the personal, experiential, emotional, or the sentimental. Music took on the nature of a sacrifice for the glory of God. Thus, it had to be the finest that could be offered, of the highest quality, and at the same time devoid of secular connotations like the strong rhythms and chromatic harmonies associated with secular music. Solos, duets, trios, and quartets, even in the course of an anthem, were to be ruthlessly suppressed. Davison's fine sieve screened out favorite hymns of the time and anthems that were well-loved staples of most church choirs' libraries.

Davison's ideal in choir repertoire was unaccompanied literature, primarily from before 1700, supplemented with later pieces in the same style and works from the Russian repertoire. Similarly, proper congregational song was to be primarily German chorales, along with some of the more austere early (and contemporary neo-classic) English hymnody.

On one hand, Davison's analysis of the situation, though cutting and severe, was largely accurate. On the other hand, his remedies, as he himself recognized, were for the most part difficult, given the resistance they invariably met in congregations. Still, he yielded nothing:

> The good that has transpired has come from individuals largely endowed with *faith, courage, persistence*, and a *clear purpose*. These individuals working quietly, in a small way, and without the handicap of publicity, have given demonstrable proof of the superiority of a high standard over a low one. It is not through the shirkers or the discouraged or the indifferent that improvement will come, but by the efforts of those sincere and consecrated persons who realize that

---

[24] Archibald T. Davison, *Protestant Church Music in America* (Boston: E. C. Schirmer, 1933).

"good" is better than "poor," and that those who come after may achieve the "best."[25]

Davison's views on church music became the ideal, and many young musicians of the next generation struggled—often with disastrous results for their careers—to implement them at least to some degree. Marginally more success was gained in improving the repertoire of choirs (at least in churches with a representation of educated and sophisticated individuals in the congregation) than in congregational hymnody, where personal associations with certain hymns by individuals invariably frustrated all but the most tactful and gradual reforms.

In 1952, Davison again surveyed the church music landscape, once more with a marked lack of enthusiasm for the seeming improvements that had transpired since his first book. For the most part, he reiterated his objections from twenty years earlier, calling the run of anthems and church music in general routine, mild, and essentially a subset of nineteenth-century vernacular music. He wrote:

> The present state of church music is one to call forth neither pride nor optimism. Representing an amorphous confusion of styles and practices, resolutely excluded from serious thought, beset by whims of personal preference and subjected to the demands of unreasoned purpose, church music, both as an art and as an accompaniment to worship, has become a self contradiction.... It no longer responds to the influences which affect the rest of music, but has fallen into a sleep from which there is, surely no prospect of an early awakening.

But if Davison was still a cynic, he was also still a mystic: "The finest church music suggests the church and nothing outside of

---

[25] Davison, *Protestant Church Music in America*, 3–4.

it...one of the thin places where the other world shows through."[26]
The volume concludes with a list of appropriate anthems, again,
primarily unaccompanied repertoire dating from before 1700 and
pieces arranged from the Russian liturgy.

Had a vote been taken, Davison's view would have been shared
by a far smaller group than in 1933. By the 1960s, church work had
been a recognized option within the profession of music for some
years. More churches now offered full-time employment to career
church musicians, and more institutions offered undergraduate and
graduate majors in church music than ever before. More fine church
music by the major composers of the past was now available, and new
music at all levels of difficulty and of considerable quality (if
sometimes uneven inspiration) was available in cheap octavo editions.
In fact, what appeared to be the dawning of a golden age for
professional church music was actually a moment of stability before
the unprecedented and largely unexpected upheaval of the late 1960s
and early 1970s.

---

[26] Archibald T. Davison, *Church Music: Illusion and Reality* (Cambridge: Harvard
University Press, 1952) 81–82, 129–30. This slender book was actually based on
three sets of lectures delivered in 1935, 1940, and 1948. Although the first set of
lectures—and possibly the second—followed too close on the heels of Davison's
earlier book for any significant change in his views to be formed, that he had not only
not moderated those views by the 1948 set and, in fact, reiterated them when he
turned them into a book, over a decade later, is worthy of note and food for thought.

11.

Conflict and Diversity

Any time as unsettled as the second half of the twentieth century presents special problems. Not without reason did Charles Morris title his study of America during the years from 1960 to 1980, *A Time of Passion*.[1] At one level, the period after 1960 is still rather close for any kind of historical perspective. At another, that era was characterized by conflicts and convergence of forces and philosophies such as to yield varied results in church music. The men and women who lived and worked during those years were not unaware of the situation. As early as May 1963, the English clergyman, musician, and scholar of church music Erik Routley (1917–1982) characterized the period presciently, if somewhat optimistically, as an "age of creative conflict":

> In church music, there has been no age so full of surprises, and so full of creative promise, as our own.... Music has at last begun to catch up with the other arts in a process in which for fifty years the visual arts have been in the lead—a process of radical experiment, or deep and ruthless questioning, and of the sacrificial exploration of its relation to

---

[1.]Charles R. Morris, *A Time of Passion: America, 1960–1980* (New York: Penguin, 1986).

life.... Had this book been written even ten years ago, its subject would have been far less interesting.[2]

Perhaps the most significant cultural factor driving the trends of the era was the changing make-up of America's population. The first wave of the post-World-War II "baby boom" generation, habituated to television as its own distinctive medium, came of college age during the 1960s. The sheer number of teenagers—the group increased fifty percent between 1960 and 1970—drove both social and market forces and popular musical tastes, as had no cohort before. The idealism of their youth and their unprecedented media-conditioned awareness focused the weight of their numbers on social issues: justice, civil rights, the environment, and peace—even as the nation became increasingly enmeshed in yet another war, this one of far less moral clarity than the one their fathers fought.

Mainline churches, Protestant and Catholic, felt compelled as never before to address this populous youth culture. In so doing, they ratified and institutionalized its idealism by shifting emphases from the theology of the transcendental that had characterized the previous decade to issues of politics, peace, and civil justice: a newer version, as it were, of what had been called the "Social Gospel" a century before. All seemed to be swept before a generation that was better schooled and healthier than its forbears, made aware by television both of its own market power and of societal inequities, and possessed of the youthful hubris that impelled it to right the wrongs it saw.

Conflict

American religion was also faced with two other phenomena in reaction to the post-war euphoria of the 1950s. American egalitarian pragmatism asserted itself against what was perceived as a decadent and defeated European "elitism." At the same time, American intellectuals—particularly the clergy and theologians—felt a need to compensate in some way for the sense of alienation and

---

[2.] Erik Routley, *Twentieth Century Church Music* (London: Oxford, 1964) 7.

disillusionment with human nature, especially as a greater awareness of such wartime horrors as the Holocaust and nuclear weapons was realized. Here again, a resolute effort to avoid "elitism" on one hand and existential loneliness on the other led to a worship style that deemphasized mysticism, aestheticism, and theological distinctions in favor of social issues, an emphasis on community participation, and an attempt to accommodate a pragmatically broad span of tastes.[3]

Few American church musicians in 1960 could have anticipated the depth and breadth of changes to come over the next two decades. In his New Year's editorial in the guild's official periodical, *The Diapason*, Frank Cunkle exhorted church musicians to strive for even greater artistic quality: "The A.G.O. and this journal are faced with the same necessity; we must not merely hold to our present standards, but must strive to raise them higher."[4] In December that year, *The Diapason* reaffirmed Cunkle's words by publishing a "Guide for Church Music Relations" prepared by the Southern California Chapter of the guild, the purpose of which was to advance church music, in part, "by recommending that high standards in church music be maintained through the use of works that are reverent in both text and music."[5]

Seth Bingham, organist and choirmaster of St. Paul's Chapel at Columbia University, told delegates at the convention of the American Guild of Organists during summer 1960 that he foresaw a "notable advance" and "a bright and shining future" for quality (by which Bingham meant "elite") church music. Crediting the guild examinations for raising standards, he declared, "If our church music

---

[3.]For two distinctly different but nevertheless perceptive views on the changes in worship and music, see Russell Schulz-Widmar, "Hymnody in the United States Since 1950," in *The Hymnal 1982 Companion*, ed. Raymond F. Glover (New York: Church Hymnal Corporation, 1990) 600–30, and Donald P. Hustad, *Jubilate II* (Carol Stream IL: Hope, 1993) 265–71. See also John Ogasapian, "American Guild of Organists Centennial AGO Conventions," *The American Organist* 30/8 (August 1996): 52–55.

[4.]Frank Cunkle, "Looking forward to the Future," *The Diapason* 50/2 (January 1960): 20.

[5.]"California Sends Guide for Church Music Relations," *The Diapason* 51/1 (December 1960): 8.

repertory shows a slow but steady gain in excellence, so also, with some exceptions, do the standards of church performance."[6]

Bingham's New York was the capital of American church music. The finest could be found at any one of a dozen of its large fanes; among the most notable was the great Episcopal cathedral on Morningside Heights, St. John-the-Divine, where Alec Wyton (b.1921) maintained an impeccable level of English cathedral excellence with his choir of men and boys. Not far away from Wyton's St. John-the-Divine was Union Seminary's School of Sacred Music, headed by Dickinson's student, Robert Baker (1916–2005), where some of the finest graduate training in church music was to be had.

Fifteen years later, the School of Sacred Music was gone from Union Seminary,[7] and Alec Wyton and his choir of men and boys from St. John-the-Divine Cathedral and school had become parables for their time and paradigms for the decline of many equally excellent, but far less visible, centers of what had been regarded as fine church music in America.

A similarly profound musico-liturgical change swept Roman Catholicism in the wake of the Second Vatican Council. Even so, in the matter of liturgy and church music, Vatican II was less the cause than an excuse for change. If the council accorded Gregorian chant "pride of place" in Catholic music, such was honored more in the breach than in the observance. Chant was accorded neither pride nor place among those who sought to be either progressive or trendy. Indeed, the rush to use vernacular liturgies begged the question of adapting chant from the Latin as a practically viable,[8] if not historically faithful, compromise, or of using chant with its original

---

[6] Seth Bingham, *The Diapason* 51/10 (September 1960): 26–27.

[7] As noted above, the school did not go out of existence, but rather it moved to Yale. But the point is not measurably lessened thereby. The School of Sacred Music—and by extension, the professional study of church music—would henceforth no longer have an unassailable and distinctive place at one of America's most visible institutions for the training of Protestant ministers.

[8] It had, after all, been used in vernacular translation by Anglican and Episcopal churches for a century, more or less.

Latin texts, satisfying the rubric by providing translations for the congregation to accommodate the goal of full participation by the laity.

In fact, most American Catholic churches, and the hierarchy as well, had long resisted both chant and the traditional Catholic corpus of continental polyphony. Not even the Caecilian movement of the nineteenth century, which had set forth an ideal of Catholic liturgical practice at least at some level, had availed much in the end.

Vernacular Styles

Outside the Roman Catholic Church, straws of upheaval were in the wind well before Bingham's overconfident prediction to 1960 convention attendees, let alone Routley's prophetic words. Some years earlier there had circulated among some Episcopal clergy and musicians a tape recording of a peculiar piece of service music from England, indifferently performed by a nondescript group of amateurs to the throbbing accompaniment of an electric organ. Composed by an English priest named Geoffrey Beaumont, who called it "A Twentieth-Century Folk Mass," the piece was repetitious[9] and full of musical clichés. Nevertheless, it caused a brief stir out of proportion to its substance. Indeed, Alec Wyton made mention of the setting at the close of his address to the 1959 convention of the Royal Canadian College of Organists, in which he pleaded for a major contemporary composer to turn his or her talents to writing church music:

> At this time a too-large number of people are listening to a work known as "A Twentieth Century Folk Mass," a setting of the Anglican Eucharistic Liturgy by an English priest, designed originally to bring recalcitrant teen-agers into church. The embarrassment of this work is compounded by a recent announcement that the composer (if "composition"

---

[9] In fact, the repetitiousness was intentional. Beaumont intended the piece to be immediately singable by a congregation, without rehearsal. Accordingly, its structure consisted in the main of short lines sung by a soloist ("cantor" in the current parlance) and then repeated by the whole group.

can accurately be said to be the process by which such a setting came into existence) has resigned his London parish to devote his whole time to the type of church music with which his name has become associated.[10]

Routley first saw the score in proof during the last week of 1955, and he quickly recognized the flaw in Beaumont's explication of his purpose in writing the piece. Beaumont had written in the preface to the score: "The theory behind this setting is that the music used at the Holy Eucharist in apostolic days was the normal music of the day, and only became 'church music' when it arrived with definite church associations in Western Europe, where it developed itself into the plainsong we know." Rather than take the easy shot at Beaumont's misapprehensions about plainsong history and origins. Routley met his thesis head-on:

> Nothing—this is the point here, and it is pivotal to the whole of our argument on this subject—was further from the apostolic mind than that Christians should make any concessions whatever to the "normal" and "everyday" standards of the non-Christian world.... What we can be assured of is that although the idea of bringing the popular music of secular life into the church may nowadays be an admirable one, it was not an apostolic one.
>
> Still less was it a likely notion to be entertained by the church of the fourth and fifth centuries, when the Fathers of the Church consistently wrote of church music as a thing that must be separated from pagan standards.[11]

Notwithstanding either the criticisms of Wyton and Routley or the hackneyed and insipid character of Beaumont's "mass," it served

---

[10] Alec Wyton, "English Church Music: Can the Golden Age Return," *The Diapason*, 51/7 (June 1960): 8–9.

[11] Routley, *Twentieth Century Church Music*, 152–53. The chapter is titled "The Vexation of 'Pop.'"

to energize a measure of interest among at least some professional church musicians in the possibilities of vernacular and other non-traditional styles of music in worship. Five years later, Wyton himself was exploring the possibilities of vernacular church music style.

The 1962 convention of the American Guild of Organists included a program called "Frontiers in Worship" and characterized it in the program as an "experiment in jazz." *The Diapason* reported, "No single program of the week was so controversial, so much discussed and so misunderstood." The music itself was well received; however, its effect was marred by the poor choice of texts and prayers that accompanied it.[12]

The "Frontiers" experiment had been a special event in the 1962 convention, but in 1964, the vernacular movement made its appearance in the hitherto circumspect environs of the guild service, a convention event traditionally exemplifying the elite in professional state-of-the-art church music. The combined choirs of men and boys of two Philadelphia area churches and New York's Cathedral of St. John-the-Divine, under the direction of newly elected guild president Alec Wyton, presented the première of Malcolm Williamson's *Ascendit Deus*, a cantata in commercial vernacular style that offended a large number of the attendees. One reviewer characterized it as "a cheap imitation of the Beaumont," an especially damning indictment since Williamson, unlike Beaumont, was a recognized composer who had produced a respectable body of work in a progressive and formal idiom. Although Williamson's cantata, like Beaumont's folk "mass," had but a fleeting moment in the musical arena, its introduction into the heretofore elite and exclusive precincts of a guild convention service served to focus the church music profession's attention on the issue of vernacular musical styles in worship.[13]

---

[12] *The Diapason* 53/9 (August 1962): 24.

[13] *The American Organist* 47/8 (August 1964): 19. Routley, cognizant of Williamson's talents as a composer, preferred to consider the idiom "Mr Williamson's Dialect," (as he titled the chapter in *Twentieth Century Church Music* (176). In other words, as he put it, Williamson's vernacular style reminded Routley of a "good writer of English...writing in dialect." (182).

Wyton, conductor of that controversial performance of the Williamson, was and is clearly one of the major figures in mid- and late-twentieth-century church music. Born in London and educated at Oxford, he came to the United States in 1950, served in the Midwest, and was appointed organist and choirmaster at St. John-the-Divine in 1954. Ten years later, he was elected to a five-year term as president of the guild, heretofore a largely ceremonial office.

A highly respected musician, composer, philosopher, essayist of church music, and a deeply committed man, Wyton came to see the customary barrier between sacred and secular musical styles as permeable and sometimes even illusory. During his twenty-year tenure at St. John-the-Divine, the repertoire ran the gamut from Byrd and Gibbons to Sowerby; Wyton's own pieces; the music of Duke Ellington; and pieces by Galt McDermott, composer of the Broadway rock musical *Hair*, whose mass setting, used in 1972 during a Eucharist at the cathedral, included a rock band.[14]

As president, Wyton led the guild down a number of new paths. If those paths were not always such that all members could follow him, his vision of appropriate church music one that not all members could share, and his vision and flexibility of a kind that not all members could affirm, nobody doubted his commitment and sincerity. And few could resist his infectious good will to all, especially those who disagreed most vehemently with him and the direction in which he had taken the guild and mainline American church music.[15]

Some of the best attempts at innovative worship music took the idiom of fine jazz. Both jazz geniuses, Edward Kennedy "Duke" Ellington (1899–1974) and Dave Brubeck (1920–) wrote sacred music. Indeed, Brubeck's oratorio *The Light in the Forest* was featured at the 1968 guild convention. The success of Brubeck's work among the traditionally oriented church musicians in attendance was more a

---

[14.]See Alec Wyton, "Twentieth Century American Church Music," in *Duty and Delight: Routley Remembered*, ed. Robin Leaver, James Litton, and Carlton Young (Carol Spring: Hope, 1985) 83.

[15.] In retirement as this is written, Wyton still casts a shadow.

function of its quality than its idiom. Jazz services of lesser quality fared far less well in similar contexts. A jazz-rock environmental "celebration" titled "Bless This World," for instance, found far less of a welcome at the 1970 convention. One reviewer was moved to declare, "Most of us have had it as far as degenerative worship is concerned." At a somewhat more existential level, another reviewer described the piece as "weak in spiritual depth and, thereby, contemporary in a way its poet and composer never intended."[16]

The reality, in retrospect, was that jazz at any level—let alone the progressive jazz of the 1960s, at anything approaching the level of such geniuses as Ellington and Brubeck—made technical demands that most church musicians had neither the talent, training, nor inclination to meet. In the end, the complex art of jazz did not make significant inroads in regular worship at the level of the usual parish church because it simply could not be done in the manner that most people were accustomed to hearing it outside of church.

Diversity

The introduction of vernacular idioms was but one of the results of new pressures bearing on churches and church music. The ecumenical movement attenuated a number of differences in worship among the Protestant denominations. Many mainstream and liturgical churches adopted a less formal worship atmosphere, even to the point of making room for gospel and folk-style music. At the same time, by the late twentieth century, Catholic congregations embraced Lutheran chorales and even Genevan psalms that were once rallying cries for the same Protestant reformers their Catholic forbears burned.[17]

[16.]Respectively, Morgan Simmons and Alan Cowle. See Morgan Simmons and Alan Cowle, "Bless This World," *Music: The A.G.O. Magazine* 4/8 (August 1970): 25.

[17] On the matter of Gospel, see Virginia Lieson Brereton, "White Folks 'Get Happy': Mainstream America Discovers the Black Gospel Tradition," in *Wonderful Words of Life: Hymns in American Protestant History and Theology*, ed. Richard J. Mouw and Mark A. Noll (Grand Rapids: Eerdmans, 2005) 164–78; on Catholics and Protestant hymnody, see Felicia Piscitelli, "Protestant Hymnody in Contemporary Roman Catholic Worship," in *Wonderful Words of Life*, 150–63.

New denominational hymnals reflected this diversity. On one hand, the widening of the repertoire resulted in the inclusion of a number of commercially conceived and ineptly written pieces in folk and popular commercial styles. On the other hand, multiculturalism and openness to other traditions enriched the shared repertoire of mainstream Protestant hymnody to include such genres as black spirituals and white folk hymns alongside traditional English hymns and Lutheran chorales. As Erik Routley put it in 1977, "Nowadays, hymnals borrow freely from each other's traditions, and look much less like the private declaration of self-sufficient sects."[18]

Perhaps the prime example of this new openness to other traditions was the Episcopal *Hymnal 1982*, successor to *The Hymnal 1940*, itself a classic of its genre and standard against which other mid-century denominational hymnals were measured. The bulk of the material in the 1940 collection, as already noted, was heavily English. The 1982 hymnal contained a much more eclectic repertoire: an expanded number of Lutheran chorales and chant, but also folk hymnody, spirituals, and vernacular pieces of varying quality.

A number of new hymns and tunes were written especially for the collection, and some, like the beautifully crafted, infectiously singable music of Richard Proulx, the subtly haunting, exquisitely harmonized modal hymn tunes of David Hurd (1950–), and the variegated melodies of Calvin Hampton (1938–1984) quickly found a permanent place in American hymnody. A later supplemental volume, *Lift Every Voice and Sing*, provided Episcopal congregations with a selection of evangelical gospel songs and African-American hymnody and service music.[19]

---

[18] Erik Routley, "Contemporary Hymnody in Its Wider Setting: A Survey of Materials," *Church Music* 77/2 (1977): 4.

[19] Hurd is professor of music at the General Seminary in New York. Hampton, at the time of his death, was organist and choirmaster of Calvary Church, also in New York. For a preliminary critique of the collection, see John Ogasapian, "Some Notes on the Episcopal Hymnal 1982," *Journal of Church Music* 30/9 (November 1987): 4–7, 30. Episcopal Church, *Lift Every Voice and Sing II* (New York: Church Hymnal Corp., 1993).

Technology and the Electronic Church

During the early 1970s, more advanced idioms and technologies also made inroads into American church music. The ascetic elegance and sinewy mastery of Daniel Pinkham (b.1923) bridges the gap between church music and concert stage and has earned him a following, even though his music can make demands on the listener. Pinkham has occasionally made use of electronically synthesized tone.[20]

Electronic sound generation, practiced experimentally in university laboratories in the years after World War II, began to play an increasingly important part in serious musical composition as relatively inexpensive sound synthesizers became available in the 1970s. Indeed, the 1974 guild convention featured demonstrations and lectures on the use of electronic music synthesizers by Donald Erb (b.1927) and William Albright (1944–1998).

But technology played a wholly other part in church music during the late 1970s and especially the 1980s. The period saw increased employment, especially experiential evangelical worship but occasionally even in the "mainstream" Protestant denominations, of musical devices and genres heretofore associated with popular music and the mass media. Interestingly, evangelicals had at first resisted associating themselves with what they viewed as "worldly" popular musical styles, preferring to stick with vernacular gospel songs in the manner of the early-twentieth-century crusades. By the mid-1960s, more evangelicals began adopting commercial styles, and since the late 1970s, an increasing number of Evangelical Christian radio stations have broadcast and publishers and recording companies issued "contemporary Christian music," cast in popular styles— usually akin to country-and-western and soft rock.[21]

More exuberant idioms, such as hard rock, entered the evangelical churches and even some mainline Protestant congre-

---

[20.]On Pinkham's early choral music, see Marlowe W. Johnson, "The Choral Music of Daniel Pinkham" (Ph.D. diss., University of Iowa, 1968).

[21.]There is a pronounced and palpable connection between the musical devices of authentically rural sacred and secular music; for instance, the improvisational devices in so-called bluegrass and in hymn-singing from the same area.

gations via charismatic worship, which became a presence in American Christianity from the 1960s on. Such worship is highly charged, emotional, and ecstatic, with congregational singing of repeated praise choruses and the physical activity of dancing and clapping. The instruments are usually those of a popular dance and rock bands: drums, electric guitars, pianos, and electronic instruments.[22]

Television became the vehicle of the so-called electronic church, especially as part of the varied offerings possible on cable with its dozens of channels. Media services aimed at a mass of viewers combined the format of the revival meeting with the flavor of a secular variety show. Musical "acts" warmed up the congregation—analogous to a studio audience—for the message of the preacher. The music was intentionally cast in the mold of popular entertainment and was calculated to appeal to a broad taste, again with country-and-western and soft rock styles predominating.

Historicism and the Organ Revival

At the other end of the continuum, so to speak—at the opposing pole from the vernacular movement in twentieth-century church music—the early music movement enjoyed significant growth during the same years. Interest was mounting in the historically informed performances of Renaissance and Baroque music. Although the main exponents of the early music movement were professional performers and academics, there was considerable natural overlap with the practice of church music. Organists' techniques adapted far more easily to the playing of the harpsichord than did pianists; and in any event, the lion's share of the organ's best repertoire—much of it written for church use—dated from the years before 1750. Moreover, an increasing amount of sacred choral music from the same period was coming into print, the fruit of post-war European and American musicological scholarship.

The years after 1960 saw the flowering of the classic organ revival and cased instruments with mechanical or tracker key action,

---

[22] Hustad, *Jubilate II*, 265–73.

rather than electric. A handful of modern European and domestic trackers had been built—or rebuilt from existing nineteenth-century instruments—during the 1950s; however, what had been a trickle became a tide so that by the bicentennial convention of American Guild of Organists, held in summer 1976 in Boston, approximately half of the organs heard in recital were recent tracker-action instruments, something that would have been inconceivable—and in any case, practically impossible—only sixteen years before.[23]

Antithesis and Synthesis

From the initial introduction of new idioms and styles into church music, their suitability for church use was being debated, sometimes heatedly. In 1968, James Boeringer defined the positions: on one hand, that music should be sacred and that it should be good; on the other, only that it should be part of the cultural language of the people. He tried to place the musical innovations into perspective: "This movement is not going to sweep through the Christian Church any more than Bach is likely to; but the shock of this music is going to have a salutary effect on the placid ineptitude and conservatism of many church musicians."[24] In a panel discussion at the 1972 guild convention, Carl Schalk declared, "We have pandered to those who view church music as entertainment." In response, Alec Wyton cautioned against viewing musical innovation as either bane or blessing. He said, "The great past is with us, but we must all clean house."[25]

The next year, composer Ned Rorem (b. 1923), a Quaker-born agnostic, took an existentialist, almost nihilistic, view of church music, both traditional and vernacular : "Neither [poets] nor God can finally stop wars, nor even change our life in smaller ways. During

---

[23.]The best source on the subject, although by now it is nearly twenty years out-of-date, is Uwe Pape, *The Tracker Organ Revival in America* (Berlin: Pape-Verlag, 1977).

[24.]James Boeringer, "Experimental Liturgies," *Music: The A.G.O. Magazine* 2/1 (January 1968): 10–12.

[25.]Alec Wyton, moderator, "Contemporary Trands in Church Music, a Panel," *Music: The A.G.O. Magazine* 6/8 (August 1972): 27.

periods of strife when we need them most, both God and the poets disappear." He then injected a dose of hard reality into the discussion: "To experiment with music in the church is to fight a losing battle.... Luring youth to church via rock concerts is asking them to accept a diluted version what they can get better at home."[26]

With the bicentennial, the tide of innovation seems to have crested and ebbed, at least in mainline denominations. Beginning in the late 1980s and 1990s, church musicians paused to take stock of the profession and to consolidate and reappraise the events of the previous twenty years. Clearly, worship has changed, but as the smoke clears, that change appears less profound in many ways, and certainly less intimidating, than once it seemed.

[26.] Ned Rorem, "Notes on Sacred Music," *Music: The A.G.O. Magazine* 7/1 (January 1973): 44–45.

Bibliography

Aaron, Amy. "William Tuckey, A Choirmaster in Colonial New York." *Musical Quarterly* 64/1 (January 1978): 79–97.

Ahlstrom, Sidney E. *A Religious History of the American People*. New Haven: Yale University Press, 1972.

Alderfer, Everett Gordon. *The Ephrata Commune: An Early American Counterculture*. Pittsburgh: University of Pittsburgh Press, 1985.

Allwardt, Anton Paul. "Sacred Music in New York City, 1800–1850." SMD dissertation, Union Theological Seminary, 1950.

American Musical Directory. New York: Thomas Hutchinson, 1861; Reprint, New York: Da Capo Press, 1980.

Anstice, Henry. *A History of St. George's Church in the City of New York*. New York: Harper Bros., 1911.

Appel, Richard G. *The Music of the Bay Psalm Book*, 9th edition. Brooklyn: Institute for Studies in American Music, 1975.

Armstrong, William H. *Organs for America: The Life and Work of David Tannenberg*. Philadelphia: University of Pennsylvania Press, 1967.

Blume, Friedrich. *Protestant Church Music*. New York: W. W. Norton, 1974.

Boyer, Horace Clarence. *How Sweet the Sound: The Golden Age of Gospel*. Washington DC: Elliott and Clark, 1995.

Brink, Emily R. "Metrical Psalmody: A Tale of Two Traditions." *Reformed Liturgy and Music* 23/1 (Winter 1989): 3–8.

Britton, Allen Perdue. "Theoretical Introductions in American Tune-Books to 1800." Ph.D. dissertation, University of Michigan, 1949.

———, Irving Lowens, and Richard Crawford. *American Sacred Music Imprints, 1698–1810*. Worcester MA: American Antiquarian Society, 1990.

Broyles, Michael. *A Yankee Musician in Europe: The 1837 Journals of Lowell Mason*. Ann Arbor: UMI Research Press, 1990.

Brunner, Raymond J. *That Ingenious Business: Pennsylvania German Organ Builders*. Birdsboro: The Pennsylvania German Society, 1990.

Buechner, Alan C. "Yankee Singing Schools and the Golden Age of Choral Music in New England, 1760–1900." Ph.D. dissertation, Harvard University, 1960; published Boston: Boston University, 2003.

Bushnell, Vinson. "Daniel Read of New Haven (1757–1836): The Man and His Musical Activities." Ph.D. dissertation, Harvard University, 1979.

Charlton, Peter. *John Stainer and the Musical Life of Victorian Britain.* North Pomfret VT: David & Charles, 1984.

Clarkson, David. *History of the Church of Zion and St. Timothy.* New York: G. P. Putnam's Sons, 1894.

Cobb, Buell E. *The Sacred Harp: A Tradition and Its Music.* Athens: University of Georgia Press, 1978.

Cooke, Nym. "William Billings in the District of Maine, 1780." *American Music* 9/3 (Fall 1991): 243–59.

Covey, Cyclone. "Puritanism and Music in Colonial America." *William and Mary Quarterly.* 3rd series. 8/3 (July 1951): 378–88.

Crawford, Richard. *Andrew Law, American Psalmodist.* Evanston: Northwestern University Press, 1968. Reprint, New York: Da Capo Press, 1981.

———. *The Core Repertory of Early American Psalmody. Recent Researches in American Music* 11–12. Madison: A-R Editions, 1984.

———. "William Billings (1746–1800) and American Psalmody: A Study of Musical Dissemination." *The American Musical Landscape.* Berkeley: University of California Press, 1993.

Cuthbert, John A. "Rayner Taylor and Anglo-American Musical Life." Ph.D. dissertation, West Virginia University, 1980.

Daniel, Ralph T. *The Anthem in New England before 1800.* Evanston: Northwestern University Press, 1966. Reprint, New York: Da Capo, 1979.

Dean, Talmage W. "The Organ in Eighteenth Century English Colonial America." Ph.D. dissertation, University of Southern California, 1960.

———. *A Survey of Twentieth Century Protestant Church Music in America.* Nashville: Broadman Press, 1988.

Dix, Morgan and John A. *A History of the Parish of Trinity Church in the City of New York* . 5 volumes. New York: G. P. Putnam's Sons, 1898–1906, 1950.

Ellinwood, Leonard. *The History of American Church Music.* New York: Morehouse-Gorham, 1953.

Fischer, David Hackett. *Albion's Seed: Four British Folkways in America.* New York: Oxford University Press, 1989.

Foote, Henry Wilder. *Three Centuries of American Hymnody*. Cambridge: Harvard University Press, 1940. Reprint, Hamden CT: Shoe String Press, 1961.

Frankiel, Sandra Sizer. *Gospel Hymns and Social Religion: The Rhetoric of Nineteenth-Century Revivalism*. Philadelphia: Temple University Press, 1978.

Gatens, William J. *Victorian Cathedral Music in Theory and Practice*. New York: Cambridge University Press, 1986.

Gaustad, Edwin Scott. *Historical Atlas of Religion in America*. Revised edition. New York: Harper and Row, 1976.

Gould, Nathaniel. *Church Music in America*. Boston: A. N. Johnson, 1853. Reprint, New York: AMS Press, 1972.

Green, Joseph. *Diary of the Rev. Joseph Green of Salem Village*. Edited by Samuel P. Fowler. Salem: Essex Institute Historical Collections 10, 1869.

Grimes, Robert R. "'How Shall We Sing in a Foreign Land?': Music of Irish-Catholic Immigrants in the Antebellum United States." Ph.D. dissertation, University of Pittsburgh, 1992.

———. *How Shall We Sing in a Foreign Land?: Music of Irish-Catholic Immigrants in the Antebellum United States*. Notre Dame IN: University of Notre Dame Press, 1996.

———. "John Aitken and Catholic Music in Federal Philadelphia." *American Music* 16/3 (Fall 1998): 289–310.

Haraszti, Zoltan. *The Enigma of the Bay Psalm Book*. Chicago: University of Chicago Press, 1956.

Hatch, Nathan O. *The Democratization of American Christianity*. New Haven: Yale University Press, 1989.

Hodges, Faustina H. *Edward Hodges*. New York: G. P. Putnam's Sons, 1896.

Hood, George. *History of Music in New England: with Biographical Sketches of Reformers and Psalmodists*. Boston: Wilkins, Carter & Co., 1846. Reprint, New York: Johnson, 1970.

Howe, Jacob F. "Chanting in the Protestant Episcopal Church and Its Author." *American Historical Record* 3/25 (January 1874): 19–20.

Hustad, Donald P. *Jubilate II: Church Music in Worship and Renewal*. Carol Stream IL: Hope Publishing, 1993.

Inserra, Lorraine, and H. Wiley Hitchcock. *The Music of Henry Ainsworth's Psalter*. Brooklyn: Institute for Studies in American Music, 1981.

Jackson, George Pullen. *White Spirituals in the Southern Uplands*. Chapel Hill: University of North Carolina Press, 1933. Reprint, New York: Dover, 1965.

Kaufman, Charles H. "George K. Jackson: American Musician of the Federal Period." Ph.D. dissertation, New York University, 1968.

Kelpius, John, and Anthony Aston. *Church Music and Musical Life in Pennsylvania in the Eighteenth Century.* 3 Volumes bound as 4. Philadelphia: Publications of the Pennsylvania Society of the Colonial Dames of America, 1926–1935. Reprint, New York: AMS Press, 1972.

Knauff, Christopher W. *Doctor Tucker, Priest-Musician.* New York: A. D. F. Randolph Co., 1897.

Kreider, Harry J. *History of the United Lutheran Synod of New York and New England.* Philadelphia: Muhlenberg Press, 1954.

Kroeger, Karl. *American Fuging Tunes, 1770–1820: A Descriptive Catalogue.* Westport CT: Greenwood Press, 1994.

———. "William Tans'ur's Influence on William Billings." *Inter-American Music Review* 11/2 (Spring–Summer 1991): 1–12.

Leaver, Robin A. *"Goostly Psalmes and Spirituall Songes": English and Dutch Metrical Psalms from Coverdale to Utenhove, 1535–1566.* Oxford: Clarendon Press and New York: Oxford University Press, 1991.

Le Huray, Peter. *Music and the Reformation in England, 1549–1660.* New York: Oxford University Press, 1967.

Lindsley, Charles Edward. "Scoring and Placement of the 'Air' in Early American Tunebooks." *Musical Quarterly* 58/3 (July 1972): 365–82.

Logan, Kenneth. "Living Issues in Early American Psalmody." *Reformed Liturgy and Music* 23/1 (Winter 1989): 9–12.

Lowens, Irving. *Music and Musicians in Early America.* New York: W. W. Norton, 1964.

MacDougall, Hamilton C. *Early New England Psalmody.* Brattleboro: Stephen Daye Press, 1940. Reprint, New York: Da Capo, 1969.

Marini, Stephen A. *Sacred Song in America: Religion, Music, and Public Culture.* Urbana: University of Illinois Press, 2003.

Martin, Betty Jean, "The Ephrata Cloister and Its Music, 1732–1785: The Cultural, Religious and Bibliographical Background." Ph.D. dissertation, University of Maryland, 1974.

Mason, Lowell. *Musical Letters from Abroad.* New York: Mason Brothers, 1854. Reprint, New York: Da Capo Press, 1967.

Mather, Cotton. *The Accomplished Singer.* Boston: B. Green for S. Gerrish, 1721.

———. *The Diary of Cotton Mather.* 1912. Collections of the Massachusetts Historical Society. Series 7, Volume 8. Massachusetts Historical Society Collections, Boston.

————. *Magnalia Christi Americana. London, 1702.* Edited and Abridged by Raymond J. Cunningham. New York: Frederick Ungar, 1970.

————, and Increase Mather. *Ratio Disciplinae Fratrum Nov-Anglorum.* Boston: S. Gerrish, 1726.

McCormick, David W. "Oliver Holden, Composer and Anthologist." SMD dissertation, Union Seminary, 1963.

McDaniel, Stanley Robert. "Church Song and the Cultivated Tradition in New England and New York." DMA dissertation, University of Southern California, 1983.

McKay, David. "William Selby, Musical Émigré in Colonial Boston." *Musical Quarterly* 57/4 (October 1971): 609–27.

————, and Richard L. Crawford. *William Billings of Boston, Eighteenth-Century Composer.* Princeton: Princeton University Press, 1975.

Meeter, Daniel. "Genevan Jigsaw: The Tunes of the New-York Psalmbook of 1761." In *Ars et Musica in Liturgia: Essays Presented to Casper Honders on His Seventieth Birthday.* Edited by Frans Brouwer and Robin A. Leaver. Metuchen NJ: Scarecrow Press, 1994.

Messiter, Arthur. *A History of the Choir and Music of Trinity Church, New York.* New York: Edwin S. Gorham, 1906. Reprint, New York: AMS Press, 1970.

Metcalf, Frank J. *American Writers and Compilers of Sacred Music.* New York: [Abington], 1925. Reprint, New York: Russell & Russell, 1967.

Morgan, Edmund S. *Visible Saints.* Ithaca: Cornell University Press, 1975.

Mouw, Richard J., and Mark A. Noll, *Wonderful Words of Life: Hymns in American Protestant History and Theology.* Grand Rapids: William B. Eerdmans, 2004.

Murray, Sterling E. "Timothy Swan and Yankee Psalmody." *Musical Quarterly* 61/3 (July 1975): 433–63.

Music, David W. *Christian Hymnody in Twentieth-Century Britain and America: An Annotated Bibliography.* Westport CT: Greenwood Press, 2001.

————. "The Diary of Samuel Sewall and Congregational Singing in Early New England." *The Hymn* 41/1 (January 1990): 7–15.

————. "Josiah Flag." *American Music* 7/2 (Summer 1989): 140–58.

Nelson, E. Clifford, editor. *The Lutherans in North America.* Philadelphia: Fortress Press, 1980.

Ochse, Orpha. *The History of the Organ in the United States.* Bloomington: Indiana University Press, 1975.

Ogasapian, John. "American Guild of Organists Centennial: AGO Conventions." *The American Organist* 30/8 (August 1996): 52–55.

————. *English Cathedral Music in New York: Edward Hodges of Trinity Church*. Richmond: Organ Historical Society, 1994.

————. *Henry Erben: Portrait of a Nineteenth-Century American Organ Builder*. Braintree MA: Organ Literature Foundation, 1980.

————. "Lowell Mason as a Church Musician." *Journal of Church Music* 21/7 (September 1979): 6–10.

————. *Music of the Colonial and Revolutionary Era*. Westport CT: Greenwood Press, 2004.

————. *Organ Building in New York City, 1700–1900*. Braintree MA: Organ Literature Foundation, 1977.

Osterhout, David. "Note Reading and Regular Singing in Eighteenth-Century New England." *American Music* 4/2 (Summer 1986): 125–44.

Owen, Barbara. "The Bay Psalm Book and Its Era." *The Hymn* 41/4 (October 1990): 12–19.

————. *The Organ in New England*. Raleigh: Sunbury Press, 1979.

————. *The Organs and Music of King's Chapel*. 2nd edition. Boston: King's Chapel, 1991.

————. "The Other Mr. Selby." *American Music* 8/4 (Winter 1980): 477–82.

Parker, John Rowe. *Musical Biography, or Sketches of the Lives and Writings of Eminent Musical Characters*. Boston: Stone and Fovill, 1825. Reprint, Detroit: Information Coordinators, 1975.

Pemberton, Carol. *Lowell Mason: A Bio-Bibliography*. New York: Greenwood Press, 1988.

————. *Lowell Mason: His Life and Work*. Ann Arbor: UMI Research Press, 1985.

Perkins, J. Newton. *History of St. Stephen's Parish in the City of New York, 1805–1905*. New York: Edwin S. Gorham, 1906.

Pratt, Waldo Selden. *The Music of the Pilgrims*. Boston: Oliver Ditson, 1921.

Rasmussen, Jane. *Musical Taste as a Religious Question in Nineteenth-Century America*. Lewiston NY: Edwin Mellen Press, 1986.

Reese, Gustave. *Music in the Renaissance*. New York: W. W. Norton, 1959.

Ridgeway, Neville. *The Choristers of St. George's Chapel*. Slough, Berkshire: Chas. Luff & Co., 1980.

Ritter, Abraham. *History of the Moravian Church in Philadelphia*. Philadelphia: Hayes and Zell, 1857.

Ruffin, Bernard. *Fanny Crosby*. Westwood NJ: Barbour and Co., 1976.

Rutman, Darrett B. *American Puritanism*. New York: W. W. Norton, 1977.

Sachse, Julius Friedrich. *Justus Falckner*. Philadelphia: n.p., 1903.

————. *The Music of the Ephrata Cloister*. Lancaster PA: n.p., 1903. Reprint, New York: AMS Press, 1971.

Sankey, Ira D. *My Life and the Story of the Gospel Hymns*. New York: Harper Brothers, 1907.

Scholes, Percy. *The Puritans and Music in England and New England*. Oxford: Clarendon Press, 1934, 1969.

Sewall, Samuel. *The Diary of Samuel Sewall*. Collections of the Massachusetts Historical Society. Series 5, Volumes 5–7. Massachusetts Historical Society Collections, Boston.

Siek, Steven. "Benjamin Carr's Theatrical Career." *American Music* 11/2 (Summer 1993): 158–84.

Silverman, Kenneth. *A Cultural History of the American Revolution*. New York: Thomas Y. Crowell, 1976.

———. *The Life and Times of Cotton Mather*. New York: Columbia University Press, 1985.

Skardon, Alvin W. *Church Leader in the Cities: William Augustus Muhlenberg*. Philadelphia: University of Pennsylvania Press, 1971.

Smith, Ronnie L. "The Church Music of Benjamin Carr." DMA dissertation, Southwestern Baptist Theological Seminary, 1970.

Sonneck, Oscar G. T. *Francis Hopkinson, the First American Poet-Composer (1737–1791): and James Lyon, Patriot, Preacher, Psalmodist (1735–1794): Two Studies in Early American Music*. Washington: McQueen, 1905. Reprint, New York: Da Capo Press, 1967.

Southern, Eileen. *The Music of Black Americans*. 3rd edition. New York: W. W. Norton, 1991.

Spencer, Jon Michael. *Black Hymnody: A Hymnological History of the African-American Church*. Knoxville: University of Tennessee Press, 1992.

Stetzel, Ronald. "John Christopher Moller (1755–1803) and His Role in Early American Music." Ph.D. dissertation, University of Iowa, 1965.

Stevenson, Robert. *Patterns of Protestant Church Music*. Durham: Duke University Press, 1953.

———. *Protestant Church Music in America*. New York: W. W. Norton, 1966.

Stiles, Ezra. *The Literary Diary of Ezra Stiles, D.D., LL.D.* Edited by Franklin Bowditch Dexter. New York: Charles Scribner's Sons, 1901.

Stocker, Harry Emilius. *A History of the Moravian Church in New York*. New York: n.p., 1922.

Stoeffler, F. Ernest, editor. *Continental Pietism and Early American Christianity*. Grand Rapids: William B. Eerdmans, 1976.

Stoutamire, Albert. *Music of the Old South, Colony to Confederacy*. Rutherford: Fairleigh Dickinson University Press, 1972.

Stowe, David W. *How Sweet the Sound: Music in the Spiritual Lives of Americans*. Cambridge: Harvard University Press, 2004.

Swanson, Jean P. "The Use of the Organ in the Church of England." Ph.D. dissertation, University of Minnesota, 1969.

Symmes, Thomas. *The Reasonableness of Regular Singing*. Boston: B. Green for Samuel Gerrish, 1720.

———. *Utile Dulci, or, a Joco-Serious Dialogue Concerning Regular Singing*. Boston: B. Green for S. Gerrish, 1723.

Temperley, Nicholas. *Bound for America: Three British Composers*. Urbana: University of Illinois Press, 2003.

———. "John Playford and the Metrical Psalms." *Journal of the American Musicological Society* 25/3 (Fall 1972): 331–78.

———. *The Music of the English Parish Church*. New York: Cambridge University Press, 1979.

———. "The Old Way of Singing: Its Origins and Development." *Journal of the American Musicological Society* 34/3 (Fall 1981): 511–44.

Thompson, James W. "Music and Musical Activities in New England, 1800–1838." Ph.D. dissertation, George Peabody College for Teachers, 1962.

Traupman-Carr, Carol A., editor. *Pleasing for Our Use: David Tannenberg and the Organs of the Moravians*. Bethlehem PA: Lehigh University Press, 2000.

Walter, Thomas. *The Grounds and Rules of Musick Explaineed; or, an Introduction to the Art of Singing by Note Fitted to the Meanest Capacities*. Boston: J. Franklin for S. Gerrish, 1721.

Wansey, Henry. *The Journal of an Excursion to the United States of North America in the Summer of 1794*. Reprint, New York: Johnson Publishing Company, 1969.

Ward, Andrew. *Dark Midnight When I Rise: The Story of the Fisk Jubilee Singers*. New York: Amistad, 2001.

Warner, Thomas E. "European Musical Activities in North America before 1620." *Musical Quarterly* 70/1 (Winter 1984): 77–95.

Weadon, David A. "Clarence Dickinson (1873–1969) and the School of Sacred Music at Union Theological Seminary in the City of New York (1928–1973)." Ph.D. dissertation, Drew University, 1993.

Webb, Guy B. "Timothy Swann, Yankee Tunesmith." DMA dissertation, University of Illinois, 1972.

Weinandt, Elwyn A. *Opinions on Church Music*. Waco: Baylor University Press, 1974.

————, and Robert H. Young. *The Anthem in England and America*. New York: The Free Press, 1970.

Weiss, Joanne Grayeski. "The Relationship Between the 'Great Awakening' and the Transition from Psalmody to Hymnody in the New England Colonies." DA dissertation, Ball State University, 1988.

Williams, George W. "Charleston Church Music 1562–1833." *Journal of the American Musicological Society* 7/1 (Spring 1954): 35–40.

————. "Jacob Eckhard and His Choirmaster's Book," *Journal of the American Musicological Society* 7/1 (Spring 1954): 41–47.

————. *St. Michael's Charleston, 1751–1951*. Columbia: University of South Carolina Press, 1951.

Willis, Richard Storrs. *Our Church Music*. New York: Dana & Co., 1856; Reprint, New York: AMS Press, 1973.

Wilson, Ruth Mack. "Anglican Chant and Chanting in England and America, 1660–1811." Ph.D. dissertation, University of Illinois, 1988.

————. *Anglican Chant and Chanting in England, Scotland, and America*. Oxford: Clarendon Press, 1996.

Wilson-Dickson, Andrew. *The Story of Christian Music from Gregorian Chant to Black Gospel*. Minneapolis: Fortress Press, 2003.

Wolf, Edward C. "Justus Henry Christian Helmuth—Hymnodist." *German-American Studies* 5 (1972): 117–47.

————. "Lutheran Church Music in America during the Eighteenth and Early Nineteenth Centuries." Ph.D. dissertation, University of Illinois, 1960.

————. "Music in Old Zion, Philadelphia, 1750–1850." *Musical Quarterly* 58/4 (October 1972): 622–52.

————. "Peter Erben and America's First Lutheran Tunebook in English," In *American Musical Life in Context and Practice*. Edited by James R. Heintze. New York: Garland Publishing, 1994.

Wolverton, Byron A. "Keyboard Music and Musicians in the Colonies and United States of America before 1830." Ph.D. dissertation, Indiana University, 1966.

Wulstan, David. *Tudor Music*. Iowa City: University of Iowa, 1986.

Yellin, Victor Fell. "Rayner Taylor." *American Music* 1/3 (Fall 1983): 48–71.

Young, Carlton R. "John Wesley's 1737 Charlestown Collection of Psalms and Hymns." *The Hymn* 41/4 (October 1990): 19–27.

Ziff, Larzer. *Puritanism in America*. New York: Viking Press, 1973.

Index